TIME & SPACE

*Lid of a snuff box, with a watch
and chime, in the style of Louis XVI*

Photographs

by Pierre Devinoy

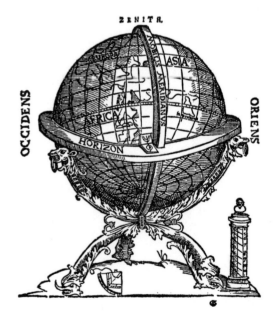

Terrestrial globe of 1530

TIME & SPACE

Measuring Instruments
from the 15th to the 19th Century

by Samuel Guye

and Henri Michel

Praeger Publishers

New York · Washington · London

Translated by Diana Dolan
in collaboration with Samuel W. Mitchell,
F.R.A.S.

Praeger Publishers, Inc.
111 Fourth Avenue, New York, N.Y. 10003,
  U.S.A.
5 Cromwell Place, London, S.W.7, England

Published in the United States of America in
  1971
Originally published as *Mesures du Temps et de
  l'Espace*
© 1970 by Office du Livre, Fribourg

Library of Congress Catalog Card Number:
  77-111070

Printed in Switzerland

Contents

ACKNOWLEDGMENTS 7

PART ONE

Clocks and Watches

INTRODUCTION 11

MONUMENTAL CLOCKS 15
Components and Working 15
Clocks with Bells and Automata 19
Historical Outline 21
Fourteenth Century 21
Fifteenth Century 23
Sixteenth Century 24
Development of the Hour Mechanism in Clocks 26
Description of the Three Monumental Clocks shown in the
Illustrations 28
The Town Hall Clock, Prague 28
The Monumental Clock in the Piazza San Marco, Venice 31
The Clock on the Zeitglockenturm, Berne 32
Conclusions 32

THE GOTHIC CLOCK 35
Types of Gothic Clocks 40

THE RENAISSANCE 41
Inventions and Discoveries 41
Renaissance Clocks 43
Different types of Renaissance Clocks 43
Fantasy in Spring-driven Clocks 44
Table Clocks 53
Monstrance Clocks 54
Crucifix Clocks 56
Small Lantern Clocks 56
Celestial Globes 56
Traveling Clocks 65
The Emergence of the Pocket Watch 66
The Movement of the First Pocket Watches 68
Adaptation of the Foliot Oscillator to the Pocket Watch 78
The Train of Wheels 80
General Remarks 85

THE SEVENTEENTH CENTURY 87
Enamelled Watches 87
Clockmakers of Lyons, Blois and Geneva 89
The Beginnings of Precision Clockmaking 92
Christian Huygens (1629-1695) 98
The First Pendulum Clocks: 1657-1659 100
Pendulum Clock 1658 102
Pendulum Clock 1659 103
The Invention of the Oscillator Balance-Spring 104
Evolution of the Watch 106

CONTENTS

THE EIGHTEENTH CENTURY. 109

The Struggle for Precision 109

Clockmakers' Jewels 110

Escapements 112

Compensation 115

Methods of Adjustment 116

Invention of New Types of Watches 122

The Great Watchmakers of Western Europe 123

The Decline of Craftsmanship and the Rise of Mechanization . 132

THE MARINE CHRONOMETER 139

John Harrison, Pierre le Roy and Ferdinand Berthoud 142

The Nineteenth Century 144

DECORATIVE CLOCKS 151

The Louis XIII Period 152

The Louis XIV Period 152

The Régence and Louis XV Periods 161

The Louis XVI Period 164

The Empire Period 174

The Post-Empire Period 189

PART TWO

Ancient Measuring Instruments

INTRODUCTION 193

MEASURING INSTRUMENTS BEFORE THE
RENAISSANCE 201

TERRESTRIAL AND CELESTIAL GLOBES . . . 205

Terrestrial Globes 205

Celestial Globes 207

ARMILLARY SPHERES AND PLANETARIA . . . 213

ASTROLABES 221

SUNDIALS 233

Sundials Measuring Height 233

Sundials Measuring Direction 238

Style-axis Sundials 245

Lunar Dials 257

Night Dials, or Star Dials 258

CLEPSYDRAS AND HOUR-GLASSES 261

TOPOGRAPHICAL INSTRUMENTS 267

Measurement of Surface Angles 270

Measurement of Vertical Angles 278

Measurement at Sea 283

CONCLUSION 285

Index 287

Acknowledgments

We gratefully acknowledge all the help so freely given in the preparation of this book especially by the Directors and Keepers of the following museums and librairies:

— Musée des Arts décoratifs
— Musée de Cluny
— Palais de Fontainebleau
— Garde-meuble national, Paris
— Musée d'horlogerie, La Chaux-de-Fonds
— Musée national d'histoire naturelle
— Observatoire de Paris
— Musée du Petit Palais, Paris

and to all the collectors—MM. Andrée and Hipola, J. Bernard, Brault, Arthur Davidson, J. Fremersdorf, R. Gest, Nathan, as well as those who, whilst preferring to remain anonymous, have allowed us to reproduce the finest examples in their collections; and also to the following dealers:

P. Bernard, Ben Simon, Charliat, Kugel, Laforet (Au Vieux Cadran), Samy Chalom, Gilbert Suc.

The photographs in this book are by Pierre Devinoy with the exception of Pl. 3 (Tourist Agency, Berne).

PART ONE

Clocks and Watches

The clock merchant; after an engraving by D. Herli-
berger, Zurich, 1720

Introduction

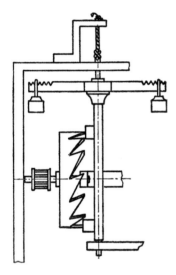

Foliot oscillator

Clocks are time-keepers, that is they are mechanisms which mark the length of time passed from the moment when they were set in motion. This length of time is composed of simple elements.

In monumental clocks, the huge clocks made from the end of the thirteenth century, the unit chosen was the period of oscillation of a mechanism called the *foliot*. The Latin word *folio* means the page of a book, and in the same way the foliot of a clock describes the passage of a small, clearly defined length of time. The foliot consists of a horizontal bar *(balance)* which carries two weights *(regulators)*, one at each end of the bar. This bar is fixed at its central point to a vertical rod *(verge)*, on which are two *pallets*. These engage with a toothed wheel, which pushes the verge first one way and then the other, causing the foliot to oscillate. The wheel itself advances by one tooth for each double oscillation.

These pieces of mechanism together form an *oscillator* and constitute the original realization of a mechanical unit of time.

Adjustment to the speed of the oscillation is made by altering either the weight of the regulators or the distance between their respective points of suspension and the verge. Heavy weights suspended at the ends of the arms give the maximum period of rest to the foliot and consequently a slower speed, whilst lighter weights, or weights suspended nearer the verge, shorten the period of rest and increase the speed. Although the oscillator constitutes the principal part of every time-measuring instrument, it is only valid when in movement, and there are other and better systems.

A clock must also have other parts capable of initiating and maintaining this movement whilst counting the number of periods accumulated by the oscillator since the start of the day.

A clock is therefore made up of two distinct but complementary machines:

(1) The oscillator, which decides the length of the unit of time.
(2) The collection of other mechanisms which initiate and maintain the movement and count the periods of oscillation.

These general principles hold good for all the mechanical instruments for measuring time discussed in the other portion of this work. The history of mechanical clocks is two-sided. It can be viewed from the scientific or the artistic angle, both of which will be discussed here, including the technical aspect which is related to the methods of construction.

Since the chief characteristic of clocks and watches is their capacity to measure and their artistic qualities are secondary, the scientific nature of their mechanism will form the main thread of this work.

Starting with the monumental clock, we shall follow the evolution of measuring instruments through to the middle of the nineteenth century. And it will be seen that in the course of five and a half centuries the general principles have not changed, even though scientific progress can be seen to have affected one or other, or sometimes all, of the following five categories:

(1) Reduction in size.
(2) The development and improvement of the form of the oscillating mechanism, so that its period became more regular and more or less independent of all the factors capable of altering its length.
(3) The development of all the other parts forming the complementary machine, so that they function without upsetting the oscillating mechanism.
(4) The addition to these essential parts of every clock of one or two additional pieces, such as automata or mechanism for a bell, a calendar, or astronomical calculations.
(5) The adaptation of the case and shape of the instrument, and of the hands and face, to the taste of the period.

Very few people realize the immense effort and igenuity that went into creating these instruments.

"Clock-making," wrote the scholar Jean Bernouilli in the middle of the eighteen century, "touches on a very delicate skill and a profound science."

Indeed it was not enough for the clockmaker to know how to work metal and hard materials: these had to be made to conform exactly to the requirements of their different mechanical functions, which the clockmaker had to combine to make them work.

The true collector will not be satisfied with buying a number of antique clocks and watches at whatever cost, but will want to know when each one was made, its original role and the progress to be seen in its design.

Such witnesses to the past, once classified, constitute a comprehensive history of the knowledge, art, skill and customs of their time. Only thus does a collection become a source of pleasure, interest and use.

If this work helps its readers towards this end, it will have fulfilled the task envisaged by its authors.

Oriental clockmaker

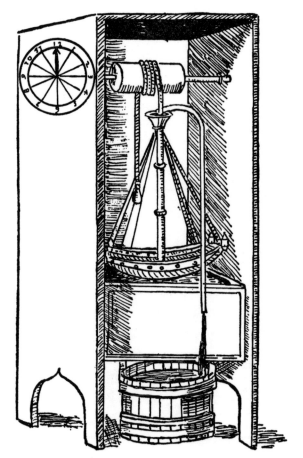

Water-clock (mechanical clepsydra) by Oronce Fine

Monumental Clocks

COMPONENTS AND WORKING

The first mechanical instruments for measuring time were monumental or architectural clocks. They date from the thirteenth century and were responsible for a great improvement in public time-keeping. Whereas the sundial, which had been used as a time-keeper from 500 B.C., only functioned during the hours of daylight and in sunshine, the mechanical clock told the hour of day or night independently of the sun.

The first monumental clock to be invented was composed of the same parts that are used in every mechanical clock today:

(1) A source of driving power.
(2) A train of wheels for carrying the motive power and the movement to the next part and at the same time for reducing the tension of the driving force and for driving the movable parts of the face.
(3) An escapement for allowing the systematic escape of power to the next component part.
(4) An oscillator providing, by means of its regular and intermittent alternating movement, a unit of time that serves as a base for measuring.
(5) A system of reading the measured time.
(6) A winding device for recharging the motive power.

The plan below shows the order in which these six parts were placed in the metal casing of the clock.

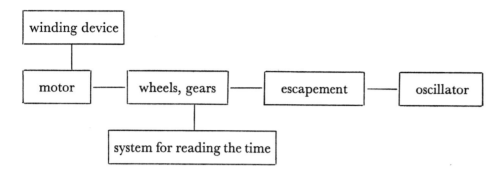

The source of energy came from a weight, usually a huge stone, hanging on the end of a rope wound round a wooden shaft. The train of wheels was originally composed of two large driving wheels and two much smaller driving wheels, known as *pinions*. The first driving wheel, carried on the axis of the cylinder of the motor, was impelled by means of a ratchet-wheel as the weight descended.

The escapement consisted of a large toothed wheel and two pallets borne on the axis of the oscillator, that is the verge. The foliot oscillator has been described in the foreword, to which reference should be made. It is useful to add that the period of oscillation corresponds to a complete cycle of the movement, that is to the amount of time separating two consecutive passages of the foliot past the same point and moving in the same direction. The oscillation consists of two alternating movements, one in which the foliot turns one way, and the other when it is reversed.

The system of reading the time measured was either on a disc graduated into hours, which turned beneath a fixed needle carried on the casing, or by a moving needle borne by the axis of the second driving-wheel of the gear-wheels, which turned round a graduated fixed face.

The winding mechanism was composed of a pinion turned by a handle, pulling against the weights on the cylinder of the drive. This mechanism worked like a winch and served to raise the weight when the cord had nearly run out. While this was being done the ratchet-wheels allowed the cylinder to run freely without engaging the first of the gear-wheels.

With the exception of the escapement and the foliot oscillator, all these parts were already known and used on clepsydras and other mechanical constructions from classical times. It was the scholars of the Schools of Alexandria who had first postulated the basic principles of geometry and mechanics. The most outstanding were Euclid (306–283 B.C.) and the geometrician Archimedes (287–212 B.C.), an extraordinary mechanical genius. Archimedes wrote a treatise on levers, and invented the toothed wheel, the work-screw

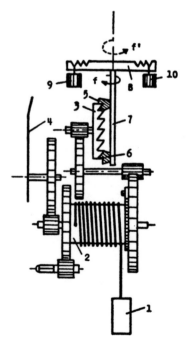

Diagram of the works of a primitive clock

and the pulley-block. Another Alexandrian, Ctesibios (third century B.C.) perfected the clepsydra by adding ratchet-wheels and a dial with hour-marks on a cylinder turned beneath a fixed pointer by a cord round its body.

This mechanical clepsydra is an important stage which was not passed till the thirteenth century A.D., when the first monumental clocks were made.

The basic principle of the construction of the first clock was in fact quite new. It consisted of the building of a machine capable of maintaining the movement of an oscillator for several days, of counting and adding together the periods of oscillation and of telling the time. It was a brilliant invention which could not have been achieved without the two new parts already mentioned. Both are far more advanced than any that had gone before. The name of the inventor is unknown, but since these clocks appeared towards the end of the Middle Ages they should be regarded as an important step forward in the progress of mechanical science during the long medieval period.

The successive impulses given by the pointed teeth of the crown-wheel against the surface of the pallets on the verge assure and maintain the oscillating movement of the foliot. Nothing would stop the driving-weights from falling, nor the wheels from freely turning, if the pallets of the balance did not periodically arrest their movement. As they pass through the highest point of their trajectory, the teeth of the crown-wheel come into contact with the upper pallet of the balance and at their lowest meet the lower pallet of the balance. These two pallets are so shaped that they engage alternately between the teeth of the wheel.

When the upper pallet is pushed by the tooth of the wheel, the foliot and its weights, driven by the verge, turn in the same direction, describing an arc in a horizontal plane. Then the foliot is slowed down and stopped in its movement by the lower pallet, which has passed between two of the lower teeth on the wheel and has come into contact with the point of one of these teeth. Thus a slight slowing-down of the wheel is achieved. Then the pallet is pushed again by the wheel, causing a reverse movement of the foliot. The escapement goes on working in this way until the energy from the drive is exhausted.

To sum up, when one of the teeth has impelled the upper pallet, contact between them is lost. At that moment the lower pallet of the balance encounters a tooth at the base of the wheel giving another impulse, followed by a hesitation in the wheel impelled by the pallet while the arc of oscillation of the foliot is completed, and then a change in the direction of the rotation of the foliot caused by the impulse of the wheel against this same pallet. The lower tooth is freed in turn and a similar action—hesitation, then impulse—is produced by the movement between the wheel and the upper pallet.

It will be seen that during every oscillation the foliot is moved successively by a movement of acceleration followed by a hesitation, and that the pallets

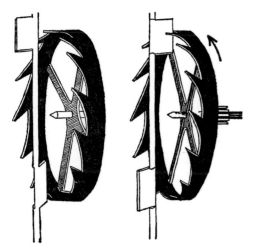

Verge escapement

are almost continuously in contact with the balance-wheel. In these conditions the oscillations of the foliot are far from being free, but are continually and firmly checked by the escapement.

Although it had many defects the verge escapement had admirable qualities: it was exceptionally strong and almost impervious to wear, and as long as the moving parts were kept well oiled they never caused the clock to stop.

It should also be noted that, in order to make the oscillator as free and durable as possible, the upper end of the verge was suspended by a fine, supple cord, so that the range of the pivot at the lower end of the verge was maintained at a small height above the fixed piece which was pierced with a hole and which served as its only guide.

Until the eighteenth century the gearing of clock wheels was crude, and the movement very irregular in consequence. This is the reason for the strong variations in the impulses given to the foliot-balance despite the steadiness of the drive. The real imperfections in these three principal parts, gear-wheels, escapement and verge, seriously upset the period of the foliot. The unit of time it was supposed to supply varied considerably and consequently the measurement of time was faulty. The error of monumental clocks could be as much as half to one hour a day despite the adjustment made possible by moving the regulators along the horizontal bar. Thus the clockmaker had to set them right at frequent intervals, using a sundial as a regulator, and as we shall see below, the sundial itself was a very inaccurate time-measuring instrument. These monumental foliot clocks, ranging from one and a half to two square meters in size, were made of wrought iron in large numbers by clockmakers who must also have been skilled blacksmiths. The clocks were excessively strong and many of them worked for centuries. Nowadays they are very rare and much sought by collectors. During the eighteenth century many of these clocks were converted to a pendulum drive.

The design of the foliot verge escapement in monumental clocks touches on ideas of kinetic and dynamic mechanics which were certainly far beyond the knowledge of a skilled craftsman of the period. This first mechanical instrument for measuring time must therefore be regarded as a collaboration between the scholars, or engineers, as they would be called today, who invented the two original parts to go with others already known, and the clockmaker-blacksmiths who realized their designs.

The close collaboration between the scholars and the skilled craftsmen is a fundamental characteristic recurring throughout the history of clock-making. If it exists in other industries and human activities there are few instances where such close, constant and indispensable collaboration are present.

When astronomical calculations and then automata were added to monumental clocks, the influence of scholars increased as did the demands on the craftsman's skill. Several of these men, as we shall see, became in their turn extraordinarily skilful clock-builders and scholars.

At the same time the finest cabinet-makers, painters, bronze-casters and other artists were called upon to make their contribution to the building of the magnificent monumental clocks of the early Renaissance. Even today they are still the finest witness to the scientific, technical and artistic progress of that period, as well as to the economic development and wealth of many European cities.

CLOCKS WITH BELLS AND AUTOMATA

In the Middle Ages cathedrals and churches told the hours with hand-bells —prime, terce, sext, none, vespers, compline at nine in the evening and so on till mattins at midnight. These canonical hours were marked by burning candles, oil-clocks, clepsydras, sundials or astrolabes.

In the fourteenth century, as mechanical inventions progressed, a method was devized of connecting to the clock a special train of wheels which caused a hammer to strike bells. This train of wheels worked, like the clock, by a weight, and consisted of two large driving wheels and two pinions. A large cam, called the count-wheel, was worked by means of an interior set of gear-teeth from a pinion fixed to one end of the axis of the drive, and carried on its periphery twelve hollow sectors of different lengths to control the number of strokes. The release of the bell-system was controlled by a system of levers worked by a pin mounted on the cylinder of the second wheel in the hourly wheel-train. The ringing gears were thus set free and began to turn at a speed held steady by a fly-wheel with small vanes called the regulator which was carried on the axis of the last pinion. The hammer was worked by a lever, itself raised and allowed to fall by lifting-pins arranged regularly round the rim of the second wheel in the bell-gear. When the halves and quarters were sounded as well as the hours, the ringing mechanism became more complicated.

The addition of other mechanical systems similar to those of the bells resulted in the development of automata to adorn the more complicated monumental clocks. Varying with the degree of elaboration of their movements, these constructions consisted, apart from a weight-driven motor, of one or two trains of wheels, combined with a very varied system of cams, levers and gear-wheels.

The skilful blacksmiths who made the clocks usually built them on the spot. A master clockmaker was helped by a team of assistants and apprentices and this team travelled from town to town, because at first only towns were rich enough to acquire such priceless instruments, though occasionally they were made for monasteries.

It is interesting to note that the wheel-rims of these clocks were made from a single piece of iron forged together with a strong crosspiece instead of spokes. The cogs were measured by hand with the aid of a pair of compasses, as shown by the dividing point on every tooth. They were then cut with a saw and finished with a file. Skilled modern smiths have expressed their amazement at the sureness of hand, beauty of line and perfect mechanical accuracy of pieces made so long ago. It is rare that a master directing such work ever aspired to a signature. The most one ever finds, hidden away in a corner, will be a small stamped seal, insufficient evidence to help in tracing the provenance of the clock.

Clock-jacks on the cathedral at Dijon

HISTORICAL OUTLINE

Although many books have been written on monumental clocks authors differ on the dates when the clocks were built. The only known clocks dating from the thirteenth century were, however, built in England and France. The following are recorded:

1284 The cathedral clock at Exeter.
1286 The cathedral clock in St. Paul's London.
1292 The cathedral clock at Canterbury.
     The cathedral clock at Sens repaired in 1319.

During the fourteenth century numbers grew fairly rapidly and after that date they are also found in Germany and Italy. The work by Tardy, *Du Gnomon à la Montre (From Gnomon to watch)* gives a list of seventy-three clocks, mostly installed in bell-towers, but occasionally found elsewhere, as for instance the ones at Caen in Normandy, in Dover Castle and in the town hall at Bologna.

Basing my researches on the most important and accurate work, *Les horloges astronomiques et monumentales les plus remarquables de l'Antiquité à nos jours* written by Alfred Ungerer and revised by the author in 1931 at Strasbourg, I have drawn up the following list:

FOURTEENTH CENTURY

France

1300–1325 Clock with a carillon in Beauvais cathedral, built by the Italian Canon Etienne Musique.
1313 Cathedral clock at Nevers.
1314 Clock on the bridge of the city of Caen.
1352–4 The first astronomical clock with automata built inside Strasbourg cathedral.
1370 Clock with a ring of bells in the square tower of the Palais de Justice in Paris, built by Henri le Vic.
1370 Clock in the Abbey of Cluny.
1382 Clock in the cathedral of Notre-Dame in Dijon, first installed at Courtrai in Belgium. An automaton was added in 1500.
1383 Astronomical clock in the cathedral of St.-Jean in Lyons.

1392　First clock in the cathedral at Chartres.

1398　Clock with a ring of five bells for the hours and the quarters, known as *Le gros horloge* in the belfry at Rouen.

　　　Fourteenth century: Clock with bells, phases of the moon and automata in Rheims cathedral.

England

1317　Astronomical clock in the church at Ottery Saint Mary, Devonshire.

1320　Clock in Peterborough cathedral.

1327　Astronomical clock, showing the ebb and flow of the tide in St. Alban's Abbey constructed by Richard of Wallingford.

1340　Astronomical clock built for the church at Ottery St. Mary, and constructed by John de Grandisson, Bishop of Exeter.

1386　Clock with a ring of bells for the hours in the Minster at Wimborne in Dorset.

1386　Clock striking the hours at Salisbury cathedral.

1392　Clock striking the hours and quarters at Wells cathedral.

Germany

1361　First clock made for the church of Our Lady in Nuremberg and replaced in 1509 by a clock with automata.

Italy

1303　Clock in the campanile of St. Eustorgio in Milan.

1344　Clock on tower of Carrara palace, Padua, designed by Jacopo de Dondi.

Belgium

1372　Clock in Malines cathedral replaced in 1560 by a clock with four faces and a carillon of forty-five bells built by Pierre Engels.

Sweden

1380　Astronomical clock with automata built for Lund cathedral.

Switzerland

1365   Clock in Basle cathedral built by Heinrich Halder.
1368   Clock in the church of St. Peter in Zurich.

FIFTEENTH CENTURY

France

1400   Clock with automata in the Hôtel de Ville at Compiègne.
1407   Second clock for the cathedral tower of Chartres.
1411   Astronomical clock striking the hours and the quarters of the Tour Gaillarde at Auxerre.
1417   Clock in Avignon cathedral.
1423   Astronomical and striking clock in Bourges cathedral built by Canon Jean Fusoris.

England

1480   Clock in Exeter cathedral, attributed to Peter Lightfoot.

Germany

1400   Astronomical striking clock with automata in the church of St. Mary, Lübeck.
1408   Astronomical clock striking the hours and the quarters and with automata made for Münster cathedral and built by J. Lange.
1470   Astronomical clock made for the church of St. Mary, Danzig, by Duringer.
        Fifteenth century: the astronomical striking clock with automata on the town hall in Jena.

Italy

1434   Clock of the Palazza del Capitano at Padua built by Giovanni della Caldiere.

1473   Clock in Mantua cathedral.

1499   Astronomical striking clock with automata in the Piazza San Marco, Venice, built by J. P. Raineri and his son, Carlo.

Belgium

Fifteenth century: clock with automaton called *Jean de Nivelles*, first built in the town hall and then moved to the collegiate church of Nivelles.

Austria

1432   Astronomical clock with automata and a carillon of sixteen bells on the town hall at Olmutz, built by Anton Pohl.

Czechoslovakia

1490   Astronomical clock with automata in the town hall at Prague built by Hanus.

Switzerland

1452   Clock with a jack striking the hours on the Tour Rouge at Soleure, built by H. Meckling and replaced in 1543 by a similar clock built by Laurent Liechti and finished by Joachim Habrecht.

1480   Astronomical striking clock on the belfry of the town hall in Zug. It was replaced in 1570 by a new astronomical clock constructed by W. Müller.

SIXTEENTH CENTURY

France

1500   Clock with a carillon and automata on Le Mans cathedral.

Jack with a red beard on the clock of the Red Tower at Soleure

1512 Clock with two automatic figures representing Moors on the town hall at Cambrai and built by Jean Pureur.

1520 Clock on the town hall at Calais.

1554 Clock on the gateway of the château at Anet, built by Mathurin Benoist.

1558 Clock on St. Omer cathedral built by Pierre Engueran.

1571–4 Second astronomical clock, known as that of Dasypodius, on Strasbourg cathedral constructed by Isaac Habrecht.

1577 Clock with automata, striking the hours and the quarters on Clermont Ferrand cathedral.

England

1540 Astronomical clock striking the hours and the quarters at the Palace of Hampton Court.

1558 Clock with automata striking the hours and the quarters in the church of St. Mary at Rye.

Germany

1505 Clock on the town hall at Ochsenfurt.

1525 Astronomical clock with automata on the town hall at Heilbronn, built by Hans Paulus and finished in 1580 by Isaac Habrecht.

1543 Clock on the church of St. Mary at Wismar, built by Michael Saygher.

1549 Clock on the town hall at Ulm replaced in 1580 by an astronomical clock with a ring of bells built by Isaac Habrecht.

1578 Astronomical clock with automata in the cathedral of Osnabrück, built by the priest Jost Bodecker.

Italy

1546 Astronomical clock with two automata striking the hours in a palace in the Piazza della Loggia at Brescia.

Sixteenth century: Clock in the Vatican at Rome ordered from Isaac Habrecht by Pope Sixtus V. The movement is in the British Museum.

Denmark

Sixteenth century: clock in Rosenborg castle, Copenhagen.

Clock by Hans of Jena, mid 16th century

Switzerland

1525 Astronomical clock with automata and a jack in the clock tower in Berne built by Caspar Brunner.

1543 Second astronomical clock with automata and a jack in the Tour Rouge at Soleure, built by Laurent Liechti.

1570 Second astronomical clock in the belfry of the town hall of Zug built by W. Müller.

1564 Astronomical clock striking the hours at Schaffhausen, built by Joachim Habrecht.

Development of the Hour Mechanism in Clocks

No major improvement emerged in clock movements until the mid seventeenth century. In 1602 the Italian scholar Galileo Galilei (1584-1642) discovered the laws and properties of the pendulum, which he thought could be applied to the control of fixed measuring instruments. However, it was not until 1657 that Salomon Coster, a clockmaker from the Hague, constructed the first pendulum clock following the designs and instructions of Christian Huygens, the great Dutch master of physics, geometry and astronomy (1629-1695). It was not a monumental clock but a small weight-driven chamber clock.

The new system of oscillation brought such an immediate improvement in the measurement of time that it was soon generally adopted for every kind of clock. But the pendulum, although a great step towards the achievement of an invariable unit, was liable to malfunction because of the irregularities in the escapement. Clockmakers therefore now turned their attention to the design of the escapement.

The anchor escapement was invented in England about 1670 by Joseph Knibb or William Clement. This consists of two pieces, a wheel with pointed teeth and an anchor carrying, at an equal distance from its axis, two pallets of tempered steel. These pallets, curved in shape, form an obstruction catching the teeth of the wheel in succession as they escape form the action of the other pallet. At their lower end they are curved so as to give an impulse to the same points as they move, transmitting to the anchor the force supplied by the drive and carried through the wheels. A metal tube ending in a small fork between the teeth of which the stem of the pendulum passes is firmly fixed to the axis of the anchor, ensuring steady oscillations. The suspension of the pendulum which was at first designed like a simple knife was corrected by Huygens's principle, by incorporating a short flexible blade which made the period of the oscillations less dependent on their size. These alterations to the monumental clock brought so great an improvement in precision that clocks became accurate to within half a minute per day.

The pin-wheel escapement invented by Amant in France in 1730 and improved by Lepaute, also in France, in 1753, consists of a wheels with a series of cylindrical steel pins on the rim attached parallel to the axis. These pins are hooked on alternately by a double "comma" attached to the pendulum. This simple yet robust device was soon applied to a large number of monumental wheel clocks in which the foliot was replaced by a pendulum. It was not a very satisfactory mechanism until the pins were made of very hard steel and the pallets of gem stones.

The dead-beat escapement for pendulum clocks, which was invented by the English clockmaker George Graham (1673-1751), gave even better results. This consists of two pieces, a wheel with pointed teeth and an anchor carrying, at an equal distance from its axis, two pallets of tempered steel. These pallets, curved in shape, form an obstruction catching the teeth of the wheel in succession as they escape from the action of the other pallet. At their lower end they are curved so as to give an impulse to the same points as they move, transmitting to the anchor the force supplied by the drive and carried through the wheels. A metal tube ending in a small fork between the teeth of which the stem of the pendulum passes is firmly fixed to the axis of the anchor, ensuring steady oscillations. The suspension of the pendulum, which was a first designed like a simple knife, was corrected by Huygens's principle, by incorporating a short flexible blade which made the period of the oscillations less dependent on their size. These alterations of the monumental clock brough so great an improvement in precision that clocks became accurate to within half a minute per day.

For a long time wrought-iron was still used for the manufacture of the frame for the movement and the levers but the other parts were affected by new processes resulting from the use of different machine tools. Lathes, milling-cutters, drills, machines for dividing and cutting the teeth on the wheels all brought mechanization and, as a result, simplification of much of this work.

DESCRIPTION OF THE THREE MONUMENTAL CLOCKS SHOWN IN THE ILLUSTRATIONS

The Town Hall Clock, Prague

The town hall of the city of Prague has two monumental clocks. One is an astronomical clock which was built in 1486 into the tower jutting out against one of the façades of the building. The dials and mechanical parts are protected by a roof in the form of a dais. Seen from below the parts of the clock are, at the base a calendar; halfway up, an astronomical dial and above that again, the automata (Pl. 1).

The calendar is a dial 2·8 meters in diameter with the arms of the city in the center, whilst the days, dates, ecclesiastical dates, the names of the saints and the fixed festivals are all shown round the rim. An angel on the left with a large sword used to indicate the date with a sceptre, but now only its index finger remains. Three figures of scholars stand beside the angel on the right side of the calendar, which is decorated with painted medallions, the twelve smallest of which represent the signs of the Zodiac. The astronomical dial placed above it measures 3.1 meters in diameter. It is interesting as it still shows the Bohemian method of measuring time used in Prague till 1582.

The center of the dial has the northern hemisphere of the earth painted on it and the pointers to solar, lunar and sidereal time perform their revolutions round it. Below the center is a round surface painted green, the edge of which represents the horizon at Prague. This is encircled by a pink band representing twilight and dawn. The upper part of the dial, azure blue in color, represents the hours of daylight, the lower part the hours of night. The bottom is divided into two series of Roman numerals from I to XII, representing the hours. The part of the dial corresponding to the daylight hours is subdivided into twelve hourly time-zones by gilt arcs in relief. This divides the path of the sun into twelve parts indicated by number, corresponding to the planetary or Babylonian hours used in the Middle Ages.

Sidereal time is indicated by a pointer ending in a silver star. The twelve signs of the Zodiac, placed eccentrically on the dial, are to be seen on the circle of the ecliptic.

The solar hand, which turns once in twenty-four hours, has a gilt hand at its tip showing the Bohemian hours on the outer band, and is, furthermore, furnished with a flaming sun which slides radially along the stem of the pointer so that it remains within the ecliptic.

The apparent movement of the moon is represented in a way analogous to a lunar globe, half black and half silver, turning once in a lunar day

Abbreviations used in the captions:

D. = Diameter   W. = Width
H. = Height   T. = Thickness
        L. = Length

Where three dimensions are given, height precedes width and thickness.

Pl. 1   The Town Hall Clock, Prague. This clock was constructed by Hanus in 1490 and comprises a calendar on the lower part, an astronomical clock flanked by several automata in the central part with animated figures, and rows of apostles and a cock.

Pl. 2   Monumental clock in the Piazza San Marco, Venice. Built in 1499 by J. P. Raineri and his son Carlo, the clock comprises a large astronomical dial surmounted by a statue with automata. On the terrace surmounting the tower two male figures known as the Mori strike the hours on a large bell.

1

2

3

(24 hours 51 minutes) and sliding along the lunar needle. This movement apart, the lunar globe describes a complete rotation in 29 days, 12 hours, 16 minutes around its axis, to represent the phases of the moon.

The astronomical dial is flanked by four wooden figures, each of them one meter in height, disposed two on the right and two on the left. On the right are Death and Envy. Death holds a sandglass in his left hand and with his right tolls the bell of the campanile. The second pair is Vanity, with a glass in her hand and Avarice, holding a purse and a cane.

On every hour of daylight figures of the Apostles pass between the two windows above the great dials, while the small bell rings in the campanile. At this sound the figure of Death nods its head and invites the three other characters to follow; they, however, shake their heads and Avarice lifts the cane and purse. As the two windows from which the Apostles emerge open, Death turns the hour-glass. At the end of the movement the cock perched above the windows crows and flaps his wings. His song is produced by three reed instruments through which air is forced by pressure. After the cock has crowed the clock strikes the Bohemian hours on a cymbal in the form of a skull-cap hanging in the campanile above the clock.

On top of the façade is a bust representing the Angel of Christ's Agony in the Garden.

The Monumental Clock in the Piazza San Marco, Venice

In the Piazza San Marco there is a private house built over a public way and furnished with a tower. The façade of this tower is divided into three large panels, of which the lowest is entirely occupied by an astronomical dial, 4·5 meters in diameter and composed of three concentric rings. The external band is part of the masonry and is painted with Roman numerals from I to XXIV. Within this circle of the hours a disc turns, bearing the twelve signs of the Zodiac and completing a sidereal day in one revolution. An hourly disc in the shape of a human face with an aureole, revolves once in twenty-four hours and represents the apparent movement of the sun. It passes through the twelve signs of the Zodiac in one year and its indicator, extending to the hourly zone, marks the hours. In the central part the moon and the five planets, represented by small gilt globes, turn round the earthly hemisphere according to the periods determined by Ptolemy: Mercury in 88 days, Venus in 224 days, Mars in 688 days, Saturn in three years and Jupiter in twelve years. A panel above the dials shows the Virgin seated in a niche with the Infant Christ on her knee, flanked by the two doorways whence the Three Kings emerge, passing in front of the Virgin and returning by the other door (Pl. 2).

Pl. 3 Monumental clock on the Zeitglockenturm at Berne. Constructed between 1525 and 1530 by Caspar Brunner, it has a dial on the two principal faces of the tower. Halfway up one of these façades is an astronomical dial with a niche and several different automata. A jack is in the lantern forming part of the steeple

31

At the top of the tower above the palisade there hangs a huge bell with two jacks each 2·7 meters in height, that strike the hour alternately. These bronze figures clad in simple goatskins are known as the *Mori*. The hammers are moved by a rotary, angular movement in the torso of the jacks.

The present clock has seen many mechanical changes.

The Clock on the Zeitglockenturm, Berne

The clock tower stands in the center of the modern town, not very far from the cathedral. It formed part of the ramparts of the old city and protected the western gate.

At the top of the two principal façades of the tower is a large dial, 5 meters across, with two hands indicating the hours and the minutes (Pl. 3).

On the front of the tower just above the city gate, is an astronomical dial, 2·5 meters in diameter, on which a solar pointer indicates the hours and a lunar pointer the apparent movement of the moon and its phases. A stellar circle with the signs of the Zodiac, the months and the 365 days of the year makes one turn in a sidereal day so as to show the relative positions of the sun and moon on the ecliptic, and also the eclipses. Above the astronomical dial the days of the week appear through an opening in the wall.

To the right of the astronomical dial is a niche with a set of automata functioning every hour; a cock crows and flaps its wings, a buffoon strikes the hours on two bells, a king waves his scepter and a group of bears—the symbol of the city—dances.

In the lantern, halfway up the steeple hang two bells which sound the hours and the quarters; a jack of about 2·5 meters in height in the form of an armed warrior is placed at one side making as if to strike the hours with a hammer.

CONCLUSIONS

Man has always been deeply preoccupied by measurement of time, but solar, lunar and sidereal days are the smallest units of time offered by nature and they are much too large for practical requirements. The true solar day, which alone constitutes a manageable unit, suffers from the grave inconvenience of being variable in length.

Sundials, although they have been used since remote antiquity to mark the daily path of the sun and by means of fixed points to follow its movement across the sky were useless at night and in cloudy weather.

To overcome these shortcomings recourse had to be made to methods that relied on more regular physical phenomena working artificially. The monumental clock solved this problem, a solution that remained, however, far from perfect from the end of the thirteenth to the second half of the seventeenth century because the oscillating period of the foliot, although it had the great advantage of being a very small fraction of the solar day and of being independent of a clear sky, was susceptible to considerable variation. The appearance of the oscillator with a pendulum, by allowing precise measurement of time in any place and at any hour of day or night, really marked the start of a new era for mankind in social as well as scientific environment.

The monumental clock made a great contribution to the world of art. The three examples described here make one realize that the builders of these instruments were just as preoccupied with the architectural and esthetic aspects as the mechanical and scientific. Those great clocks furnished with hourly and astronomical dials, automata and bells played their part in giving the splendid cathedrals, town halls and palaces of the late Middle Ages and the Renaissance an attraction which even today arouses interest and admiration.

In his preface to Ungerer's book on monumental clocks Camille Flammarion (1842–1925), astronomer and founder of the Astronomical Society of France, says of the cathedral clock at Strasbourg: "What a splendid thing it is! It is living proof of the strength of the human will, and as you study its ingenious mechanism you feel an admiration equal to the experience of sharing the thoughts of Copernicus, Galileo and Kepler as they gazed upon the system of the universe. Invention is close to creation."

Clock of the Samaritaine, Paris, 17th century

The Gothic Clock

In the period after the mid-fourteenth century when the great monumental clocks were being constructed, a fashion for similar but smaller iron clocks spread through all the countries of Western Europe.

Charles V of France, for instance, who died in 1380, ordered from Henri le Vic of Lorraine, the clock called *L'horloge du Palais* in Paris, and also other clocks for his houses, Beauté, Hesdin, Plessis du Parc, Vincennes and Montargis. Charles VI's uncle, the Duc de Berry, had also ordered clocks for the châteaux of Mehun-sur-Yèvres, Nonette and Lusignan.

In an interesting essay published in 1966 *, my co-author Henri Michel describes the clock-building industry in Belgium at the time of the Dukes of Burgundy. "The sons of Jean le Bon were by tradition interested in mechanical curiosities. Charles V was a collector of all kinds of instruments for measuring time, including clocks. Philip the Bold, seeing his nephew, Charles VI, set fire to the Belgian town of Courtrai, seized the opportunity to carry off the clock from the Market Hall with its bell-tower and automata to his capital, Dijon. The third Duke of Burgundy, Philip the Good, seems to have had a great interest in automata; it is said that his banquets in the château de Hesdin were famous for the strange chimeras that walked across the table moving jaws and tails, while Dianas of silver and precious stones drew their bows, to the wonder and amazement of the guests. To be the owner of such objects at that time, perhaps a hundred years after the appearance of the first monumental clocks, was a source of great pride."

After studying the accounts and inventories of the Dukes of Burgundy and the archives in Bruges, Louvain and Mons, Michel cites seven fourteenth-century and five fifteenth-century clocks made in Flanders which he describes, giving the names of their makers. He also discusses the medieval clock on the town hall of Damme, which dates from 1459 and which was made by the Master Clockmaker, Brixus Vleesch of Ypres. As far as can be ascertained this clock, still working today, is the last relic of the flourishing Belgian industry.

The day inevitably came when noblemen, rich monasteries and cities were no longer alone in wanting a clock. Several very skilled craftsmen, in pursuit of the passion for things miniature, started to make smaller iron clocks for interiors such as halls or anterooms, and the fashion soon spread.

The first wall-clocks probably came from Italy, and although still in the Gothic period, were furnished with an alarm and perhaps an hourly chime. The art of making them passed along two distinct routes: one through France, Burgundy and Flanders and the other along the Danube as far as Augsburg, a city which became one of the most important clockmaking centres in the world in the sixteenth century.

At first chamber clocks were the prerogative of noblemen, but later were kept by rich bankers and merchants and the bourgeoisie. The earliest ones were used in monasteries and convents where they told the hours of the office. They may even have been invented by a monk with a talent for clockmaking.

In any case the church was largely responsible for their spread. The first chamber clocks were no more accurate than monumental clocks, but the demands of luxury and the necessity for accuracy gradually brought improvements. It was observed that mechanisms exposed to dust and damp wore out quickly and very often went wrong. So the makers enclosed the movement of chamber-clocks in a box which protected the clock whilst lending itself to decoration. Other improvements appeared in due time. The first clocks had only one hand and sometimes even lacked a dial. Later on a small, independent minute-dial was added to that of the hours. The two concentric hands date from about the same period. These clocks, constructed by skilful locksmiths or armourers, soon followed the example of monumental clocks by the addition of rings of bells and astronomical information, ranging from the simple phases of the moon to a complete astrolabe.

Every Gothic clock has a verge escapement and a foliot with regulators or a ring balance. At first they worked by weights which had to be pulled up two or three times daily. Replacement of the weights by a driving spring did not take place till the late fifteenth century and the fusee, attributed to Leonardo da Vinci (because a sketch of this device was found in his sketchbook), appeared about the same period.

The real improvement in chamber clocks did not, however, come till the second half of the seventeenth century when the foliot oscillator was replaced by a pendulum (the first was in 1657) followed by the replacement of the escapement by a mechanism with no backward movement, but which fulfilled the same function. This was the anchor escapement which has been mentioned

Pl. 4 Iron clocks. Left: *with phases of the moon, dated 1638. H. 45 cm.* Right: *clock with two tones, dated 1643. H. 45 cm. Collection Dr. Gschwind, Basle*

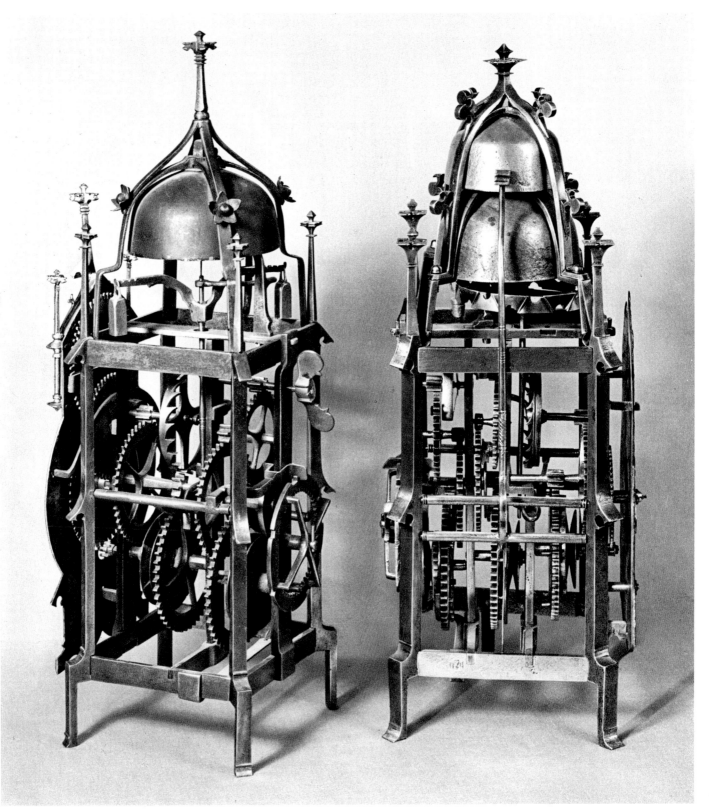

First printed illustration of a mechanical clock by Bertholdus, Basle, 1492

Pl. 5 Iron clock, with carillon, 17th century. H. 75 cm. Through the open door the mechanism can be seen: a drum with studs which control the hammer-levers as they pass. Collection Dr. Gschwind, Basle

above, and was invented by Joseph Knibb or William Clement about 1670. In 1666 a French astronomer, Jean Picard, first observed the variations in temperature of pendulum clocks and in 1726 John Harrison, a famous English clockmaker invented the gridiron pendulum to correct the variations noted by Picard sixty years before. Finally in 1676 two English clockmakers, Barlow and Quare, invented a repeater ringing mechanism for chamber-clocks.

TYPES OF GOTHIC CLOCKS

It is possible to distinguish six types of Gothic clock as they appear chronologically. They are all weight-driven, usually by two weights, except in the case of the last.

(1) Clock with a single iron frame to contain the movement.

(2) Chamber-clock in which the movement, surmounted by the foliot and the ringing mechanism, has an oblong shape.

(3) Chamber-clock of a more refined appearance than the foregoing. Its casing consists of four carefully worked pillars surmounted by an ogival bell-chamber.

(4) An even more luxurious version of the preceding type. It has an hour-dial and several dials giving astronomical information while its ogival bell chamber, decorated with wrought-iron motives, sounds two or even three different notes.

(5) The so-called lantern clock is to be distinguished by its large dial and a semi-circular, rather than ogival, bell-chamber. English and French examples are made of brass.

(6) Portable clock with a spring drive. The body of the clock is oblong with a pediment surmounting its principal face and its two side dials. The whole is surmounted by an ogival bell-chamber.

It is their wrought-iron ornament that gives these Gothic clocks their special character. Spirals, volutes, curling leaves and rosettes, ornamental pediments enclosing plant forms, crockets, grotesques, pinnacles, scrolls and stems, all feature among the decorative motives applied by the skilled ironsmiths who made these clocks. Plates 4 and 5 show three superb examples of this style.

The Renaissance

THE POLITICAL AND ECONOMIC LIFE in the Italian City States provided a fertile soil for the flowering of the Renaissance. Leonardo da Vinci is the personification of its spirit. His astonishing genius explored every field and excelled in everything he undertook, his curiosity about the natural world led him to a profound study of anatomy, botany, geology, mathematics and astronomy. In a sketchbook of more than five thousand pages he made drawings anticipating the great inventions like the helicopter, the submarine, the machine-gun and the car. At the bottom of one page he proudly signed his name: Leonardo da Vinci, pupil of Experience.

INVENTIONS AND DISCOVERIES

Several inventions and discoveries affected the intellectual and artistic movement of the Renaissance which, although born in Italy, spread rapidly all over Europe. The most influential was the discovery of printing with movable type which could be set at will by the compositor. The invention is credited to Johan Gutenberg of Mainz (1400–1467) and, some believe, to Coster van Haarlem.

The spread of books and pamphlets in large numbers made an enormous contribution to the flowering of the arts and sciences. At that time many subjects were being disputed with passionate interest by scholars and literate men. One of the most heated questions at stake was Nicholas Copernicus's

(1473–1543) theory of the solar system. The solar system so hotly debated in the fifteenth and sixteenth centuries was not the one familiar to us. Round a stationary sun the planets turned, describing circles at a constant speed, according to the theory of Aristotle. In order to fit the observed movements of the planets into the theory, Copernicus, like Ptolemy, had been forced to use epicycles; probably his theory was easier because of the central position of the sun, but Kepler declared that Copernicus had explained only Ptolemy, not the universe.

Tycho Brahe's system was less revolutionary; in his scheme the planets circled the sun, the whole being centred on the immobile earth.

The system accepted today, first postulated by the German astronomer, Johannes Kepler (1571–1630) retained the central position of the sun whilst discarding the Aristotelian circular trajectory and constant speed of the planets.

He demonstrated that they described ellipses with variable speeds. The German scientist formulated Kepler's Law, whence Newton was able to deduce the theory of gravity, although even great men of his day could scarce follow his swift flight of thought.

Clock workshop in south Germany ; print by Jost Ammann, 1568

At the same time Christopher Columbus (1436–1506), a native of Genoa, discovered the New World (Central America), the Portuguese navigator, Vasco de Gama (1469–1524) sailed round the Cape of Good Hope to India and Ferdinand de Magellan (1470–1521) passed from the Atlantic to the Pacific Ocean through the Straits which now bear his name at the southernmost tip of America and Tierra del Fuego.

RENAISSANCE CLOCKS

The late Middle Ages was a very inventive period for mechanical clocks, making great strides in the scientific, technical and artistic fields. The advance from the monumental to the chamber-clock, from the clock responsible for telling the time to the public, to the family clock, is the first step in the swift and artistic development of the following years. Clock movements became smaller and smaller, portable clocks were designed of a different type; then came the travelling clock and at last, at the beginning of the sixteenth century, the watch.

DIFFERENT TYPES OF RENAISSANCE CLOCKS

The Gothic clocks and tower-clocks came first. The latter were clearly inspired by monumental clocks, for they are in fact miniature versions of them, small enough to be placed on a chimney piece or table.

The case was gilded brass and can be distinguished from Gothic clocks by a total absence of wrought iron. The Gothic clock was wrought by a smith but this was not the case with the tower-clock, because although the frame and parts of the movement were still made of iron, the rest was brass or copper. They give the impression of being made, not so much by blacksmiths, armourers or iron workers specializing in clock movements, as by skilled craftsmen who had created a new profession, the clockmaker proper—with his own methods of working and more than likely his own tools as well.

One very important invention in the first quarter of the fifteenth century brought an immense improvement to clocks. The name of its author is lost.

This was the spring-driven motor to replace the older weights. Henceforward the driving-gear became an accumulator of energy capable of storing the motive power to ensure the clock's movement for a period of about eight to fifteen days.

The spring is a simple, long, thin, tempered steel blade which is rolled, by alternate heating and cooling, onto a cylinder, the axis of which carries the first wheel in the train.

The external end of the spring is attached to a fixed point on the framework, whilst the internal end is attached to the cylinder. When the clock is wound, by means of a key hollowed into a square, the spring tightens round the cylinder and is subjected to pressure which accumulates energy.

When the clock is set in motion the spring begins to uncoil and so to move the cylinder, which also turns the first wheel of the gearing. A system of ratchet-wheels enables the cylinder to be wound on its axis, and at the same time to move independently of it when the clock is going.

The motor-driven spring brought two great advantages. On the one hand a much less clumsy mechanism, and on the other ease of movement. Its motor was no longer dependent on weights and the clock could then be placed anywhere and be quite portable, as we shall see with the later carriage-clock.

One of the earliest spring-driven clocks belonged to the Dukes of Burgundy and is now in the Germanisches Nationalmuseum in Nuremberg. The clock is in gilded copper and the case, which is highly decorated and measures about 40 cm. is in the shape of a Gothic cathedral with two towers surmounted by lions, one of which bears the arms of Philip the Good (1398–1467) and the other the torch of Burgundy, the emblem of the Order of the Golden Fleece, created by Philip the Good in 1429. Four hounds support the base.

Plates 6, 7, 8 and 9 are all clocks of this kind. Some of them have elaborate additions: hourly and quarterly chimes, alarms, automata, astronomical calendars and even astrolabes, but this was only to be expected because many fifteenth-century monumental clocks also had these elaborations.

Fantasy in Spring-driven Clocks

Rare types of this kind of clock will be found illustrated in plates 10–13. The little clock with the arms of Marie de Médicis which also bears the signature of Nicholas Lemaindre of Blois and the date 1619 is a particularly remarkable model. So is the hexagonal table clock with an astrolable signed Jean Naze illustrated in pl. 12. Another type made both at Augsburg and Strasbourg is illustrated in pls. 15 and 17, whereas nos 18–22 and color plate I are all of more or less bizarre shape, though not all have automata. These clocks give a

Pl. 6   Octagonal table clock in engraved copper, pierced and gilt. Ornament of palm leaves and rosettes. The dancer on the top shows the quarters; the clock strikes the hour and has an alarm. D. 12, H. 17 cm. Private Collection, Paris

Pl. 7   Rectangular table clock in gilt copper, with engraved silver dial. Late 16th century. It strikes the hours and quarters and has an alarm. 25 × 12 × 12 cm. Private Collection, Paris

Pl. 8   Double faced table clock, mid 17th century. Perhaps made in Strasbourg. Gilt copper, complicated iron movement, five winders. One face shows the hour, phases of the moon, date, annual feasts; the other face has an astrolabe. The case is contained within very simple pillars without ornament. A balustrade and obelisks surround the pierced roof. The whole is placed on an ogee base engraved with scrolls. 43 × 33 × 23 cm. Private Collection, Paris

Pl. 9   Detail of the astrolabe in Pl. 8. The figures and letters on the astrolabe are engraved, not punched

Pls. 10 & 11 Clock with the arms of Marie de Medici by Nicolas Lemaindre, Blois. Signed and dated 1619. N. Lemaindre was clockmaker to the Duke of Orléans and to Louis XIV. He is well known for his clockcases made of rock crystal (10), D. 11, H.19 cm. View of same clock from below: gilt copper with ornament in blued steel (11). Private Collection

Pl. 12   Hexagonal table clock by Jean Naze. Third quarter of the 16th century. The upper part contains an astrolabe giving the position of the sun, the moon and its phases, and of the planets. Gilt copper, chiselled with damascened doors and Renaissance base and colums. Leather hexagonal case of the period. D. of the circle containing the hexagon 8 cm, H. 17 cm. Musée du Petit Palais, Dutuit Collection, Paris

Pl. 13   Astronomical clock by Nicolas Feau à Mercelle (Marseilles), clockmaker to Henrietta Maria, sister of Louis XIII who was married in 1625 to Charles I of England. 17 × 11 × 11 cm. Musée du Petit Palais, Dutuit Collection, Paris

Pl. 14   View of the upper plate of the same clock and of the astrolabe carrying the sun on the ecliptic, and a pivoting arm to show the phases of the moon. Punched letters and figures

6

7

8

9

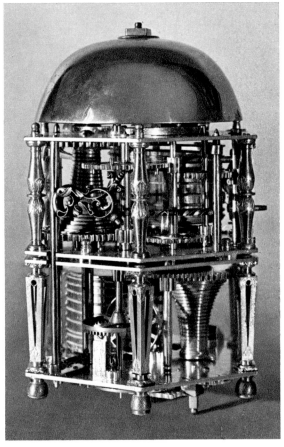

10

11

12

13

14

15

16

17

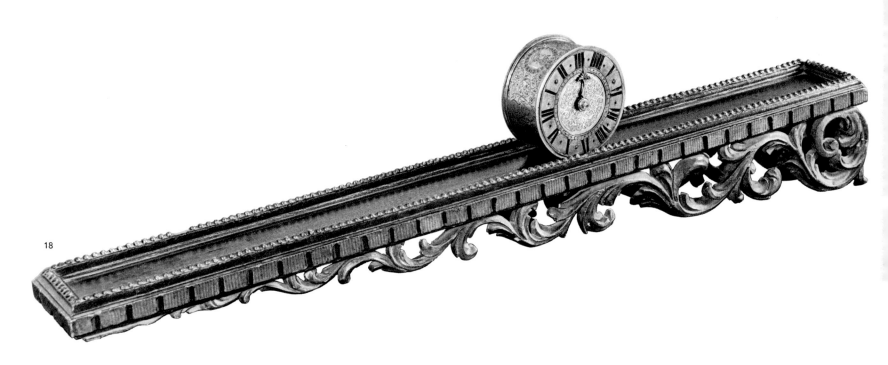

18

20

21

22

good idea of the immense variety made at the time; the artists who fashioned them were no longer satisfied with a tower-clock in miniature, but combining taste and imagination, set about inventing new forms.

Table Clocks

Table clocks are always finely designed often with very simple forms. Round, square or polygonal, they vary in diameter from about 23 to 10 cm and from 13 to 6 cm in height.

The examples illustrated here in pls. 23–26 are among the finest known, as interesting in their movements as in their decoration. A full description of the round clock shown in plate 23 will give the reader a better idea of the type.

The movement has an escapement and toothed wheel, balance-wheel and a cylindrical spring-case with fusee and cat-gut cord. It has gilt wheels, brass plates and carved pillars. The movement chimes hours and quarters and is provided with an alarm. This clock was probably made for Italy where attention was centered in the sixteenth century on recording the hours from one to six and thus dividing the day into four parts. The hourly division with Roman figures in relief and small ornaments to show the halves and quarters is on the border of the dial. The face is completely covered with vine tendrils, birds and serpents, finely chiselled into the metal. The single hand has the form of a serpent twined round a vine-stock and its central pin is a rosette encircled by vine leaves.

The box is in gilded bronze with finely chased and chiselled relief decoration. On the base Orpheus plays a viol and Eurydice turns back to Hades, whilst between them stands Cerberus, the three-headed dog. Many kinds of beasts surround this group: cockerel, stag, monkey, ostrich, ram, a bear eating honey, horse, elephant, camel, lion, fox, beaver, snail, slug and fledglings, all against a wooded ground. A large astronomical table surrounded by leafy arabesques is engraved on the base plate.

Wenzel Jamnitzer (1508–1585), who is said to have made this table clock, lived in Nuremberg. He worked for four emperors, the king of France and several princes. Influenced by many artistic currents he skilfully combined them into the most dazzling fantasies to make some of the finest masterpieces of Renaissance goldsmith's work. His creative inspiration was used to enrich the *cabinets de curiosités* and the personal treasure of his noble patrons.

The square table clock in pl. 26 is an outstanding example of scientific, technical and artistic excellence and merits a detailed description.

The iron movement consists of an escapement with crown-wheel and balance, the cylinders have fusee cords of cat-gut to control the hourly chimes

Pl. 15   Double-faced clock, early 17th century. Gilt copper, pierced and engraved with biblical subjects. Mounted on four lions. Fine movement in iron. It has mechanisms for striking the hour, an alarm, shows the days of the month and phases of the moon. Private Collection, Paris

Pl. 16   The same clock as Pl. 15 showing the opposite face.

Pl. 17   Rectangular table clock marked I. F. of Augsburg. Late 16th century. Bronze and copper engraved and gilt, pierced base, striking mechanism on the hour. 13 × 20 × 9 cm. Private Collection, Paris

Pl. 18   Clock made about 1660. Iron hands on both faces. This clock is described in the "Recueil d'ouvrages curieux de Mathématiques et de Mécanique" of M. Grollier de Servière, written by his grandson Grollier de Sevière, one of the 25 members of the Académie des Sciences et Belles Lettres; published by David Forey, Lyons in 1733. Ramp: 88 cm long, 11 cm wide; clock: D. 11, T. 6 cm; weight 2·61 kg. Nathan Collection, Binningen

Pl. 19   Detail of Pl. 17. Stackfreed, the balance movement controlled by a vertical adjustable horsehair, the shadow of which can be clearly seen on the plate. Private Collection, Paris

Pl. 20   Clock with an automaton. A monkey playing the clown by Carl Schmidt, about 1600. Ebony case with glazed openings. Enamelled silver dials with flowers and birds. Hours are marked from 1-12 and 13-24. The monkey looks in the glass and eats the apple on the hour, whilst the eyes roll perpetually. H. 32 cm. Formerly Percy Webster Collection; Nathan Collection, Binningen

Pl. 21   Clock and automaton, early 17th century. Gilt copper on an ebony base. The elephant rolls its eyes, its tail forms the balance, and in the case below the elephant, a menagerie moves on the hour. Charliat Collection, Paris

Pl. 22   Clock with automaton, made in Nuremberg, chiselled and gilt copper with six iron movements. The eyes of the ostrich flaps perpetually. On the hour the ostrich waves its wings and opens its beak; on the quarters the bear turns its head and for the alarm it beats the drum. 50 × 39 × 52 cm. J. Fremersdorf Collection, Lucerne

and the ringing mechanism. The clock has an alarm and an hourly and quarterly chime on two notes. The movement is housed between two large iron plates linked by four turned pillars. The astrolabe occupies the whole of the centre of the dial and is worked by planetary sets of gears linked to the lateral dials by several sets of gears and by articulations to the cardan shaft.

The dial with the astrolabe tells solar and lunar time whilst a hand in the shape of a dragon indicates solar and lunar eclipses. The hour-dial has the numerals 1-12 twice in Roman numerals. A calendar showing all the saints'-days encloses the whole circle containing the hour-dial and the astrolabe.

Eight dials, some in enamelled silver, others in pierced and chiselled copper, are arranged in pairs on the four lateral faces, each angle of which is decorated with pilasters. The dials tell the time, the signs of the Zodiac, exact solar time, the orbit of the moon, the dominical letters throughout the year, the epacts, with a record of the calendar since 1592, and the days of the week represented by Saints.

The case is made of chased and gilded copper. The feet are decorated with fruit and volutes. On the base, astronomical data tell the different dates of four polar heights and there is a list of towns in these latitudes.

The creator of this splendid clock was Jacob Reinhold, a native of Liegnitz in Saxony. He also designed several celestial spheres with clock movements which are signed jointly with Georg Roll. One of these dated 1584, is in the Victoria and Albert Museum in London, the others, dated 1586, are in the Center for Physics and Mathematics in Dresden and the Astronomical Observatory, Naples, respectively. It should also be noted in passing that the Astronomisch-physikalischer Kabinett des Hessischen Landesmuseums in Cassel has a large square table clock very similar to the one we have just described, built by Jost Burgi in 1591. Its rich and ornate casing is the work of Hans Jacob Emck of Cassel.

Monstrance Clocks

Before the close of the Middle Ages goldsmiths were making portable reliquaries, to contain and exhibit small relics. In the sixteenth century clockmakers were inspired to use the same way of displaying their small spring-driven clocks. These were the so-called monstrance clocks of which the finest can be seen in plates 28–30. The one in plate 28 measures 16·5 cm high and its case is carved from a piece of rock crystal 5·7 cm thick. It was made in Augsburg about 1630 by Martin Zoller and is exceptionally lovely.

Pl. I A group of old clocks and watches from a private collection, (see plates 6, 16, 17, 24, 41).

23

24

25

26

28

29

30

30 a

31

32

33

34

36

37

38

39

40

Pl. 31 Clock in the form of a gilt bronze crucifix. Movement by Pfaff (probably Pfaff of Augsburg) worked in the second half of the 17th century. H. 52 cm, W. of cross 15·5 cm. Kugel Collection, Paris

Pl. 32 Cross of black wood by Bury of Paris, the movement signed by Guéroult of Avranches. The body of Christ and the plaques on the base are silver. Above it indicates : the time, the signs of the zodiac, the months, days and below, the date (Jacob Bury, Paris 1686-1722). H. 42 cm, base 12·5 × 12·5 cm. Formerly Collection Anthon Feill ; Nathan Collection, Binningen

Pl. 33 Wall clock with weights. End of the 16th century. Finely engraved and gilt copper. Iron movement, showing the hours, the date, lunar phases; alarm bell. 24 × 10 × 10 cm. Formerly Arquembourg Collection ; Private Collection, Paris

Pl. 34 Table clock. Engraved and pierced gilt copper. H. 24 cm, including the domed lantern. The movement H. 13, T. 8·7 cm. Dial 5 cm. Musée du Petit Palais, Dutuit Collection, Paris

Pl. 35 Clock with clockwork celestial sphere. Copper and gilt brass. D. 11, H. 22 cm. Private Collection, Paris

Pl. 36 Celestial sphere with clockwork movement by Jost Burgi (1552-1632). Conservatoire national des arts et métiers, Paris

Pl. 37 Astronomical clock comprising a case with four dials not shown surmounted by an Atlas carrying a globe. The mechanism is attributed to Ph. Math. Hahn. Overall height 72 cm. D. of the sphere 18 cm. Andrée and Hipola Collection, Madrid

Pl. 38 Bottom of a table clock of the late 16th century, with a solar dial. Iron movement and regulator with weights. D. 11, H. 6 cm. Nathan Collection, Binningen

Pl. 39 Table clock by Volant, Paris, who was made Master in 1612. Gilt brass with engraved allegorical subjects, the upper part pierced and engraved. Brass movement with a verge escapement. Striking mechanism for the hours and original case. D. 17, H. 8 cm. Musée d'Horlogerie, La Chaux-de-Fonds

Pl. 40 Table clock by N. Plantart, a "compagnon" at Blois in 1619. Gilt brass, brass movement and balance wheel escapement. Spiral balance, "à tact" dial. D. 9·3, H. 16 cm. Musée d'Horlogerie, La Chaux-de-Fonds

angled on the vertical axis so that when the globe is properly sited by means of the compass in the base, the axis of the poles is parallel to the earth. Originally it was possible to raise or lower the pole along the line of the meridian to adapt its position to the desired latitude.

The mechanism within the sphere comprises sets of gears for keeping the hours and the chimes. The hours can be read on the two upper drums set above the capital and on a dial on the north Pole. The two drums turn below fixed pointers; one is divided into twelve hours, the other into six parts, subdivided into five periods of five minutes. The dial is divided into two periods of twelve hours and sixty minutes.

The sphere is furnished with the equator, the ecliptic, the twelve broad bands corresponding to the signs of the Zodiac, the colures, the tropics and the polar circles. The sphere makes one rotation in a sidereal day; the solar index makes one revolution in the same direction in a mean day and passes through the ecliptic in one year. The calendar is carried on a horizontal annular ring, the rim of which is divided into three hundred and sixty five days with the months, the day of the month and the principal saints'-days: it progresses continuously and the date is read by a pointer in the shape of the tongue of a lizard which leaps a day every four years. The mechanism of the sphere has a great many features that were quite new at the time, among these, a Maltese Cross.

Traveling Clocks

During the Renaissance, clockmakers adapted their designs to many new demands. Whilst the government of the most advanced countries of Europe was usually situated in their respective capitals, kings and noblemen, who made up the court, were frequently absent. The kings of France, for instance, used Versailles and Fontainebleau as their winter residences, whereas the châteaux of Blois or Chambord on the Loire were occupied in Spring or Summer. All these journeys were made in a carriage and many merchants, bankers and scholars also used this method of traveling. So it is not surprising that the first portable, individual clock should be a carriage-clock. It dates from the fifteenth or early years of the sixteenth century.

Clocks of this type are illustrated in pls. 38–40. They are cylindrical in shape and a good deal smaller in diameter than table clocks. To protect them from the hazards of a journey over rough roads these clocks were always housed in a strong leather case with iron locks. The chiming clock shown in plate 39 is still in its original case, the one in plate 40 has no chimes and is signed N. Plantard à Blois, 1619. It is 9·3 cm in diameter, and 7 cm in height.

A cylindrical alarm, smaller in diameter, supported on three feet and sur-mounted by a skull is removable. It is intended to be fixed on the dial of the clock and to be released by the hand as it passes. The dial of the clock is designed to be felt; that is to say, a small pin is set above the surface beside each numeral, allowing the time to be told in the dark by touch alone. When the alarm is attached this carriage-clock measures 16 cm overall.

From the middle of the sixteenth century carriage-clocks took on the form of large, round, thick watches housed in metal boxes attached to a pendant or ring. Usually these watches had both chimes and alarms. To make the sound louder the box was often decorated along the edge with pierced and engraved garlands.

The evolution of the carriage-clock to the carriage-watch is particularly important because it took place only a short time before the first pocket watches. Plates 41–44 show three remarkable examples of carriage-clocks of the period; numbers 43 and 44 are in their original cases.

THE EMERGENCE OF THE POCKET WATCH

The historical development of the clock during the Renaissance can be looked upon as a journey towards miniaturization, at the end of which the clock emerged in the form of the pocket watch. From the design of the carriage-clock it was only a short step, first to the carriage-watch and then to an even smaller portable watch—the pocket watch. It has been suggested that it was only after they had reduced the size of the carriage-clock to a flat cylinder between six and eight centimetres in diameter that the watchmakers thought of adding a ring to the side of the instrument so that it could be worn hanging like a pendant. Indeed several portraits of noblemen of the period depict the sitter magnificently dressed and wearing a watch suspended on a chain. At a time when pomp and display was the rule among the nobility it is not surprising that this useful and decorative invention should become fashionable, nor that everyone who had, or wanted to appear as if he had, the means, hastened to possess one.

The first pocket watches date from the sixteenth century. Bassermann-Jordan, the German author and collector, found and published the fol-lowing document dated 1511: "In Nuremberg Heinlein is renowned for very small clocks which will go for forty hours either in the pocket or worn on a chain." Another earlier German historian, Cochlæus, in a supplement to the *Cosmography of Pomponius Mela*, described the Nuremberg artists: "Every

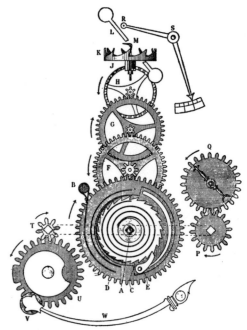

Diagram of the movement of a primitive watch with stackfreed and foliot oscillator

day they invent new and more refined pieces. For instance, Peter Hele, who is still a young man and whose work is the admiration of scholars and mathematicians, can make a watch from a small piece of iron and furnished with many wheels. This kind of clock goes, whatever its position, without weights, for forty hours. It tells the time and chimes the hour whether it is carried in the pocket or worn as a pendant."

This document makes it clear that the watch was not always worn on a chain and that from the beginning the pocket-watch was carried in a purse or sometimes in a pocket on the belt round the breeches.

The following extract comes from a manuscript in the Bibliothèque Nationale written by Jean Sapin, Receiver General of the Languedoc. It is dated the last day of December, 1518.

"To Julien Coudray, Master Clockmaker of Blois, paid the sum of two hundred gold écus for two excellent daggers, each set with a watch, all gilded, in the handle, ordered by the king for his own use."

Until 1950 horologists generally agreed that the first pocket watches were all made about the same time, 1515, both in Germany and France. As this type of watch was not a new invention but a development of the travelling clock which had been familiar in Europe for the past thirty years at least, to find the name of the first watchmaker looked like an impossible task.

However, Professor Morpurgo, working among archives in Italy was fortunate to discover documents which prove that Pietro Guido of Mantua, known to have been a very skilful small clockmaker, constructed pocket watches before 1500. A letter dated 7 May 1506, sent by Doctor Bernardus Bembo to Her Highness the Marquise Isabella of Gonzagues, mentions "small clocks and very tiny ones constructed by Pietro Guido and sent for repair."

There are few collections containing watches that can be definitely dated to the early sixteenth century, but after that date they were made and sold widely in many countries of western Europe. All the great museums of Europe and America and many private collections possess watches of this period, and the movement is usually signed with the name of the maker.

There were watchmakers in many French towns: they are recorded at Paris, Lyon, Blois, Strasbourg, Dijon, Rouen, La Rochelle and Metz; in Germany at Nuremberg, Augsburg, Cologne and Bremen; in Switzerland at Geneva, Zug and Basle and also in London, Amsterdam, Brussels and the Hague.

At different times, the chief watchmaking centres were Paris, Lyons, Blois, London and Geneva.

Plates 45–49 show pocket watches that were derived from the carriage watch. Protection of the dial and the single hour hand was assured by a hinged lid, artistically engraved and pierced with tracery so as to form a grille through which the time could be told.

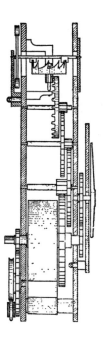

Section of the movement of the same watch

Plates 50–71 are examples of pocket watches, round, oval or polygonal in shape. As every owner of one of these extravagant jewels wanted the finest, goldsmith-watchmakers of the period had to use all their creative ingenuity. Competition was greatly increased when women of fashion also began to wear a pendant watch and this accounts for the appearance of magnificent small watches of all shapes with cases of rock-crystal, agate, jasper and semi-precious stones about the middle of the sixteenth century. Some were gold while others, to be discussed below, were decorated with ornamental motifs or enamelled. From 1590 till about 1630 the oval shape predominated. Many of these watches also have a small sundial and a compass, a very necessary precaution, for their beauty was not matched by accuracy so that it was quite usual to have to correct them by the sundial.

The Movement of the First Pocket Watches

The first watches were round, the movement being entirely of iron and fixed with cotter-pins or bolts. Screws first appeared about 1550.

The spring, forged by hand and smoothed on a file, was held by four pillars serving as a brace between the two plates. Its outer end was fixed to one of the pillars while the other was rolled round a drum or plug of an axis. About 1550 the spring was sometimes housed in a cylindrical box, usually pierced and called the drum. The axis, driven by the spring, carried the first wheel of the gear: its teeth engaged with those of the first pinion which had seven wings (or teeth) whereas the second pinion had five. The axis of the wheels pivoed in holes bored in the two metal plates. This hole was not pierced through and covered by a counter-pivot of steel until a later date.

The wheels are of iron, hollowed out. The teeth are cut on a file and very irregular. It was not till the publication in 1675 of the works of Olaf Roemer (1644–1710), a Danish astronomer and physicist, and of the French scholars Girard Desargues (1593–1662) and Philippe de la Hire (1640–1695) that the epicycloidal curve was applied to clock gears, and a machine for dividing and cutting the wheels invented in 1741 by Nicholas Fardoil, clockmaker of Paris, who also invented a tool to make fusees. The tool for cutting the pinions was presented before the Academy in 1744 by an English clockmaker, William Blakey, living in Paris, but this had been used in England for forty years.

The first problem for the watchmakers, already encountered by the makers of small spring-driven clocks, was how to regulate the power produced by the spring.

Pls. 41 & 42 Carriage watch by H.G. (Hans Gruber), hallmark of Nuremberg, master in 1552. Engraved, pierced and gilt copper, the dial below the pierced cover. Stackfreed movement. D. 8·5 cm. Formerly Arquembourg Collection; Private Collection, Paris

Pls. 43 & 44 Travelling watch by Jean Grégoire, of Blois, first third of the 17th century. Silver case pierced and engraved with lilies, tulips and narcissi; striking mechanism. Contemporary leather case. D. 10 cm. Musée du Petit Paris, Paris

Pl. 45 Flat watch, German work, signed; 1560. Gilt copper with allegorical scenes of astronomy in the center and hunting scenes round the edge. Mechanism: foliot, verge, stackfreed. D. of case 6·5, D. of movement 5·1 cm. Private Collection, Paris

Pl. 45a View of the mechanism of Pl. 45. Stackfreed, foliot regulating device

Pl. 46 Watch by Cameel, Strasbourg, about 1610. The gadrooned case is in copper and silver; striking mechanism on the hour, alarm. Formerly Gélis Collection; Private Collection, Paris

Pl. 47 Watch-case of the period of Francis I, first half of the 16th century. Gilt brass. D. 7, T. 3 cm. Au Vieux Cadran, Paris

Pl. 48 Watch recording the days of the month and the phases of the moon. Au Vieux Cadran, Paris

Pl. 49 Puritan alarm watch, German work, 1560. Alarm hand is on the counter-end of the hour hand, the alarm dial in arabic numerals. Gilt brass. H. of dial 6, W. 4·8, T. 3 cm. Au Vieux Cadran, Paris

42

41

43

44

45

46

45-a

47

49

48

51

52

53

54

55

56

57

58

59

60

Pl. 50   Left: *Watch by Ballard of Bourd. Gilt copper case 7·9 × 4·9 cm. It shows the days of the week and the phases of the moon.* Right: *Watch by Salomon Chesnon, Blois, 1620. Solar dial in the lid. 7·7 × 5 cm. Collection Dr. Gschwind, Basle*

Pl. 51   *Astronomical watch by the famous Pironneau of Blois, 1620. The engraved silver watch shows the days of the month, days of the week and phases of the moon, the zodiac and the calendar. On the edge of the case the time of sunrise and sunset. Oval 6 × 4·7 cm, T. 3·5 cm. Formerly Gélis Collection; Private Collection, Paris*

Pl. 52   *Small watches with covers made of rock crystal. The one on the left from the Soltykoff Collection; H. 3·5 cm; the one on the right with a wavy rim, signed by J. Rousseau, 1590, or his son, mid 17th century. Musée du Petit Palais, Dutuit Collection, Paris*

Pls. 53 & 54   *Small watch in the shape of a shell (not recorded by Britten). Silver, the dial engraved gilt copper. Gilt cock. H. 4 cm. Au Vieux Cadran, Paris*

Pl. 55   *Watch by Hubuer of Bremen, early 18th century. Engraved silver, four dials, showing the hours, the phases of the moon and the date. The phases of the moon appear in a window above the crescent. Oval 4·7 × 3·5 cm. Formerly Gélis Collection; Private Collection, Paris*

Pl. 56   *Oval watch with a striking mechanism by G. Rumuault of Abbeville, late 16th century. Verge escapement, silver and gilt brass, 5·5 × 4·7 cm. Musée d'Horlogerie, La Chaux-de-Fonds*

Pl. 57   *Musical watch by John Archambaud, London, about 1740. Five-tone chime for the hours and the quarters. D. 6 cm. Nathan Collection, Binningen*

Pl. 58   *Round silver watch by Davis, London. The balance is in the form of a small pendulum. Verge escapement, minute hand. D. 5, H. (glass open) 3·1 cm. Musée d'Horlogerie, La Chaux-de-Fonds*

Pls. 59 & 60   *Large traveling watch, with a silver case by Flant, clockmaker at La Rochelle. Late 16th, early 17th century. Four sundials, calculated for four different latitudes. D. 9·5 cm. Musée du Petit Palais, Dutuit Collection, Paris*

In Germany the problem was solved by the stackfreed, or brake. This was a fixed auxiliary spring carried on the upper plate with a pulley at its end resting on a spiral cam. This cam was carried on a toothed wheel turned by a pinion fixed to the axis of the drum. It was so arranged that when the mainspring was fully wound up the pulley of the stackfreed pressed strongly against the salient part of the spiral and gave a braking effect. On the other hand when the spring was partly run-down the pulley exerted only a moderate pressure against the narrowest part of the spiral, thus offering less braking effect. It even gave some slight assistance to the mainspring when it was nearly run-down.

By 1530 the stackfreed was replaced by the fusee, which is attributed by some historians to Leonardo da Vinci, about 1500. The fusee consists of a drum with a spiral track cut in the form of a cone, on which a cat-gut cord or fine chain is wound. In fact Leonardo's sketch books do contain a drawing of four cylinders working, with four fusees mounted on the same arbor. The springs of the four cylinders unwind one after another so that the clock goes more slowly. In 1953 Professor Morpurgo found a remarkably interesting document: a letter from the assistant bishop of Mantua, Comino da Pontevico (a man who was interested in clocks and owned a laboratory) to the Marquis of Mantua, written on 21st August 1482. The following passage is an extract;

"The clock has a steel spring, concealed in a brass cylinder, round which is wound a cat-gut cord, so as to make it (the spring) invisible; and if this steel spring were not there, despite the cord, the machine would not work. The cord is tied to the cylinder, united with the steel spring so as to provoke the pull of the thread (fusee) to which it is fixed; this movement of the thread sets all the wheels of the clock in motion. Such are the clocks which I have shown Your Grace; all the Masters who make clocks without weights use this method and several examples are to be seen here in Mantua."

In the fusee method the power of the coiled spring, transmitted by the cat-gut, pulls on the smallest diameter of the fusee when the spring is fully wound. But as the spring unwinds the pull of the cord works on a larger and larger diameter of the fusee. By suitable shaping of the fusee cone the power transmitted can be made quite uniform for all states of the spring. The fusee mechanism is still used in mechanical marine chronometers today.

About 1540 the fusee method was also adopted for pocket watches. The form of the movement was modified and, so as to be able to house the mechanism more easily, an oval, somewhat deeper shape was adopted.

On fusees the stop is a very important part. Its action ensures the stopping of the mechanism at the top of the winding gear so as to prevent the cord being torn off at one end or the other. The cat-gut was used till about 1650. After 1650 it was replaced by a small chain of steel links, invented by Gruet, a Genevan clockmaker. This invention allowed deeper grooves to be made in the fusee and so reduced the size of the watch. In oval pocket watches the first brass movements appeared, of which the balance cock, (which covered and protected the oscillator, or wheel-balance) the coqueret and the pillars were ornamented with gilding. The escapement with the crown-wheel was the same in large, medium and small clocks. The oscillator, however, had some peculiarities.

Adaptation of the Foliot Oscillator to the Pocket Watch

In very early clocks the verge escapement with ratchet-wheel, pallets and foliot was suspended by a thread which also served as a method of torsion. The pull on this cord set the reverse movement of the foliot and helped it to pass the "dead" point of the system.

In portable clocks and watches the suspension-thread and torsion had to be altered to allow the upper edge of the verge to pivot on a bridge called the cock. The regulators also had to go, and were replaced by small cup-shaped weights which could be moved along the arms, or by simple weights fixed at the end of the arms of the foliot.

The balance would now be an inert mass with no means of changing the point of inertia. It was necessary to find a way of adjusting the period and of regaining the impulse so as to pass over the dead point.

The first of these two problems was resolved by the use of a short pig's bristle. The bristle was fixed either to the plate or to one end of the foliot. In the first case the free end of the bristle encountered an arm of the foliot. In the second the path of the foliot was limited by two adjustable blocks, arranged perpendicularly to the plate.

Towards the middle of the sixteenth century the foliot was replaced by a circular balance formed by a metal rim attached to the verge of the escapement by spokes and a hub. The size of the oscillations of the balance were regulated by an elbowed lever with one or two bristles set between the spokes of the balance. The position of these bristles could be changed; if they were placed near the rim of the balance the duration of the oscillation was increased and the movement of the watch in consequence retarded. If, on the other hand, the bristles were moved nearer the centre, the duration was decreased and the watch consequently advanced. The other end of the bristles, arm had a pointer, which was moved over guide lines to control regulation.

The resulting movement was fairly regular but the fact that the oscillator was in continuous contact with the wheel of the escapement made the balance very sensitive to shock so the watch stopped. From its invention till the last

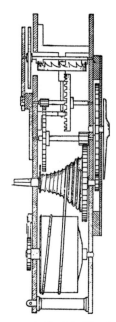

Section of the movement of a primitive fusee watch

61

62

63

64

65

66

67

68

69

70

71

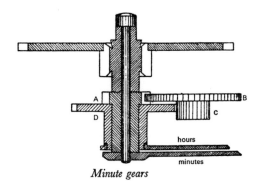

Minute gears

Britten, the English horlogist, illustrates a very fine Renaissance clock in his *Old Clocks and Watches*. It dates from 1587 and has a minute hand on the same axis as the hour hand. The two hands were controlled separately by the gearing of the movement. All these clocks are in original condition and no changes or additions have been made.

The minute mechanism of two pinions and two wheels, still in use today, is described by Christian Huygens in his famous work *Horologium Oscillatorium* published in 1673. Huygens does not claim to have been the inventor, so perhaps the design existed already or was the work of one of his colleagues. About 1700, clocks and watches had become more accurate and time was regarded as more valuable, so that a minute hand was now an essential part of all clocks and watches regardless of size.

GENERAL REMARKS

Pls. 66 & 67   Watch of the Louis XIV period, engraved silver, by Formereau, La Rochelle, about 1630. Pierced case covered in leather; alarm. Formerly Gélis Collection (not recorded in Britten); Private Collection, Paris

Pl. 68   Watch of Frederick William, Elector of Brandenburg, about 1650. Rolled silver. D. 3·5, T. 1·8 cm. Au Vieux Cadran, Paris

Pl. 69   Spherical watch by Matheus Hallaycher, Augsburg, 1680. The mechanism is mounted on a universal joint. D. 5·2 cm. Collection Dr. Gschwind, Basle

Pl. 70   Side view of works of a watch by Gilles Martinot, one of the earliest enamelled dials, early 18th century. Verge escapement, engraved cock, two hands. D. 5·5 cm. Au Vieux Cadran, Paris

Pl. 71   Side view of works of a watch by Smith, London. Double gold case, chiselled and pierced, the hands set with roses. D. 5 cm. Au Vieux Cadran, Paris

In any collection of early timepieces, Renaissance clocks and watches must always, in our view, take pride of place. However, it is not on account of their accuracy that these pieces merit so much attention because at that date an oscillator capable of producing a regular and invariable unit of time was unknown.

It is the ingenious mechanism that gives sixteenth- and seventeenth-century clocks their interest, together with their fine shape and beautifully decorated cases, and the fact that they are handmade, that every piece had to be hammered and cut out of the raw material before it could be shaped, filed and fitted into a particular style. When that piece was also one of the principal parts of the clock or watch it had a precise mechanical function similar to parts of the human body. It is the combination of these different functions which constitutes the marvellous little living mechanism we have in a clock or a watch.

The clockmaker-artists who made these masterpieces were so conscientious and so absorbed in their work that they took as much care over the quality of the working parts as they did over the beauty of form. Decoration was not limited to the external parts of the instrument, the case, the dial and the hands, but was also applied to several parts of the movement. The movement of every clock or watch from the fifteenth to the seventeenth century, and even into the beginning of the eighteenth, comprises two plates linked by pillars. The decorated parts are the pillars, the cock, which serves as a bracket for the foliot, or which covers the balance wheel, several coquerets which belong to the regulator or the movement and, for very fine pieces, the outside of the drum case. Ornamental motives were generally flowering scrolls and arabesques.

From the early seventeenth century the profession of clockmaker was graced by a number of Master Horologists in Germany, especially in the regions of Augsburg and Dresden, in England in London, in France at Blois, Lyons and Paris and in Switzerland in Geneva. Usually they came from families of substance or from generations of craftsmen. They constituted groups of highly skilled workers, even with a certain degree of culture acquired through their commercial and scientific contacts with noblemen and scholars, and of a social standing which put them in the highest ranks of craftsmen.

Illustration in a work
by Henri Pentaleone, Basle, 1565

The Seventeenth Century

Initials by Kilian Lukas, copper engraving, Augsburg, 1627

THE RENAISSANCE WAS FOLLOWED by the Reformation and then by the period known by historians as the Age of Reason. In clock and watch making the period was marked, as we shall see, by new developments in the artistic field and also by two scientific discoveries made in 1583 and 1657. These marked the first step towards precise mechanical measurement of time and ultimately towards chronometry.

In the seventeenth century watches were generally made of silver, copper-gilt or carved from rock crystal or topaz, rarely of gold. Such was the taste of the period that beauty of workmanship was preferred to costly materials.

Dials were decorated with rich engraving. Etienne Delaulne, one of the most famous French decorators of the late sixteenth and early seventeenth centuries, published several collections of engraved designs for decoration of watches and goldsmith's work. These are very rare today: a complete set of Delaulne prints representing watch-cases was sold for 10,000 francs in Paris in June 1914. These collections were kept in the studios of Master goldsmiths and clockmakers, who sometimes also made their watch cases themselves. Among the rarer materials used are amethyst, cornelian, ivory and amber, carved in relief or in intaglio.

ENAMELLED WATCHES

Enamel was used from very early times in a transparent or opaque mass in the processes of champlevé and cloisonné, with a polychrome palette ranging from the palest to most brilliant tones. In Limoges enamel, monochrome, usually dark purple, forms the ground color. The artists obtained a plastic effect by applying layers of varying thickness in white enamel over this ground and producing a very delicate form of bas-relief.

About 1630 a goldsmith from Châteaudun, Jean Toutin, perfected a method of painting with polychrome enamels. He produced a series of tones rendered permanent by firing in a kiln. The piece to be decorated was first covered with a layer of opaque white enamel and fired. Then the required colors were painted on with a fine brush and the whole fired once more. Toutin spent some time in England where he met Van Dyck at the court of King Charles. Everybody wanted to emulate the king and become the possessor of one of these admirable portraits, which showed all the shades of detail of a great painting within the space of twenty to thirty millimeters.

By about 1650 Toutin's art had become widespread. Petitot, born in Geneva in the seventeenth century, was a portraitist in enamel of great renown. Painted enamel watch cases are almost always decorated on both sides of the base. The sides also are decorated with a landscape, so that the plain enamel, indispensable to the solidity of the decoration, was concealed.

Jacques Vauquer of Blois made a collection of prints which were used as models by the painters, engravers, and decorators of the period.

English cock, drawn from a movement with one hand and signed Terroux, Geneva

In 1671 a very talented miniaturist called Pierre Huaut, a native of Châtellerault, who had left France fifty years before as a Huguenot refugee, was made a citizen of Geneva along with his three sons. They later took Jean Toutin's marvellous craft to Berlin in Prussia.

All these artists enamelled many watches to be seen today in museums and private collections. These fragile toys, examples of which are seen in the following color plates were usually protected by a second case of embossed leather reinforced with gold or silver mounts.

After the Revocation of the Edict of Nantes in 1685 many French craftsmen emigrated, among them whole families of clockmakers, enamellers and goldsmiths. Many settled in Switzerland and about ten per cent of the names enrolled in the splendid clockmakers' corporation of Blois are subsequently to be found in Switzerland; Girard, Dubié, Perret, Vauthier, Rougement, Dufour, Guignard, Guillon Lamarche are now common names in Geneva and Neuchâtel and still figure in the watchmaking industry.

Sixteenth- and seventeenth-century watches are much sought by collectors especially if they are signed by one or other of the great artists of this period. It is therefore useful to append a list—albeit incomplete—of the most important of these.

The books mentioned below, with the books by Britten and Baillie, essential to all collectors, of course contain much more comprehensive lists:

Chanoine Develle, *Les Horlogers blésois* (1917).
Eugène Vial and Claudius Côte, *Les Horlogers lyonnais* (1927).
Eugène Jacquet and Alfred Chapuis, *Histoire et Technique de la Montre suisse* (1945).

Late 17th-century engraving

CLOCKMAKERS OF LYONS, BLOIS AND GENEVA

(The dates show the working life of the watchmaker)

Clockmakers of Lyons

Louis Arthaud   1612–1662
Hugues Combret   1619–1669

Pierre Combret   1570–1622
Claude du Cléron   1594–1637
(Zacharie?) Formereau   after 1626
Pierre Louteau   1603–1628
Guillaume Nourisson   1655–1700
Christophe and Pierre Noytolon   1558–1607 and 1610–1630
Abel Senebier   1638–1640
Jean Vallier   1596–1649

Clockmakers of Blois

Salomon Chesnon
Guillaume Coudray
Julien Coudray   1504–1551
Cuper
Abraham de la Garde
Jacques de la Garde   1551
Nicolas and Abraham Gribelin
Jean du Jardin
Nicolas and Louis Le Maindre
Jehan Naze   1554–1581
Piron
Vaultier

Clockmakers of Geneva

Antoine Arlaud, became a citizen of Geneva in 1617
Henry Arlaud   1631–1689
Charles Bobinet   1610–1678
Denis Bordier   1629–1708
Jean-Baptiste Duboule   1615–1694
Martin Duboule   1583–1639
Pierre Duhamel   1630–1686
David Rousseau   1641–1738
Jean Rousseau   1606–1684 (great-grandfather of Jean-Jacques)
Jacques Sermand   1595–1651
Jacques Sermand (nephew)   1636–1667

Pl. III   A group of early watches from a Private Collection. Top left: *astronomical watch by Pironneau, Blois, signed Piron. Engraved silver, counting the days of the month, days of the week, phases of the moon, zodiac and calender. The rim of the case shows the times of sunrise and sunset. Oval 6 × 4·7 × 3·5 cm (see detail plate 51). Formerly in the Gélis Collection.* Top center: *watch by Bouquet Londini, 1625. Rock crystal, double case in solid silver. Oval 4·4 × 3·7 × 2·2 cm; case 4·8 × 4·2 × 2·2 cm.* Top right: *watch by Salomon Chesnon, Blois. Decorated with rural scenes and women bathing and with ornaments and scrolls enclosing a squirrel, a rabbit and a peacock. Putti, squirrels and a hare on the gilt brass dial; in the center, Bacchus. Sundial and compass in the interior. Oval 5·6 × 4·2 × 2·6 cm.* Center: *enamelled gold watch by Lépine. Pierced case with strike release. D. 3·6, T. 2 cm.* Bottom left: *watch of chiselled and pierced silver by L. Formereau, La Rochelle. Double case of leather, dial of gilt brass, the ring showing the hours in silver; alarm. Movement, fusee with gut cord. Case, black shagreen studded with silver. Watch D. 4·8, T. 3 cm; dial D. 3·8 cm; case D. 5·5, T. 3·1 cm.* Bottom center: *gold watch by Fromanteel with pierced and engraved case. It counts the days of the month and has an alarm (see details plates 72-4).* Bottom right: *complex astronomical watch by Gautrin with dials on both sides (see plate 94)*

THE BEGINNINGS OF PRECISION CLOCKMAKING

An evolution similar to that which developed the watch out of the original monumental clock perfected the accuracy of the watch and introduced the ultimate precision of chronometry. Following the pattern of preceding centuries advances were made step by step, starting with medium-sized clocks and ending with the watch.

We must therefore turn back to the late sixteenth century to examine the scientific event which led the way to accuracy, namely the discovery of the properties of the pendulum in 1583 by the Italian scholar and humanist Galileo, and the application of that discovery to the measurement of time. Galileo Galilei, always known as Galileo, was born of a noble Florentine family in 1564. His taste for science came from his father and his love of art and letters from his mother. He was still a student of nineteen, reading medicine and philosophy at the university when he made one of his finest discoveries in physics.

One evening in the cathedral he raised his eyes to look at a large lamp suspended from the vaulted arch. The sacristan had touched it and it was swinging back and forth. Galileo noticed that the duration of the swing was always the same even though the arc gradually diminished: he had discovered that the duration of the oscillation of a pendulum is independent of the size of the arc. At that time Galileo was not a mathematician and he was studying the subject almost unaided. At the age of twenty-five he was offered the Chair of Mathematics at the University of Padua. He soon became known for his practical character and for his dislike of the long and vague dissertations, at that time too often a substitute for proof.

In the course of his life Galileo made other great discoveries and inventions, including the thermometer, and the hydrostatic balance. He discovered the laws of motion of falling bodies and formulated the principles of modern dynamics. In Venice in 1609 he constructed his first astronomical telescope with which he observed the phases of Venus. His observations led him to accept the Copernican theory of the universe which had been denounced by the Church as heretical. At the age of seventy, Galileo in collision with the Church, was forced to disclaim his "heresy" before the Inquisition in 1633. Banished to Arcetri near Florence, and forbidden to conduct any further experiments he wrote his immortal *Dialogues on the New Science*. He died, blind, on 8th January 1642, with his son Vincenzio, Viviani his youngest disciple, and the most famous of his former pupils, the natural philosopher and geometrician Evangelista Torricelli, beside him. His followers raised a monument to him soon after his death in the Basilica of Santa Croce in Florence.

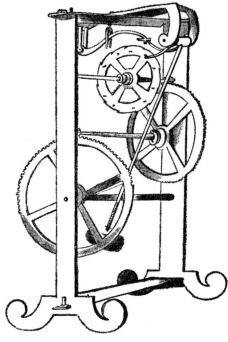

Drawing of the pendulum clock begun by Galileo and sent to Huygens by Boulliau in 1660

Pls. 72, 73 & 74 Gold watch by Fromanteel, middle or late 17th century. Engraved and pierced case and dial in gold, counting the days of the month and with an alarm. D. 4·5 cm. Private Collection, Paris

Pl. 75 Watch by Lucas, Amsterdam. D. 5 cm. Musée des Arts décoratifs, Paris

Pl. 76 Watch by Marchand, Geneva, 1700. D. 5·5 cm. Musée des Arts décoratifs, Paris

Pl. 77 Left: Watch by Cabrier, London. Days of the month. D. 4·8 cm. Right: Watch by Lestourgeon, 1680-1700. Gold dial. D. 5 cm. Musée des Arts décoratifs, Paris

Pl. 78 Left: Silver watch by Marcou, Amsterdam, 1680. D. 4·3 cm. Right: Watch by van Loon, Harlem, 1700. Date and phases of the moon. D. 4·7 cm. Formerly Olivier Collection; Musée des Arts décoratifs, Paris

72

73

74

75

76

77

78

79

80

81

82

83

84

85

87

86

Galileo formulated the following laws on the simple pendulum, that is, a pendulum consisting of a small weight hanging by a fine thread of negligible weight:

(1) The oscillation of the pendulum is isochronic; the period is independent of length of the swing.
(2) The period is independent of the size of the weight.
(3) The ratio of the periods of two pendulums is equal to the square root of the ratio of their lengths.

The first of these propositions is not exact because the duration is increased by 18 % when the swing increases above 1·90 degrees. It is strange that Galileo, who was a meticulous experimental thinker, should not have noticed this; perhaps he never thought the size of the arc could be varied so much. Galileo had the idea of applying the pendulum to measurement of time. It is said that he measured heart-beats by a pendulum held in his hand, which he regulated until the beat of the heart and the swing of the pendulum coincided. As an old man Galileo designed a pendulum clock with a new type of escapement. This machine was intended to count the oscillations of the pendulum, the movement of which was no longer maintained by hand.

Vincenzio, Galileo's son, began to build the clock conceived by his father, but it was never completed, because in 1668 the inventory, drawn up on the death of Vincenzio's widow, contains the following entry: *Un oriuolo non finito di ferro col pendolo, prima inventione del Galileo* ("An unfinished iron clock with a pendulum first invented by Galileo.")

There is further documentary proof that Galileo was the first to invent the pendulum clock. In 1658, shortly after Huygens had published his *Horologium*, an announcement was made in Florence claiming priority for Galileo. It was made at the request of Prince Leopoldo dei Medici and Vincenzio Viviani, former pupil and colleague of Galileo, and it declared that Galileo had handed on to his son the necessary details for producing a pendulum clock which he had in mind. The son followed his father's instructions and constructed the clock but it was abandoned when he died in 1649, only seven years after Galileo himself.

The astronomer Boulliau was then able to pass on to his friend Huygens the design of Galileo's clock which he had acquired from Leopoldo Medici. Huygens replied in a letter dated 22nd January 1660, now preserved in the Bibliothèque Nationale in Paris: "You have rendered me a great service in sending the design of the clock begun by Galileo. I see that the pendulum is much the same as mine but used in a different way; for one thing he was substituted a much more complicated invention for the wheel, known as the

Pl. 79 Watch by Smith, London, 1680. Gold. Engraved and lined case. Au Vieux Cadran, Paris

Pl. 80 Gold watch by Charles François Bouvier, Paris (not recorded in Britten). White enamel dial with hands in the form of snakes; the subjects of the enamel painting are taken from the life of Antony and Cleopatra: their meeting, the death of Antony, and Cleopatra and the asp. D. 6, T. 2·6 cm. Au Vieux Cadran, Paris

Pl. 81 Carriage watch by Samuel Michelin, Langres, 1680. It has only a single hand, in the center the phases of the moon and the hours arranged round the dial; the months, the day of the month and the day of the week in special openings. Strikes on the hour and has an alarm. Formerly Franklin Dennison Collection; Nathan Collection, Binningen

Pl. 82 Silver carriage watch, Breslau, showing the days of the month, phases of the moon, the hour and with an alarm and winding key of the period. D. 11, T. 7 cm. D. of dial 9 cm. Ben Simon Collection, Paris

Pls. 83 & 84 Carriage watch made by Barronneau, Paris, 1670. Gilt brass, chiselled and pierced copper, finely engraved with scenes of animals in the cartouches; engraved interior. It sounds the hours and has an alarm. The dial partly of silver, the hands of blued steel. D. 11 cm. Formerly Arquembourg Collection; Private Collection, Paris

Pls. 85 & 86 Watch with a double case, repeater and alarm by George Graham, London (1673-1751). Silver, the case pierced and chiselled. Cylinder escapement, wheel of brass. D. 6·7, H. (closed) 3·5 cm. The detail shows English chiselling for comparison with French work of the same period, as shown in plate 84. Musée d'Horlogerie, La Chaux-de-Fonds

Pl. 87 Keys from watches of the 17th and 18th centuries. The key showing the days of the week is by Tavernier; H. 5·5 cm. Collection Dr. Gschwind, Basle

crown-wheel. And secondly he has not suspended the pendulum by a cord or small ribbon, so that all its weight rests on the axis through which it moves, which is undoubtedly the reason why his model did not succeed, because I know from experience that the movement becomes slower and the clock tends to stop. Although Galileo had the same idea as I about the way to use the pendulum, it shows rather to my advantage because I have been able to achieve what he could not, and by my own efforts without aid from him or anyone else. If it should ever be found otherwise then may I be called a plagiarist, thief or any other vile name."

Comparison of Huygens's clock with Galileo's construction is proof enough that the one was a machine that worked and measured time while the other did not. Galileo had constructed a machine which counted oscillations, not time.

Galileo's escapement, however, is worthy of consideration because it is known as a "free" escapement, and was undoubtedly the first of these. Others have been made since then and they are to be found in the best mechanical clocks and watches today. They have only a very brief contact with the oscillator (either pendulum or other system) assuring its continuous movement and counting the oscillations in such a way that the movement is partially free.

Christian Huygens (1629–1695)

If the pendulum was to be a better oscillator than the foliot it had to be capable of producing a small, invariable unit of time of a determined length and capable of fine adjustment.

It was a great Dutch scholar Christian Huygens who found two solutions to this difficult problem, both of which are used in the great proportion of mechanical timepieces today.

Knowledge and social progress achieved during the Middle Ages had produced at a given moment the monumental clock; the Renaissance had encouraged magnificent technical and artistic developments in western Europe and now a new era, centered in Holland, England and France, had just begun. Primarily in scientific, but also in artistic and technical fields, it was to produce more important advances and more rapid progress in clockmaking than all the preceding centuries.

The Netherlands in the seventeenth century were a confederation of seven republics, the United Provinces. This small country played an important political role. Its soldiers withstood the combined forces of Louis XIV and the Emperor, and its fleet, commanded by de Ruyter, was able to hold its own against France and England.

Pl. IV A group of early watches from the Musée d'Horlogerie at La Chaux-de-Fonds. Top left: silver watch with turquoise champlevé enamels. D. 4·25 cm. Top center: watch in the shape of a cross in rock crystal. Engraved silver dial, gilt case with colored enamels (Museum Cat. no. 1158). H. 5·8, W. 4·1 cm. Top right: watch with enamelling on a turquoise ground. Movement by Duhamel, painting attributed to Pierre Huaud. D. 3·3, T. 1·66 cm (Museum Cat. no. 552). Center left: watch with a convex case and hinged cover without glass, counting days of the month, phases of the moon. D. 4, T. 2·16 cm (Museum Cat. no. 1119). Center right: watch with a convex case in very fine green enamel, D. 3·17, T. 1·5 cm (Museum Cat. no. 1159). Bottom left: Lépine watch made in the 18th century by T. Brown. Case early 17th century. Fine enamels with a tulip design to be compared with those of the watch opposite, in which the dial and the decoration of the case can be seen. D. 4·6, T. 2·3 cm (Museum Cat. no. 1219). Bottom right: watch enamelled with hunting scene round the case and a fine decoration of flowers in the interior. Movement by Wetzel, Strasbourg, 1636. D. 4·72, T. 1·9 cm (Museum Cat. no. 1331)

The beginning of the same century saw the expansion of the United Provinces; in 1601, the Dutch East India Company was formed and in 1619 established its headquarters in Java. The prodigious success of the Netherlands trade stirred both France and England to jealousy, and enabled the Dutch to live very comfortably: the bourgeoisie, merchants and bankers, wielded power great enough to eclipse the nobility.

Constantin Huygens (1596–1687), Baron of Zuylichem, Zeelhem and Monikeland, secretary to the House of Orange, President of the Council and Lord Treasurer of England under William III, was a person of standing and a poet of high renown. His second son, Christian, became one of the world's great scholars.

By the age of sixteen he was studying law and mathematics in the University of Leyden and proved himself to be a specially talented mathematician. He finished his law studies in France where he received the degree of Doctor of Laws in 1655 at the University of Angers. He pursued the study of mathematics and physics all his life.

But he was not satisfied with mere abstract speculation. While still a boy he worked with his father and brother on cutting and polishing spectacle lenses. After many disappointments they abandoned the hyperbolic lens recommended by Descartes, his father's friend, and turned to spherical lenses which were difficult to obtain at the time. Working glass and metal with his own hands and wrestling with raw materials taught Huygens to understand the difficulties inherent in things outside abstract concepts. Practical work forced the young mathematician to apply his mind to technical problems, to astronomical observations and questions of physics, and in particular to try to make an improved instrument for measuring time.

The First Pendulum Clocks: 1657–1659

Although Galileo had conceived the idea of applying the pendulum to clocks and measurement of time, the first working clock regulated by a pendulum was constructed in 1657 by Salomon Coster, clockmaker of the Hague, to a design by Christian Huygens. This clock is still in existence. It belongs to the Rijksmuseum of Amsterdam and can be seen in the Rijksmuseum voor de Geschiedenis der Natuurwetenschoppen in Leyden.

The pendulum consists of a metal stem with a round bead that can be moved up and down. The stem is attached to a supple cord hung at the meeting-point of two curved supporting leaves called cheeks, the point of which is explained below. The pendulum is guided by a fork or "crutch", the horizontal axis of which is also the verge carrying the pallets of a crown-wheel

Pl. V   A group of early watches from the Musée d'Horlogerie at La Chaux-de-Fonds. Top left: enamelled watch in convex form, the movement by Goullons, Paris, 1650. D. 6·1 cm (Museum Cat. no. 551). Top right: watch of convex form enamelled with the story of Antony and Cleopatra. Movement by Bonbruict, Blois, 1650. D. 6·2, T. 2·5 cm (Museum Cat. no. 553). Bottom left: watch by Huand le Puiné enamelled with subjects of Mars and Venus. Movement by Johannes van Ceulen Haghe, about 1700. D. 3·5, T. 2·0 cm (Museum Cat. no. 1160). Center: watch with a portrait of Tolstoy, Minister of Peter the Great. The diamond forming a crest on the fur hat oscillates with the balance. Movement by Debary, Geneva, 1700. D. 5·2, T. 3·4 cm (Museum Cat. no. 556). Bottom right: convex watch in fine green enamel, Geneva, late 17th century. The other face can be seen on Pl. IV (center right). D. 3·2, T. 1·5 cm (Museum Cat. no. 1159)

escapement. The movement, worked by a spring, is identical with that of clocks with a vertical foliot.

Huygens replaced the foliot with a pendulum guided by a fork and produced an immense improvement at very little cost. Many foliot clocks were altered to a pendulum movement at that time. Two coaxial hands told the time, one for hours, one for minutes. This clock was far more accurate than even the most refined foliot systems.

The Estates General accorded a monopoly for the making of this new clock on 16th June 1657; a month later the same privilege was granted by West Friesland and the Dutch Estates. Huygens ceded these rights to Salomon Coster.

The inventor had great plans for his clock; he hoped to increase its accuracy so that it could perform several tasks he noted in his *Memoirs*:

(1) To find the difference between the meridians with greater accuracy.
(2) To measure time more accurately than the sun.
(3) To be a perpetual and universal measure.

Huygens therefore began to study the isochronic nature of pendulum oscillations, then the properties of the cycloid, the theory of evolutes and determination of the centre of oscillation of a compound pendulum.

He knew that the oscillations of the pendulum were not truly isochronic and when he constructed his first clock he tried to give an equal duration to all the oscillations regardless of size. Large oscillations are slower than small and this inequality can be corrected by decreasing the length of the pendulum while increasing the size of the arc. Huygens succeeded by applying the curved leaves already mentioned as support for the suspension thread. In 1657 Huygens still did not know how to shape these leaves; they were probably bent in an arbitrary way and then modified as a result of observing the clock in motion.

Pendulum Clock 1658

It was no easy task to fashion the cheeks accurately. Huygens was capable of doing it, but this was not the case with most clockmakers. That was probably the reason which led Huygens to eliminate them on the 1658 clock. There is, however, another reason and that was that they did more harm than good if the clock was not standing properly level.

This new clock (shown, right), is described in the *Horologium* published at the Hague in 1658, which should not be confused with the classic treatise

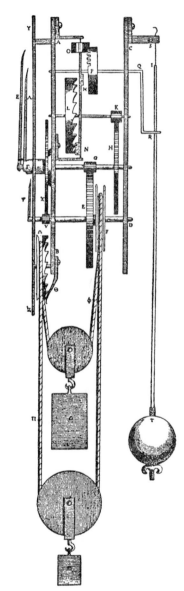

Clock by Huygens, 1658

of 1673 *Horologium Oscillatorium sive de motu pendulorum ad horlogia aptato* which will be mentioned below.

However, Huygens could not bring himself to leave the oscillations alone. Because he had decided against the use of corrective cheeks he determined to overcome the problem of isochronism by diminishing the length of the arc of the pendulum. The horizontal pinion of the verge engages in a vertical, partially toothed crown-wheel. The axis of the crown-wheel is also that of the fork.

The motive power is a weight suspended on an endless cord, which Christian Huygens invented to ensure that the clock did not stop when it was wound. The clock has three hands: the hour and minute hand are on a single central axis.

Pendulum Clock 1659

Subsequently Huygens made additional improvements to pendulum clocks. In his determination to achieve isochronous oscillations he turned back to the problem of the form of the corrective cheeks, or wings, of his first clock. He discovered that the pendulum would have to describe a cycloidal arc and detailed the method to be followed. His 1659 clock has corrective cheeks again, but these are calculated curves following a predetermined pattern and they are consequently easily copied.

In 1661 Huygens invented the moving weight which was used to facilitate the adjustment of the period of oscillation by sliding up or down the rod of the pendulum. In 1663, encouraged by Alexander Bruce, the Scottish Earl of Kincardine, who was an exile in Holland, Huygens turned his attention to the problem of longitude. Two small spring-driven marine clocks differing only from others in the suspension of the movement, and in bearing several additional devices calculated to prevent the clock from stopping or from oscillating irregularly, were made for experiment at sea. Later Huygens designed another marine clock, provided with a moveable suspension in the form of a gimbal fixed to a metal frame attached to the ceiling of the cabin, thus developing Cardano's suspension which is still in use today for marine chronometers. The box containing the movement was attached to another case well below it in which was a fifty-pound weight designed to counteract movement. The ordinary pendulum was replaced by a triangular pendulum with a lead-shaped bob and cycloidal balance cheeks. This clock was also supplied with a regulated winder or remontoire, which rendered the fusee superfluous. A small weight, lifted by a spring every thirty seconds and in direct contact with the crown-wheel, controlled the oscillations of the pendulum by a constant force.

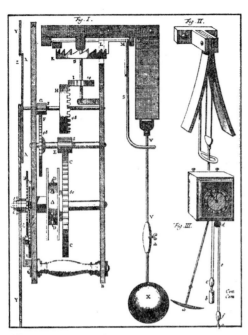

Clock by Huygens, 1673

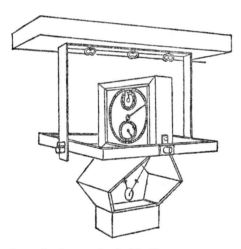

Suspension for a marine clock by Huygens

THE INVENTION OF THE OSCILLATOR
BALANCE-SPRING

The introduction of the spring into watches was similar in effect to the development of the pendulum in clocks. The spring supplied the balance with an alternating controlled movement so that the motive power no longer had any other function than to restore the energy lost by passive resistance to the regulating mechanism. Consequently it was possible to reduce the motive power or extend the moment of inertia on the balance-wheel which became, therefore, less sensitive to shocks and sudden movements.

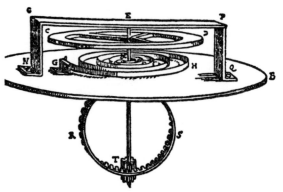

Spiral balance-spring

Christian Huygens believed he had now discovered a timepiece capable of replacing the pendulum clock and also of withstanding the agitation of the sea, because his oscillator was not dependent on gravity. The drawing Huygens sent with his inventions to the secretary of the Royal Society in France, dated 30th January 1675, is shown here.

From the moment of publication Huygens's invention was contested by several clockmakers, and principally the English scholar, Dr. Robert Hooke (1635–1703). In the end, however, it was established that, even though the idea of using the spring to regulate the movement of the balance-wheel had been advanced before by Hooke, the Duc de Roannez, Blaise Pascal and the Abbé d'Hautefeuille, not one of these inventors had, like Huygens, showed the spiral form of the spring. Furthermore this shape is essential because it allows the balance oscillations of great amplitude and puts the center of gravity of the spring on the axle of the balance. To say that the shape of the spring is of no importance is to miss the whole point of Huygens's discovery, because at that particular time the value of the invention lay solely in its special shape. It is also the only form which is still in use today.

Huygens's design is the invention of a scholar: a very simple idea which till then had evaded the skill and ingenuity of the finest clockmakers. Nevertheless they had been able to design many complicated mechanisms, among them chimes, calendars and automata, and it was a year after Huygens's invention, in 1676 that two English clockmakers, Barlow and Quare, invented a repeater chime which enabled a person to tell the time in the dark. (The watch sounds the hour and the quarters that have passed every time a lever—usually in the pendant—is pressed.)

However complicated they may be these mechanisms can be discussed in ordinary language because they are always a combination of wheels, cams and levers. The spiral regulator spring fulfills the idea of isochronic oscillations in a mechanical system consisting of a balanced volume (*i.e.* the balance) and a recoiling spring. This oscillatory system, worked by reserves of energy

Pl. VI Watch splendidly decorated with a design of the Tower of Babel in brilliant fresh enamels inspired by Breughel's famous painting. About five times actual size. D. 4·7 cm. Collection Musée d'Horlogerie, La Chaux-de-Fonds

produced by the escapement, implies the alternate transformation of kinetic into potential energy. It was by applying rational mechanical theory that Huygens and several other famous scholars of the day began to free men's minds from fumbling experimentation and the mists of metaphysics. The type of watch thus created was to last for two centuries because the verge escapement was still being made in Switzerland in the early nineteenth century.

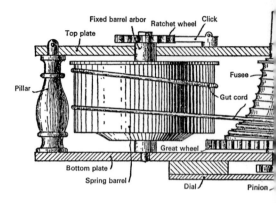

Diagram of the development of a 17th-century movement with one hand, gut fusee but no balance-spring

EVOLUTION OF THE WATCH

During the last years of the seventeenth and the first half of the eighteenth century development was restricted to details in the methods of making and reduction in the thickness of the movement. The principal innovation was the adaptation of the very small train of wheels to the watch in 1691 by Daniel Quare (1648–1724) and, as a result, the appearance of the first watches with both a minute and an hour hand. This improvement spread so rapidly that after 1700 nearly every watch had two hands.

Seventeenth-century movements are very thick and watches of this period are often known as turnip watches. The pillars separating the two plates are very long, often covered with ornament and the axles of the exposed movement are also very long. After the middle of the eighteenth century, movements became gradually flatter, the pillars less tall and cylindrical, and the crown-wheel much smaller. At the beginning of the nineteenth century lack of space between the plates led to reductions in their thickness. Like sixteenth-century watches a very important element of these late movements with pillars was the cock surmounting the upper plate which carries one end of the verge and covers the balance completely. It was therefore a means of protecting the balance when the watch was opened for winding.

The large cock was invented in mid-sixteenth century at the same time as the foliot was changed into a ring. It was not long before artists started to decorate this piece which was plainly visible and offered a good surface. So it appears pierced, engraved or chiselled in the admirable taste of the time. In the sixteenth century the most popular decoration was of flowers or strawberry plants with tiny animals playing in the leaves and eating the fruit, very similar to contemporary decoration of illuminated manuscripts. The early form of cock was fixed to the upper plate by a foot, the rest overhanging. English watchmakers long remained faithful to this design. In France and

Escapement for a clock and a watch dating from 1860

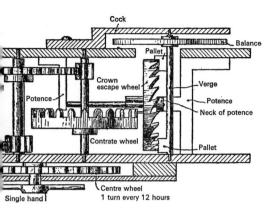

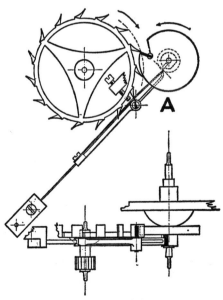

Spring-detent escapement for a marine chronometer

Switzerland at the end of the seventeenth century the cock was fixed by two feet and became almost circular. Its size increased with the curve of the balance and consequently in the eighteenth century the cock came to occupy the greater part of the plate. This whole surface was decorated in fine Louis XIV style with scrolls and varied motifs, but only rarely with figures. The cock is usually of gilt brass, though sometimes of silver; a few are decorated with enamels.

Decoration of the cock followed the changes in style from Louis XIV to Louis XVI, at last weakening into degenerate copying of earlier periods until it became more or less fixed in a pseudo-Louis XV style. After the adoption of the Lépine caliber the top plate was replaced by bars or bridges without ornament and the only point of difference was then the device it carried for adjustment of the oscillation period, that is the regulating lever held by a coqueret, in the center of which is fixed a top balance staff with rubies, sapphires or diamonds.

At the end of the seventeenth century the clockmaking industry, which had already attained an important position in England, France and Geneva, settled in another region of Switzerland. Daniel Jean Richard (1665-1741) was the promoter of this new venture. In 1706 he opened a workshop at Le Locle near Neuchâtel and was the first craftsman with a shop in the country which is now the watchmaking centre of the world.

Although the universal adoption of the pendulum movement in clocks and the spiral balance movement in watches had notably increased the accuracy of measuring instruments, it was still a far cry from the modern watch. Even the most sophisticated watches had a daily error of from five to ten minutes and during the next hundred years watchmakers made a series of improvements which produced better results.

The illustrations in plates 72–87 show seventeenth-century pieces.

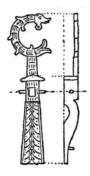

Cock of the very early period

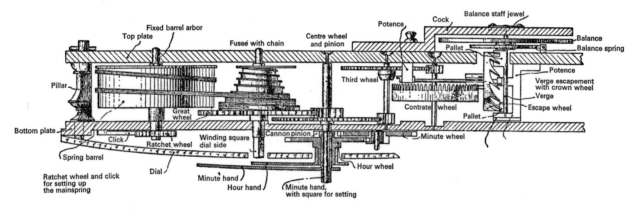

Diagram of an 18th-century movement with a verge escapement

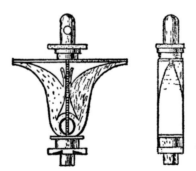

Tulip-shaped pillar from a one-handed watch by Duhamel, Geneva, 1675

The Eighteenth Century

THE STRUGGLE FOR PRECISION

Watch made for China; gold, pearls and rubies, about 1800

Before discussing the history of this period it is necessary to consider several theoretical questions.

The impulse supplied by the new oscillators was much more regular and, consequently, much easier to adjust than that of the foliot oscillator. Once clockmakers had appreciated the consequent improvement in precision they soon realized that greater precision could only be achieved by eliminating all the causes of disturbance in the impulse of the two new types of oscillator.

Successive inventions, which perfected those parts regulating and counting the period of the oscillators, enabled new and significant progress to be made during the eighteenth century.

Apart from the marine chronometer, which will be discussed elsewhere no new type of clock or watch was invented, but the precision of movements gradually attained a chronometric standard. Pocket watches continued to be made in a more or less definite style for a long time, although straightforward watches became much slimmer. In the reign of Louis XV (1715–1774) cases became round and more elegant; their outline is like a rather round and inflated lozenge. When the pierced and engraved watch is supplied with a striking mechanism it can be recognized by the very large hinge parallel to the pendant, finely carved, solid and decorative, and still known today as a Louis XV hinge. These cases are protected by an outer cover of tooled leather, of tortoiseshell or repoussé gold or silver, such as those illustrated here. Fine enamel painting, chiselling and precious stones sometimes decorate the elegant watches of this period. The watch was worn as an ornament, the watch chain displayed over brocaded dresses or waistcoats, while the keys, tassels and seals attached to it jingled together.

In the Louis XVI period watch-cases remained the same shape, but the pendant was lengthened and the diameter became slightly smaller than in the Louis XV style. The three round watches show in the color plate are of this period. While considering in a general way the characteristics of eighteenth-century watches it is of interest to point out the rare and magnificent piece shown in pls. 93, 94 and plate III. This is an astronomical watch with two faces, made in France and bearing the signature of Gautrin (1739–1799), a consummate artist.

CLOCKMAKERS' JEWELS

The Swiss mathematician Nicolas Fatio, who was born at Basle in 1664 and brought up in Geneva, discovered in 1700 how to pierce and fashion precious stones. He went to England to exploit these processes and settled in London, where he also made optical glass.

The English patent granted to Fatio for his discovery dates from 1st May 1704. He exploited it in collaboration with two French clockmakers working in London, Pierre and Thomas Debaufre. An entry in the *London Gazette* dated 11th May 1704 announced that watches mounted with pierced rubies could be examined in their workshop.

Until that time the staff pivots of the wheels moved in holes pierced through the plates. These holes gradually filled with verdigris from the oil used to prevent friction and after a while a sticky deposit was formed which

Bracelet with a gold watch, its balance visible, and with a decoration of enamel and diamonds in two rows. Geneva, about 1790

increased frictional resistance and sometimes even stopped the watch. The balance-staffs turned in holes called oil-sinks, made in the brass of the base plate and in the cock without entirely piercing the metal. Later a simple hole was pierced in which a polished steel counter-pivot was set. A small cavity made at the top of the hole below the counter-pivot served to retain the oil.

At first jewels were only set in the balance-staffs and the pivots of the escapement wheel, but subsequently in the other pivot-points of the moving parts. When different methods replaced the crown-wheel escapement hardstones were used.

The introduction of bearings with rubies and the use of jewels generally in watchmaking was a great step forward. They helped to reduce friction, motive power and wear on the staffs and also kept the oil at the pivotal points.

Until about 1770 English watchmakers alone benefited from these improvement because the manufacture of watch-jewels was kept secret. In a memorandum of 6th September 1771 the great French clockmaker Pierre Le Roy (1717–1785) wrote: "Whereas in Harrison's watch and indeed in all the good watches of England the balance-staff and the last wheels (of the train) are set and move in pierced rubies, we in France have not the secret of making these rubies."

Sent to England by the duc de Praslin, French Minister of the Marine, and charged with discovering the principles of John Harrison's marine watches, Ferdinand Berthoud, another great watchmaker of the period, wrote in a letter on the subject dated 14th March 1766: "If some parts of this watch would be difficult to make, there are others which could not be done at all in France. I mean the pierced rubies carrying the pivotal staffs," and again later: "I have become acquainted in London with all the necessary workers whom I shall make use of until I can find others to take their place. It would not then be difficult to construct this machine."

Escapement by Graham for a pendulum clock

On 3rd November Ferdinand Berthoud sent two marine clocks to the French Admiralty to be tested at sea. They comprised the use of hardstones on the moving surfaces of the cylinder-escapement with an intermediate rack gearing which was part of the design. The good results obtained gained for the designer a pension of three thousand livres and the title of Horloger-Mécanicien de Sa Majesté et de la Marine. These were probably the first two watches set with jewels to be made on the Continent.

As a result of his friendly relationship with English watchmakers, Abraham Louis Bréguet (1744–1823) was able to acquire pierced stones from England as well as different watchmakers' parts with hardstones. By this means his Paris workshop produced, about 1796, his famous Subscription watches, furnished with a ruby cylinder escapement (pl. 108).

At the end of the eighteenth century the secret was known and France, followed by Switzerland, began to manufacture watch jewels. The Master watchmakers, and particularly A. L. Bréguet, used them widely for their fine pieces. Pierced stones, counter-pivots, roller or cylinder escapements, anchor or release cams are all made of sapphires or rubies. However, until the Restoration of 1814 no stones were used in the making of watches for everyday use. It was only in 1823 that Pierre Frédéric Ingold, jewel specialist in the House of Bréguet, returned to his birthplace, La Chaux-de-Fonds in Switzerland, to make stones on a commercial scale.

ESCAPEMENTS

Other inventions, much more important for accuracy than the pierced hardstone, appeared about 1710. The most significant of these was the replacement of the verge by other escapements with improved mechanisms capable of maintaining and counting the oscillations of clock pendulums, or of balance-spring watches, without making it necessary to modify their respective periods.

The question of compensation which will be discussed below preoccupied the minds of the best European clockmakers throughout the eighteenth century. Several different types of escapement were invented, works of great ingenuity and manual skill. Apart from the few escapements still in use today there were numerous others which have since diappeared. Escapements can be classifed in three categories:

(1) *Recoil escapements*. In these an organ dependent on the oscillator describes a recoil from the crown-wheel at the moment of hesitation

Cylinder escapement

Pl. VII   A group of watches from Au Vieux Cadran. Top left: watch with a case enamelled with the Holy Family. Movement replaced by Shearwood. D. 3·7 cm. Top center: watch with a double case in silver by Lestourgeon, London. Two hands, the regulators in front, on the dial. The inside of gilt brass, the cock of silver. Below the cock several pillars of blued steel, others engraved and pierced, with a crown and two interlaced initials. In the center of the crown is a St. Andrew's cross. On the dial the lion and the unicorn. D. 5·5 cm. Watch D. 4·5, T. 2·5 cm. Top right: watch by Julien Le Roy, Paris. Enamelled with a shepherd and shepherdess and a landscape on the interior. Fusee and chain. The cock with very fine original engraving. D. 4·5, T. 2·6 cm. Bottom left: Revolutionary watch. Decimal and duodecimal dial, and the days of the month. Two hands on each dial. Fuse and chain and flat movement. D. 5·5, T. 2·2 cm. Bottom center: watch with a double case in gold by F. Roberts, London. Hercules and Mars. D. 4·5 cm. Bottom right: gold watch with a double face by François Girard, Carouges. On side records hours and minutes, the other the months and days of the week. The months are shown in the blue ring, the hands gilded. Chain and fusee movement. D. 5, T. 2·2 cm

in the train. This kind produced the greatest disturbance on the period of oscillation. The verge or crown-wheel escapement is one of these.

(2) *Frictional rest escapements.* Here the balance is constantly in contact with the escape-wheel without forcing a recoil at the moment of hesitation in the train. This type of escapement causes much less disturbance in the period of oscillation.

(3) *Detached escapements.* This type of movement is characterized by the interposition of a piece between the escape-wheel and oscillator. The escapement wheel is held immobile against this piece at the period of hesitation in the train. Except at the very brief moment of impulse the balance moves without any contact with the escapement. Detached escapements cause the least disturbance to the oscillating period and are mechanically the best. Watches and chronometers with this kind of movement have a large, heavy balance-wheel (with a large moment of inertia) coupled with a spiral spring. All these changes moved towards precision.

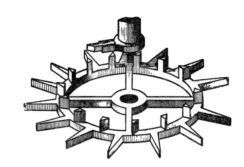

Duplex escapement

The only frictional rest (dead-beat) escapements still in use are the Graham escapements for pendulum clocks and the cylinder escapement for clocks. The earliest of these bears the name of its inventor, George Graham (1675–1751) and dates from 1715. The principle was applied immediately to making clocks with second-hands and a pendulum about a yard long. These proved accurate enough for a proper study of the variations in temperature which affected the period of oscillation and consequently the daily working of the instrument. In 1715 Graham invented the compensating mercury pendulum. Henceforward the clock showing seconds became and remained for more than two centuries the most accurate of measuring instruments and every astronomical observatory had one.

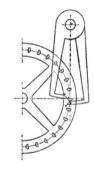

Pin-wheel escapement

The invention of the cylinder-escapement is also attributed to George Graham, although his first rudimentary model was patented in 1695 by William H. Houghton (1638–1713), Thomas Tompion's associate, and by Edward Barlow (1636–1716). Tompion was George Graham's uncle. The two frictional rest escapements mentioned above are distinguished by their extreme simplicity. Neither one had more than two parts: the anchor and wheel in Graham's experiment, the cylinder and wheel in the second.

These frictional rest escapements were also successful in the second half of the eighteenth century: the virgule escapement invented by the French clockmaker, Jean André Lepaute (1720–1789); the duplex escapement attributed to Pierre Le Roy and the double virgule escapement invented by Amant, perfected by J. A. Lepaute together with P. A. Caron de Beaumarchais.

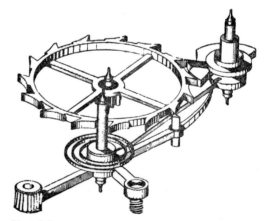

Pivoted detent escapement

The first detached escapement was demonstrated to the Académie des Sciences in Paris in 1748 by Pierre Le Roy. It was a detent escapement, intended for marine clocks with a spiral balance, one of the first being made by Le Roy.

The lever escapement which today is fitted to almost every watch of whatever size, was invented about 1754 by the English clockmaker Thomas Mudge (1715-1794). At first it comprised four pieces: the wheel, the anchor, the fork and the balance staff, which, even in miniature, was like an arbor of complicated cams. It also comprised four functional parts in hardstone and remained unique of its kind till 1782. The Swiss clockmaker Josiah Emery (1725-1796), working in London, made several modifications. Towards the middle of the nineteenth century it acquired its modern form with only three pieces.

At the same time the detent escapement was also improved in several ways. Reserved at first for marine chronometers, from the mid-nineteenth century it was used for good quality chronometric watches. The clockmakers who contributed most towards the watch in its modern form were the Englishmen John Arnold (1736–1799) and Thomas Earnshaw (1749–1829). After the beginning of the twentieth century the lever escapement allowed a greater degree of precision equal to or superior to that of detent chronometers and the detent escapement was reserved for marine chronometers.

COMPENSATION

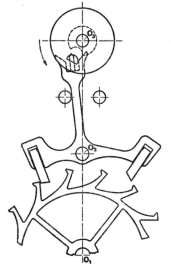

Club-toothed lever escapement

With the introduction of the pendulum oscillator in clocks, the spiral balance in watches, and the replacement of the verge escapement by others that were much less disturbing to the oscillator, the precision of chronometric instruments was such as to allowe an accurate calculation of the effect of temperature on the movement. It had been observed that heat caused a retard, and cold an advance, so first it was necessary to fine the cause for this and then the means of correcting the error.

In pendulum clocks it is the lenghthening and shortening of the rod of the pendulum by expansion that causes these variations. They are not great variations because the rod of the pendulum is steel and therefore their exact rate is about half a second per degree Celsius per day.

In the case of the spring-balance oscillator the effect of temperature is much greater, rising to eleven seconds per degree per day, because the spiral is steel and the balance brass. Expansion has the same effect here as on the pendulum, but is is much diminished because the effect on the balance and the spiral contradicts, and therefore almost exactly compensates, itself. Temperature influences the oscillating period by as much as 10.9 seconds per degree per day because of the different elastic properties of the spiral which becomes softer as the temperature rises and more rigid as it falls.

METHODS OF ADJUSTMENT

These methods aimed to correct the effect of temperature so that the period of the oscillator remained constant between temperatures of 0° and 40° centigrade. So it was necessary to find additional devices capable of producing an advance in hot, and a retard in cold conditions, of one half of a second per degree per day for clocks, and eleven seconds for watches, to compensate for the effects indicated above. Thus the precision of chronometers, independent now of variation in temperature, would be greatly increased. Watchmakers call this compensation.

For ordinary pendulum clocks the first attempted solution was to construct the rod of the pendulum of wood, thoroughly matured and protected from damp with varnish. The second solution, valid for clocks with seconds, henceforward known as "precision pendulum-clocks" or "astronomical pendulum-clocks", was Graham's mercury pendulum. Invented in 1721, it was composed of a steel rod, at the end of which is fixed a cylindrical glass bulb containing mercury. As the temperature rises the steels rod expands and lengthens, whereas the mercury, with a coefficient of expansion seventeen times greater than that of steel, rises in its bulb. These two simultaneous and contrary effects have the result of maintaining the pendulum's centre of gravity at a constant distance from its axis of suspension.

The gridiron pendulum, invented by John Harrison in 1726, has a heavy bar fixed to the stem of the pendulum by means of a series of parallel rods, some of which are steel and others brass, bronze or zinc. The rods are placed symmetrically on either side of the rod of the pendulum. The number used varies and depends on the difference between the coefficients of expansion of the metals used for the curb and the rod, increasing as the expansion difference diminishes.

Whereas the steel rods are fixed close to the axis of suspension, getting longer towards the bottom, the brass, bronze or zinc rods are kept in place

Pl. 88 Carriage watch by Julien Le Roy, late 17th century. Copper case, red lacquer with decoration and eyelets of silver. The case is pierced and shaped in the interior and there is a regulator key. The cock is decorated with scrolls and a dolphin. The chime has a fine tone. D. 15, T. 6 cm. Private Collection, Paris

Pl. 89 Japanese carriage watch in silver, engraved and pierced, with a striking mechanism. D. 7.2, H. 4 cm. Private Collection, Paris

Pl. 90 Watch-cases in studded leather. Left: Silver studs on brass; the leather has perished. D. 5.8 cm. Right: Silver studs on brass, leather still in place. D. 6.5 cm. Musée des Arts décoratifs, Paris

Pl. 91 Left: Case with gold studs on a cover of black shagreen. D. 5.5 cm. Right: Chased and chiselled silver box, German, by Augustin Rummel. D. 5.8 cm. Formerly Olivier Collection; Musée des Arts décoratifs, Paris

Pl. 92 Left: Watch-case of pierced tortoiseshell. D. 5.5 cm. Right: Watch-case. D. 5.5 cm. Formerly Olivier Collection; Musée des Arts décoratifs, Paris

88

89

90

91

92

93

94

95

96

97

98

by a cross-bar linking the ends of two steel rods and lengthening towards the top. The expansion of these rods and the rod of the pendulum counteract one another, hence the distance between the centre of gravity and the axis of suspension remains constant at temperatures between 0–40° centigrade, and consequently the oscillation period is not affected. In the case of watches the problem was more difficult. The first spiral-balance oscillator supplied with means of compensation was John Harrison's marine chronometer No. 1, which was first tested at sea in 1736. Inspired by the gridiron pendulum it was composed of a large number of laminated bars of steel and brass working by means of a system of levers, along the whole length of the spiral. This distance was shortened when the temperature rose, and lengthened when it fell. It was in effect a static, horizontal, triple gridiron.

In 1755 Pierre Le Roy invented the bimetallic balance, which became general in watches of good quality from the early nineteenth century. The rim of this balance is a bimetallic strip composed of two metals having different coefficients, steel on the inside and brass on the outside. The rim is cut near the arm, either at two points diametrically opposite, or, if the balance has three arms, at three equidistant points; it is pierced with a certain number of holes to receive large-headed brass, gold or platinum screws.

The metals of the balance-rim are soldered together, the brass being welded on to the steel. Brass has a higher coefficient of expansion so that a rise in temperature has the effect of closing the mass of the rim towards the center; the moment of inertia of the balance becomes smaller, producing a reduction in the oscillation period, which causes the watch to advance.

The opposite effect is obtained when the watch is kept in the cold: the moment of inertia is increased, the period is lengthened and the watch goes slow.

The compensation thus obtained can be adjusted so that variations in temperature have the least possible effect. To do this it is necessary to move two, four or six screws towards the cut or away from it while keeping them symmetrical, and therefore the rim always has more holes than screws.

Other systems of compensation were used for watches. A. L. Bréguet is responsible for a bimetallic strip, curved and bent, with two parallel U-shaped arms fixed to the short end of the regulator index. A salient piece attached to the end of the interior segment of the strip serves as a point of rest for the spring as it expands, whilst a pin inserted in the same arm of the index fulfilled the same function when the spiral contracted. In cold conditions these two supporting parts were very close to one another; the active part of the spiral was the shortest and resulted in the period of oscillation being diminished. In warm conditions the support of the bimetallic strip was withdrawn from the pin of the index so that the active length of the spiral was augmented

Pls. 93 & 94   Complex watch by Gautrin, mid 18th century (1739-1799). Gautrin was a well known maker who presented to the Academy a watch showing the seconds and sold one to Louis XVI. This watch has a double face; one side shows the hour, the minutes, and date; the other twenty-four hours, the months, the zodiac, the phases of the moon and the time of sunrise and sunset, seen through two slots which move so as to diminish the duration of the sun's appearance. D. 4·5, T. 2·5 cm; D. of dial 3·6 cm. Private Collection, Paris

Pl. 95   Travelling clock by Baillon, Paris, about 1770. W. 18 cm. Kugel Collection, Paris

Pl. 96   Repeater-watch with a châtelaine by Dufalga of Geneva and Paris. Enamel decoration. Another watch with châtelaine; pearls and translucent blue enamel decoration. Musée d'Horlogerie, La Chaux-de-Fonds

Pls. 97 & 98   Officers' clocks, late 18th century. The first by Hessen, H. 17 cm; the second by Le Roy, Paris. Below: Small Viennese travelling clock. H. 14 cm. Kugel Collection and Au Vieux Cadran, Paris

and hence the corresponding period of the oscillator. This method, intended only for watches of less high quality, as it allowed no adjustment of the compensation, was short-lived; only the compensated balance survived to be further developed.

INVENTION OF NEW TYPES OF WATCHES

The ingenuity and manual skill of watchmakers in inventing new escapements and compensatory systems had produced pendulum clocks and marine clocks with chronometric precision, but it did not stop there. Talented English, French and then Swiss clockmakers of the mid-eighteenth to mid-nineteenth centuries, vied with each other in designing new kinds of small watches.

About 1755 Jean Romilly of Geneva (1714–1796) was the advocate of the eight-day watch, constructing several examples, one of which had a cylinder escapement and a very large balance giving one alternation per second (two alternations equal one oscillation). He also constructed watches showing the equation of time, and a repeater second-watch which went for 378 days without being wound, which he presented to the Académie royale des Sciences in 1758. He was a skilful experimenter and the author of numerous technical articles on clocks. In a treatise published in 1887 it was claimed that no other single person made such accurate experiments as Jean Romilly.

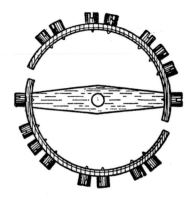

The French clockmaker Jean Antoine Lépine (1720–1814) invented watch movements with no fusee and with bars or bridges instead or pillars and upper plates in about 1775. This arrangement allowed the balance to be set on one side instead of on top of the mainspring, wheels and escapement and produced a much flatter watch. Lépine also claimed the invention of the virgule escapement.

The term Lépine caliber has been in use ever since to describe a watch movement in which the second-hand is placed in the axis of the winding-staff as opposed to the Savonette caliber in which the second-hand is placed on an axis perpendicular to the axis of the winding-staff. The term caliber had been in use since the eighteenth century—it was first coined by Sully in 1715—to describe the arrangement and dimensions of different parts of a watch movement. Then the word has been used to describe the form of the movement, the bridges, the origin of the watch or the name of its constructor.

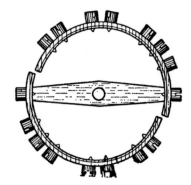

Antoine Tavan (1749–1836), of French origin, was one of the most distinguished watchmakers of Geneva. He became a freeman of the city in

Normal bimetallic balance, at normal temperature and at high temperature

1798. An expert in escapements, he made a collection of twelve different kinds, now in the Musée d'Horlogerie in Geneva. In 1808 he presented to the Geneva Society of Arts a watch with a "second beat", that is with two sets of gears. This type of watch was later the basis for an important development.

In 1816 the Society of Arts instituted a competition for the regulating of clocks and watches at the Observatory in Geneva. Its terms were as follows:

"A prize of 800 florins is offered to the man who can exhibit a watch the variations of which do not exceed three seconds in twenty-four hours, whether it be placed on a flat surface, suspended, or worn, and this must be observed in a temperature above 25 in the Réaumur scale."

Antoine Tavan carried off the prize. He also constructed a large number of chronometers remarkable for their perfection of design and precision, but often also for the complication of their mechanisms.

It would appear from the foregoing that watches had improved greatly since Huygens's invention of the balance oscillator. But after 1775 the ordinary watch remained almost at a standstill whilst the luxury watch was continually being improved.

In the first half of the nineteenth century the turnip watch was still the watch of the peasant. It was similar to those made a hundred years before but of inferior quality, because the standard of workmanship, as well as of taste, had deteriorated. In fact the manufacture of crown-wheel watches, both simple and repeating ones, had become semi-industrial with the work being farmed out. These watches are mass-produced and dull. The only jewels they contain are counter-pivots of rubies, whilst the decoration of the cock, no longer engraved and chiselled, grows ever more feeble. They are of little interest to collectors.

At the same time splendid chronometers were made for the rich and, whether simple or complicated, they achieved a standard rarely surpassed since. They mark the culminating point of the skill of the artist-craftsman and the finest ones are often unique as the watch would be ordered by a client and fashioned to his taste.

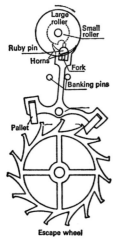

Club-toothed lever escapement

THE GREAT WATCHMAKERS OF WESTERN EUROPE

There was intense competition between all the great watchmakers of western Europe. Whilst the English craftsmen were chiefly preoccupied with improving the precision of marine and pocket watches, in France and Switzerland interest was centered on research on practical additions, as well as on new types of watches. This period is also characterized by the fact that English clockmakers, foremost until that time, were now overtaken on some points by French and Swiss designers.

Leaving aside George Graham, John Harrison, Thomas Mudge and Josiah Emery, who have already been mentioned, it is essential to list the most distinguished English eighteenth- and nineetenth-century watchmakers.

John Ellicott   1706–1772
John Arnold   1736–1799
Thomas Earnshaw   1749–1829
William Frodsham   1778–1850
Edward John Dent   1790–1853
James Ferguson Cole   1798–1880
Charles Frodsham   1810–1871
Aaron L. Dennison   1812–1895 (American by birth)
Edward Howard   1813–1904 (American by birth)

In France, apart from Pierre Le Roy, Ferdinand Berthoud, Pierre A. Caron de Beaumarchais, Jean Antoine Lépine and A. L. Bréguet were:

Jean André Lepaute   1720–1789
Antide Janvier   1751–1835
Louis Moinet   1786–1853
Joseph Winnerl   1799–1886 (Austrian by birth)

There were more watchmakers of Swiss than of other nationality at this time. Of these Ferdinand Berthoud, A. L. Bréguet and Josiah Emery developed their careers in France or England. Jean Romilly and Antoine Tavan have already been discussed:

Pierre Jaquet-Droz   1721-1790
Abraham Louis Perrelet   1729–1820
Jacques Frédéric Houriet   1743–1830
Jean Frédéric Leschot   1746–1824
Henry Louis Jaquet-Droz   1752–1791
Jean Moïse Pouzait   1753–1793
Frédéric Louis Favre-Bulle   1770–1849
Jean François Bautte   1772–1845
Urban Jürgensen   1776–1830 (Danish by birth)
Louis Benjamin Audemars   1782–1833
Pierre Frédéric Ingold   1787–1878
Georges Auguste Leschot   1800–1884
Jean Célamis Lutz   1800–1863
Antoine Le Coultre   1803–1881
Henry Grandjean   1803–1879

Pl. 99   Revolutionary watches. Right: Decimal dial counting ten to a hundred, and duodecimal twelve to sixty (ten decimal hours equal twenty-four duodecimal hours). Left: Watch showing the date. D. 5 cm. Au Vieux Cadran, Paris

Pl. 100   Watch with four dials by Bréguet, showing hours, minutes, seconds and the temperature. D. 4.4, T. O. 6 cm. Private Collection, Paris

Pl. 101   Watch with a double dial and second-hand. D. 5 cm. Au Vieux Cadran, Paris

Pl. 102   Watch by Bréguet with the date, repeating at the quarters. Hidden signature. D. 6.5 cm. Au Vieux Cadran, Paris

Pl. 103   Gold watch by Bréguet, with the date. D. 3.9 cm. Private Collection, Paris

Pl. 104   Perpetual watch by Bréguet with a pedometer winding mechanism. Gold case, anchor escapement, compensating balance and the following dials: hours, minutes, seconds, phases of the moon and a winding indicator of 60 hours. Through the slot in the seconds dial the date appears. D. 5.7 cm, H. with glass 20 cm. Bréguet, No. 28. Provenance: duc de la Force (1791). Musée d'Horlogerie, La Chaux-de-Fonds

Pl. 105   Back view of a clock by F. Berthoud H. 25 cm; D. of the dial 13 cm. Au Vieux Cadran, Paris

99

100

101

102

103

104

105

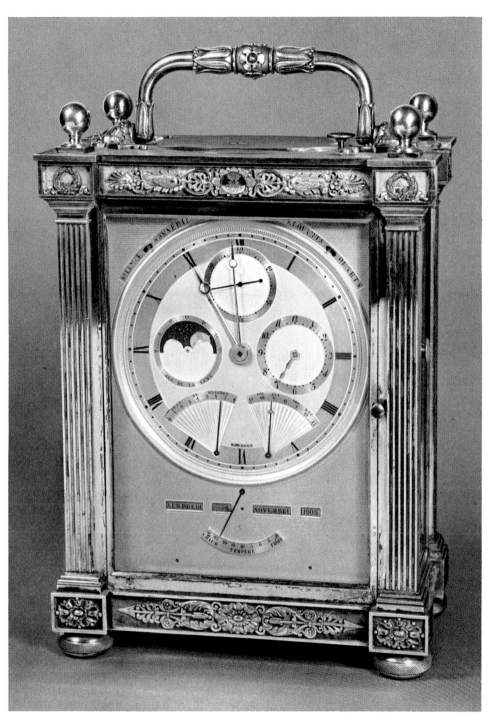

108

109

Sylvain Mairet   1805–1890
Jules Jürgensen   1808–1877
Antoine Léchaud   1812–1875
Louis Richard   1812–1895
Georges Frédéric Roskopf   1813–1889 (German by birth)
Ulysse Nardin   1823–1876
Several important clockmakers came from other countries:
Heinrich Johannes Kessels   1781–1848 (Germany)
Adolf Ferdinand Lange   1815–1875 (Germany)
Charles Fasold   1818–1898 (Germany)
Karl Moritz Grossmann   1826–1885 (Germany)
Henri Robert Ekegren   1823–1896 (Sweden)
Victor Kullberg   1824–1890 (Sweden)
Lyman W. Tompson   1825–1910 (U.S.A.)
Edward Koehn Snr.   1839–1908 (U.S.A.)

It would require a large volume to deal adequately with the work of these talented craftsmen and to show their contribution to general progress. Here we can narrate only the most important events in the history of clock-making.

1768. Jacques Frédéric Houriet spent nine years in Paris working in the studios of Julien Le Roy, Watchmaker Royal; he became friendly with his compatriots Berthoud and Bréguet and then returned to Switzerland to found a watchmaking business at Le Locle. He is usually considered to be the founder of the watchmaking industry of the Jura near Neuchâtel.

1770. Abraham Louis Perrelet at Le Locle invented the so-called perpetual watch which is wound by the movement of the wearer, the forerunner of the present-day automatic wrist-watch.

1780. A. L. Bréguet, working in Paris, perfected the perpetual watch and invented an escapement with constant motive power, which has the ability to restore to the oscillator, at every oscillation, an exact and unchanging quantity of energy whatever the quantity and variation in the motive power. He also invented several other additions and improvements of which the following are the most important:

(1) Improvement of the ruby cylinder escapement (invented by Arnold)   1790
(2) Perpetual calendar   1795
(3) Tourbillon   1795
(4) Repeating chimes   1795

Pl. 106   Mechanism of a travelling clock by Le Roi et Fils. 20×13×11 cm; T. 11 cm. Private Collection, Paris

Pl. 107   Gilt travelling clock by Bréguet. H. 18 cm. Musée des Arts décoratifs, Paris

Pl. 108   Subscription watch by A.L. Bréguet, about 1820. Cylinder escapement with ruby bearings. Cock with a compensating ratchet and shock-absorber. Musée d'Horlogerie, La Chaux-de-Fonds

Pl. 109   Swiss watch of the Empire period in the form of a bonbonnière. The movement strikes boldly on the hours and the quarters. Formerly G. Loup Collection; Collection H. Wilsdorf, Geneva

(5) Sympathetic clock which reset itself 1795
(6) Watch to be read by touch 1796–1800
(7) Sympathetic clock which reset and rewound a watch 1805–1810
A. L. Bréguet was also the inventor of the parachute which is the first form of a device for protecting the staff pivots of the balance against shock. He was the first to construct flat and extra flat watches. Bréguet is considered to be the greatest watchmaker of all time. With his competitors and contemporaries he reached the heights of complicated work.

Watch with a visible escapement in a glass and metal case, about 1830

In the Revolutionary period watches were made in France to count decimal hours (for a day of twice ten hours) and if they included monthly calendars, the names of the months were the Revolutionary names. Wrist-watches and ring watches (which were soon abandoned on account of their fragility) appeared in the First Empire and it was at this period that the cylinder escapement was developed.

Towards the end of the First Empire there was a fashion for ladies' watches with cases in the shape of flowers, mandolines, lyres or hearts (Pl. VIII). It was only a passing fancy. From 1820–1830 watch movements scarcely changed at all. The old crown-wheel escapement was still in use but the cylinder escapement was more usual. Flat and extra flat watches became very fashionable about 1830. They were engraved according to the taste of the time with romantic subjects or with transparent enamels over a low relief engraving.

During the period 1780–1820 enamelled watches had a great vogue in Geneva and talented painters decorated pocket watches with fine enamel painting. They can be distinguished from older, similar watches by their brilliant appearance which is due to the coat of translucent enamel painted over to protect the design.

The so-called Chinese watch also appeared at that time. As soon as trade with China was well established the mandarins and overlords began to collect complicated and richly-decorated watches. All the best Geneva watchmakers and artists and some from the cantons of Jura, Neuchâtel and Vaud, turned their resources to satisfy this demand. They constructed splendid enamel watches with twisted bridge movements and decorated all over with engraving, sometimes even enriched with cloisonné enamels.

Pl. 99 shows two French watches from the First Republic (1792–1795), one showing both ten- and twelve-hour time, the other, twelve-hour time and the day of the month. Pls. 100–104 are all different kinds of watch designed by Bréguet. The last is specially interesting as it comprises the following complicated work: automatic winding; an up-and-down dial; free anchor escape-

Pl. VIII A group of watches from Au Vieux Cadran. Top left: *movement by Fabron, Geneva. H. 4 cm.* Top center: *small watch with stackfreed; in the interior of the case, a royal crown surrounded by a laurel wreath. H. of case 1·6, T. 1·3 cm; H. of watch 1·4 cm.* Top right: *enamelled watch by J. Jolly, Paris. Fusee and gut cord. The interior and all the parts enamelled. D. 4·4, T. 1·8 cm.* Center left: *watch in the shape of an apple by J. Leroy. Green enamel. D. 3, T. 2·2 cm.* Center: *watch with an emerald case in the shape of a heart by J. Barberet, Paris. The emerald D. 3·4, T. 1·4 cm.* Center right: *enamelled watch in the shape of a cockle shell decorated with pearls and enamels in beige, reddish brown and black.* Bottom left (above): *Montre à tact by Leroy. Greyish blue enamel on a chequered ground. D. 3·7, T. 0·5 cm.* Bottom left (below): *enamelled watch in the shape of a basket of flowers. H. 3·5, W. 2·8 cm.* Bottom center: *watch with automata in which the characters actually strike the hour on the bell. D. 6, T. 2·3 cm.* Bottom right (above): *watch in the shape of a heart on a scent bottle. Framed in pearls, with a musical case. H. 3, T. 2·8 cm.* Bottom right (below): *watch in the shape of a mandoline, part of arms of Marie Antoinette and Louis XVI. Enamels, diamonds and a musical case. H. 8·7 cm*

ment; holes and levers set with rubies; dates; phases of the moon and a minute repeater mechanism. The "subscription" watch with cylinder escapement in rubies of pl. 108 is also the work of A. L. Bréguet. It is the only model which the watchmaker duplicated in about one hundred and fifty examples and these are avidly sought by collectors today. When it was made the price of this watch varied according to its casing between 600 and 1800 francs.

The magnificent repeater and chiming enamel watch of pl. 109 dates from the First Empire (1804–1814), whereas the striking watch shown in pl. 110 signed by Jaquet-Droz and dating from about 1790 is also of the perpetual type. These two watches were originally part of the Loup collection which was formed entirely in China by a Swiss businessman. Pl. 111 shows two repeater watches with automata, a fashion which continued in vogue from the First Empire until 1830.

The next two illustrations show a repeater, perpetual watch, signed *Du Bois et Fils, Le Locle,* and dating from 1812 (pl. 112); a watch with a skeletonised movement, cut away and engraved and, on the left, a slightly later watch in which the repeater striking mechanism is visible, whereas it is usually concealed beneath the dial (pl. 114).

The last illustration to this chapter (pls. 113 and 115) is an extremely complicated watch which was exhibited at the Exposition Universelle in Paris in 1878, with a dial of fifteen hands as well as a dial for the phases of the moon. It was built by the Swiss Ami Lecoultre-Piguet of Le Brassus. It has the following features: a large and small chiming movement, striking the hours and quarters and a minute repeater; an alarm; a chronograph movement with slide; a double dial showing two different hours; perpetual calendar; day, date, year and Leap Year; phases and quarters of the moon; up-and-down dial; bimetallic thermometer; triple remontoire; double form of setting by the pendant; anchor escapement with compensated balance. The watch has forty-seven rubies.

THE DECLINE OF CRAFTSMANSHIP
AND THE RISE OF MECHANIZATION

It is true to say that after the end of the eighteenth century there were far more processes and mechanical aids in watchmaking than is sometimes supposed. In 1799 an industrialist named Japy made rough working models of watches at Beaucourt in the French Jura by an already very advanced

Pl. 110 Pedometer watch by Jaquet-Droz, late 18th century. It rings the quarters and is decorated with pearls and rubies. Formerly G. Loup Collection; Musée d'Horlogerie, La Chaux-de-Fonds

Pl. 111 Watches with automata. Above: Automata; bell-tower, mill, fisherman and fish, with its original key. D. 5·7 cm. Below: Automata with fountains, lions, swans, a dolphin and a landscape background. Original key. D. 6·4 cm. R. Lecoultre Collection, Le Sentier

Pl. 112 Lépine watch with automatic winding and repeating mechanism. The oscillating weight stops when the spring is fully wound. Dial signed: Du Bois et Fils, 1812, Le Locle. Musée d'Horlogerie, La Chaux-de-Fonds

Pl. 113 Dial and movement of the highly complex watch by Ami Lecoultre-Piguet, 1870 (see plate 115). Musée d'Horlogerie, La Chaux-de-Fonds

112

113

mechanical process. Georges Leschot (1800 1878) developed the lever escapement and its manufacture by machine, and in 1794 the factory of Fontainemelon was founded, as the first step towards mechanized manufacture in Swiss watchmaking. After a slow start the advance from 1840 onward became rapid.

Another important development was the replacement of the key-winding system, still used until then for different winding systems, by the pendants invented by Adrien Philippe at Geneva in 1842 and by Antoine Le Coultre in 1847. In 1870 the first repeater watches to be mechanically made were also put on the market by the same Antoine Le Coultre of Le Sentier in the Swiss Jura.

Elsewhere improvements were made to the oscillator balance spring in an attempt to improve the isochronism of the periods and to reduce the differences in rate between different vertical positions. To do this the spring was furnished with one or two terminal curves, a technique inspired by A. L. Bréguet, but its scientific basis was a treatise: *L'Etude sur le spiral réglant*, published in 1860 by Edouard Philipps, a French engineer.

In 1862 the House of Nicole & Capt in London produced the first chronographs with a device for returning to zero, inspired by Henri Piguet of Le Brassus in Switzerland.

The use of the lever escapement was to culminate in the mechanical watch of today. It seems surprising that watchmakers waited so long before adopting this system, the perfection and simplicity of which seem obvious. It had been more or less ignored by watchmakers, who were cautious of the complexity of the different means of manufacture to which it had been subject since its invention in 1754, until the last quarter of the last century.

Pl. 114 Lépine watch with a skeleton movement cut out and engraved, 1800. Musée d'Horlogerie, La Chaux-de-Fonds

Pl. 115 Highly complex watch designed and made by Ami Lecoultre-Piguet of Le Brassus (Switzerland) and shown at the Universal Exhibition in Paris in 1878. It has the following features: chiming mechanism for the hours and the quarters, minute-repeater; alarm; stop-watch device and corrector; double hour dial showing time in different time-zones; perpetual calendar of the days and date of the month. Indicator shows when spring fully wound; bimetallic thermometer. Triple remontoir and adjustment under the ring. Musée d'Horlogerie, La Chaux-de-Fonds

Bracelet watch by Nitot, jeweller to Napoleon I, 1806

The classic treatise on the lever escapement which made a great contribution to its popularity, was written by Moritz Grossman and dates from 1867. Only after that date did the cylinder escapement begin to decline in favour of the lever escapement and be gradually relegated to watches of inferior quality.

About the same time, Georges Frédéric Roskopf, an industrialist at La Chaux-de-Fonds, constructed a very simplified watch with a lever escapement with pin pallet and without jewels; it was known as the people's watch. Its production was subsequently greatly extended and marked the end of the cylinder movement.

Henceforward, apart from marine chronometers, which were still equipped with a spring detent escapement, the lever escapement was the only kind to be used in small watches. It was made mechanically and in different qualities and was as suitable for the Roskopf or lever watch as for the most sophisticated and precise chronometers.

After about 1850 mechanization spread and brought with it a rather characterless period in which the most important factors were mechanical function in conjunction with strength and precision. The day of the craftsman was over, watch movements were no longer works of art, but manufactured objects, the finish and quality of which varied according to price. Some concern for esthetics could still be seen in the way the case, the dial and the hands were made. But only a few artist-craftsmen were engaged in constructing and regulating by hand chronometers specially built to take part in the tests of the Observatory competitions held in Neuchâtel, Greenwich, Besançon and Geneva.

The Marine Chronometer

W HEN ONE CONSIDERS the factors which contributed most to the birth of modern society one's mind naturally turns to the great navigators of the late fifteenth and early sixteenth centuries, but it was the seventeenth- and eighteenth-century clockmakers who gave navigation on the high seas the means of precise reckoning indispensable to future development.

Until the middle of the seventeenth century, that is for a period of almost 250 years, the economic repercussions of the Genoese, Portuguese and Spanish discoverers were relatively limited. Only three or four great ocean routes were known and used in the eighteenth century. At that period navigation was still so dangerous that ships driven off their intended course along the coasts and islands were often lost. The unsatisfactory means of finding position at sea were the cause of many wrecks every year till the late eighteenth century, whilst pirates on watch for vessels in distress only added to the dangers.

It was essential for navigation to establish the exact position of islands and continents and to draw accurate charts of their coasts. It was also necessary to find a means for navigators to determine the geographical position of their ship accurately by day or night.

The fundamental technical problem was how to determine the geographical coordinates of a given place. These coordinates are the latitude, that is the angular height above or below the equator, and the longitude, or angular distance between the meridian on which the observer is standing and that of a standard meridian such as Greenwich (Longitude 0º).

The latitude of a place is calculated at night by the height of the pole star above the horizon and, by day, by the same angular height of the sun as it passes over the meridian. Other means of calculating the latitude of a place measure the angular height of different stars above the horizon where

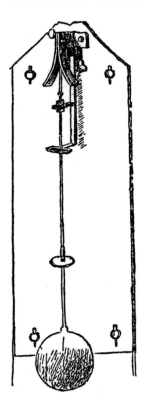

Marine clock with gimbals suspension

the pole star is not visible or the sun hidden by clouds. These methods had been known since antiquity, and in the sixteenth century the astrolabe was accurate enough to calculate the latitude.

To determine the longitude is more difficult. Until mid-eighteenth century sailors proceeded by estimation alone. Astronomical phenomena were the only guides: conjunctions of stars and eclipses of Jupiter's satellites. Over the centuries Greek, Roman and other astronomers had tried to calculate these astronomical events more exactly and by 1500 they could be predicted to within an hour. But in determining the longitude of a place a difference of an hour constitutes an error of about one thousand miles, the distance, say, from Paris to Stockholm, and is completely useless for purposes of navigation.

Philip III, who came to the throne of Spain in 1598, saw how important the problem was and offered a reward of 100,000 escudos to the man who could find a means of more exact calculation. The Netherlands soon followed his example by offering 30,000 florins for an answer to the same problem.

Gradually instruments and astronomical tables were improved and therefore produced better results. In the second half of the eighteenth century a method was evolved that enabled the longitudinal position of a ship to be calculated to within approximately thirty to ten miles. This was the method of lunars, and consists of taking a simultaneous reading of the angular distance of the moon from a known star and the height of these bodies above the horizon. Complicated formulae enabled calculations to be made using tables drawn up by observatories from which longitude could be deduced.

At that time the method which is used today to determine the longitude with great precision was already known, but the instruments necessary to apply it were so imprecise that the error could well amount to some hundreds of miles. The method, suggested by the famous Dutch astronomer and mathematician, Gemma Frisius, was by use of a watch.

In 1558 Frisius wrote:

"People are beginning to use small clocks called watches and they are light enough to be carried. Their movement continues for twenty-four hours and they offer a simple means of finding the longitude. Before setting out set your watch exactly at the time of the country you are leaving. See that the watch does not stop en route. When you have moved a certain distance calculate the hour of this place with the astrolabe; compare this with that of your watch and you have the longitude."

However, more than a hundred years had to pass before Frisius's method produced results equal to those of the lunar-distance method, and another hundred years before really vital progress was made.

The first attempts to use a watch to determine longitude were made by Huygens. The characteristics of the Huygens's marine pendulum clock have already been discussed. Two examples were made about 1665 and tested at sea in 1669. They were not entirely satisfactory and Holmes, the captain of the ship, after a voyage of 5500 km made a landfall in the Cape Verde Islands giving an error of 150 km by the watches and 600 km by dead reckoning.

In 1714 the English Parliament passed a famous act to encourage research on the problem of navigational longitude. Prizes were offered to anyone who could produce an invention which satisfied the Royal Commission Board of Longitude, set up to examine the problem. Rewards were offered on a scale laid down: £10,000 for an instrument accurate to within one degree of longitude on a voyage from England to the West Indies, £15,000 for two thirds of a degree and £20,000 for half a degree. In other words, the timepiece had to be accurate to within two minutes for a voyage of about eight weeks.

In 1718 the Académie des Sciences in Paris, with a donation from Count Meslay, offered a reward of 2,000 livres for the same invention. Henceforward the greatest English and French watchmakers competed in their attempts to construct a marine chronometer.

The English prize of £10,000 was awarded at last in 1765 to John Harrison, a man of seventy-five, who had devoted more than forty years of his life to the problem of marine clocks. He received a further £8,750 in 1773.

The French prize was awarded in 1747 to a famous mathematician and professor of physics at St. Petersburg, Daniel Bernoulli of Basle (1700–1782), for theoretical work on the subject.

JOHN HARRISON, PIERRE LE ROY AND FERDINAND BERTHOUD

Among the many great clockmakers and watchmakers of that very important period in horological and economic history, three are outstanding: John Harrison, the Englishman (1693–1776), the Frenchman Pierre Le Roy (1717–1785) and Ferdinand Berthoud (1725–1807), a Swiss. They were all famous watchmakers, creators of modern chronometry, whose endeavours made navigation far less hazardous, and stimulated the economic and demographic expansion of Europe, North America and the rest of the world which followed in the late eighteenth century.

John Harrison was born at Foulby in Yorkshire. He had been a carpenter's apprentice and seems to have taught himself the fundamentals of clockmaking. His first clocks were simple ones made of wood. In 1735 he laid his marine clock No. 1 before the Board of Longitude. It was a large and heavy machine which had cost him six years of unceasing work (Pl. 116). But it was not deemed accurate enough. He built a second, and then a third marine clock on which he worked for seventeen years. Although lighter than the first two the third still weighed nearly sixty pounds. The fourth, however, was like a large pocket-watch in size and appearance and gave better results. In 1764 his son William embarked with the watch, No. 4, on a warship bound for Jamaica. Both on the outward and inward voyage the watch showed a variation of only one minute, fifty-four seconds.

The Parisian Pierre Le Roy, the son of Julien Le Roy, clockmaker and physicist of renown, early showed a lively, analytical and inventive mind.

In his memorandum: *La Meilleure Manière de Mesurer le Temps en Mer*, Pierre Le Roy described his new longitudinal watch presented to the king in 1766. He suggested that the best way to reduce the causes of irregularity was to make these machines as simple as possible and gave his instructions:

"(1) Reduce friction and make the balance as free and as powerful as possible. (2) Aim for the highest possible isochronism. (3) Design an escapement which does not upset the isochronism. (4) Compensate for the effects of heat and cold as accurately and as simply as possible. (5) Design the regulator in such a way that there is no constraint anywhere and every part remains the same in extremes of temperature. (6) Protect the instrument from the effects of changes of position and from shock."

Pierre Le Roy's marine watch fulfilled the conditions. The movement, 81 mm in diameter, is composed of a cage containing the toothed drum and the usual train of wheels; the seconds wheel makes sixty turns an hour and works a kind of six-pointed star-wheel which drives the escapement. The movement is thus reduced to its simplest terms and isochronism of the balance is achieved without having recourse to the fusee. Every alternation is half a second and the watch therefore beats seconds. The balance-wheel restores the lost energy to the oscillator in every other alternating movement.

The balance-wheel weighs about 153 grams and is 108 mm in diameter. The arbor which carries the balance runs in roller bearings at top and bottom; the arbor itself is suspended from a fine harpischord wire three inches long. This is similar to the device used in the modern so-called "400-day" clocks. Instead of the normal spring-balance, two springs are fixed at the foot of the arbor of the balance-wheel to facilitate regulation and to make small adjustments easier. Small regulating screws are fixed on the rim of the balance-wheel to allow easy adjustment to the advance or retard position.

Pierre Le Roy was the first to achieve temperature-compensation by modifying the period of inertia of the balance-wheel, first by means of a complicated and fragile system comprising two glass tubes filled with mercury and fixed to the balance. Later Le Roy conceived the idea of compensating for temperature changes by means of a circular balance wheel composed of steel and brass rivetted together, causing the circumference of the balance to expand or contract. The bimetallic cut balance is still used today for high-grade chronometers. In fact the detached escapement, the isochronous oscillator and an advanced compensation introduced by Pierre Le Roy in his marine clock are the basis of all modern chronometers. Pls. 117 and 118 refer to Le Roy's marine clock.

Ferdinand Berthoud (1727–1807), son of an architect, was apprenticed at fourteen to his eldest brother, a clockmaker at Couvet. In 1745 he went to Paris to complete his studies, where he worked for a time with Julien Le Roy in company with his son, Pierre, later to be his great rival. Whilst still a young man he set up in Paris as a Master Clockmaker. He was a very intelligent and self-sufficient man who got on well with scientists; an indefatigable worker, he studied the mathematical sciences and was of an extraordinarily inventive turn of mind. He was a writer whose many publications soon made him influential in those circles studying the accurate measurement of time. He, too, was drawn to attempt to solve the problem of determination of longitude at sea.

His first marine clock was described in his book *Essai sur l'horlogerie* and he obtained permission from the Minister of Marine to test it in one of His Majesty's vessels. These tests proved unsatisfactory; he twice modified his chronometers and only in 1769 achieved good results with two marine clocks. He was granted the title of Horloger du Roy et de la Marine with the exclusive privilege of providing the navy with chronometers. In 1795 he was made a member of the Institut de France and also elected to the Royal Society of England. Napoleon made him a Chevalier de la Légion d'Honneur when the Order was created (See plates 119 and 120).

Whilst the marine clocks Nos. 1 and 2 produced by Ferdinand Berthoud and built respectively in 1760 and 1763, were extraordinarily bulky machines, No. 3 was only a watch in size, but a marine watch with the dimensions of a carriage clock. From 1775 he built marine watches which he sometimes called longitudinal clocks, in which the motive power used till then was replaced by a fusee-driven spring. He also experimented with a detent escapement of his invention, but retained the gridiron compensation. His model No. 52, made in 1793, was the nearest to modern mechanical chronometers. It has a detent escapement, the suspension thread of the pivot of the balance has been suppressed and it pivots in pierced rubies in association with jewelled counter-pivots. Two straight auxiliary strips, which were bimetallic with a regulating device, are fixed on the rim of the balance to ensure compensation.

THE NINETEENTH CENTURY

The use of the word chronometer to describe a portable and very accurate timepiece was first employed by Pierre Le Roy in his memorandum of 5th April 1761, to the Académie. It became an everyday term during the eighteenth century.

At that time the marine chronometer was much the same in France as in England. It was made industrially following the design of a single model,

Pl. 116 John Harrison's marine chronometer No. 1, made between 1729 and 1735 and tested at sea on the Centurion in 1736. Maritime Museum, Greenwich

Pl. 117 Marine watch by Pierre Le Roy with wire suspension. Conservatoire national des arts et métiers, Paris

Pl. 118 Marine watch by Pierre Le Roy. Detail of the escapement and the oscillator

Pl. 119 Ferdinand Berthoud's marine chronometer No. 12. Detail of the temperature-compensation mechanism

Pl. 120 Ferdinand Berthoud's marine chronometer No. 12, made in 1774. Musée d'Horlogerie, La Chaux-de-Fonds

117

118

119

120

122

123

driven by a spring, drum and fusee, with a detached detent escapement with ruby pallets, a steel and brass balance, cylindrical spring and the use of pierced rubies for all the most important pivotal points.

The clockmakers who made the greatest contribution to the development of the marine chronometer were John Arnold, Thomas Earnshaw in England, and A. L. Bréguet and Louis Berthoud, nephew and successor to Ferdinand, in France.

In France by 1800 only warships were supplied with marine chronometers and the first known inventory made in 1832 lists a total of 143. Commercial and civil navigators did not have marine chronometers until later. Things progressed more quickly in England due to the work of such eminent watchmakers as John Arnold, Josiah Emery, Thomas Earnshaw and others. It was probably the principal reason for the great growth of the British Navy and for its role in commercial and economic expansion.

Henceforward the manufacture of marine chronometers in England, France and Switzerland became a special branch of watchmaking, but it was partially mechanized after 1850. However, the detent escapement was always made by men of great skill by hand, because it does not lend itself to mass-production.

Pl. 121 shows the movement of A. L. Bréguet's marine chronometers; pl. 123, a marine chronometer made by the House of Bréguet et Fils, dating from about 1820; pl. 122, a similar chronometer, made by Winnerl about 1850.

In the nineteenth century makers of marine chronometers, apart from those already mentioned, were:

England:	William Frodsham	1778–1850
	Edward John Dent	1790–1853
	James Ferguson Cole	1798–1880
	Aaron L. Dennison	1812–1895
France:	Motel	1786–1859
	Winnerl	1799–1886
	Vissière	1822–1887
	O. Dumas	1824–1889
	Th. Leroy	1827–1899
Switzerland:	Frédéric Louis Favre-Bulle	1770–1849
	Henry Grandjean	1803–1879
	Jules Jürgensen	1808–1877
	William Dubois	1811–1869
	Louis Richard	1812–1875
	Ulysse Nardin	1823–1876

Pl. 121 Movement of the marine chronometer made by Bréguet & Fils and shown in plate 123. Musée d'Horlogerie, La Chaux-de-Fonds

Pl. 122 Marine chronometer by Joseph Winnerl, Paris, 1850. Sloping case showing the functioning of the universal joint. Musée d'Horlogerie. La Chaux-de-Fonds

Pl. 123 Marine chronometer by Bréguet & Fils, Paris, 1830. Dimensions of mahogany case 250 × 230 × 15 cm. Musée d'Horlogerie, La Chaux-de-Fonds

The annual competitions in accuracy first organized at the Observatory of Kew-Teddington, the French Observatory of Besançon and by the Swiss Observatories of Geneva (after 1873) and Neuchâtel (after 1875) contributed greatly to the advance of the marine chronometer. After the middle of the century very high standards of precision were recorded:

Mean variations in the daily rate: 0.2-0.3 seconds per day.

Daily rate of gain: + 1 to 2 seconds per day

Taking into account the other possible errors that could intervene in a determination of longitude, it was now possible to find the position of a ship at sea within one or two miles near the equator and less than a mile in temperate zones.

Decorative Clocks

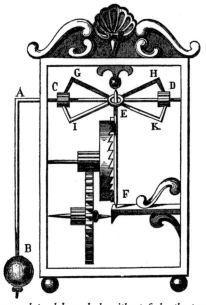

Verge and pendulum clock without fork; the pendulum receives its impulse from a system of gears

WE HAVE SEEN that richly decorated foliot clocks played a very important part in the decorative arts of the Renaissance. Renaissance clock-cases were decorated in finely-worked and sumptuous materials. The clockmaker, like the sculptor and architect, signed his original work with his name, initials and seal.

In clockmaking there is generally only one signature engraved on the upper plate of the movement, that of the master clockmaker, who usually also designed the case. Only a very few, large luxurious pieces have two signatures, that of the clockmaker on the movement and of the creator and decorator of the case on the outside.

In the sixteenth century the master clockmakers of Augsburg were the principal creators of decorative clocks; after the seventeenth century their mantle fell on the French and Swiss clockmakers.

The new school came into being at Blois, when François I was the patron of great artists, among them Benvenuto Cellini, Andrea del Sarto, Leonardo da Vinci and Primaticcio, whom he brought to his court from Italy.

His successors Henri IV and Louis XIII continued his policy of patronage and watchmakers, jewellers, engravers, bronze-workers, enamellers and silversmiths gave a new impulse to French clockmaking.

In the reign of Louis XIII (1610–1643) spring-driven chamber clocks developed rapidly in France where their history was soon linked with that of furniture. As the habit of wearing watches spread among the rich, small carriage clocks became less necessary and so they were made larger and larger to be placed on a chimney piece or commode, or fixed to the wall.

Huygens's application of the pendulum to clocks in 1657 gave a further stimulus to the industry. The first of these was presented to Louis XIV and it was not long before craftsmen and artists turned their attention to the new type of clock and set themselves to produce cases for pendulum clocks that would match the rich furnishings and sumptuous houses of the period. This was the start of the French pendulum clock and it produced a school that was to be the inspiration of the master clockmakers of Neuchâtel and of other European countries.

THE LOUIS XIII PERIOD

The influence of the Louis XIII style was soon manifest in clocks. Their long cases, rectangular with capital and cornice, were of natural wood. They were severe in outline, recalling church porches, and hence were dubbed *religieuses*. Gradually decoration became richer; at first ornament consisted of ivory, pewter or brass intended to relieve the austere effect of the wood. Then the case was covered with marquetry or paint enhanced by small applied floral designs in bronze.

Pls. 124–131 illustrate Louis XIII clocks distinguished by their simplicity and the large dial with Roman figures. These examples are French, except 126, 127 and 131 which are English.

THE LOUIS XIV PERIOD

A Louis XIV clock, richly decorated and imposing, is a fine symbol of its time. In the first part of the Sun King's reign France was all dazzling splendour and power, and many foreign artists were drawn to the magnificent court. Colbert founded great national manufactories such as the Gobelins, the now famous Ecoles and the Académie.

The Palace of Versailles was the center of artistic interest, where many superb pieces were collected together and hundreds of artists worked. The king lodged his most famous designers in the Louvre and other royal residences and every artist was ordered to create pieces in character with the majestic splendor of the Court. Symmetry was enforced because it alone expressed the sense of overwhelming power. The taste of the king was faith-

Pl. 124 Religious clock by Thuret, Paris, clockmaker to Louis XIV. The dial is laid on a velvet base with tortoiseshell, copper and brass inlay; engraved gilt bronze ornament. R. Gest Collection, Beauvais

Pl. 125 Mantel clock by Gaudron, Paris. Gilt bronze, Louis XIII. The dial showing hours and minutes. 52 × 25 × 14 cm; D. 19 cm. Ben Simon Collection, Paris

Pl. 126 Clock by Claudius Du Chesne, London, late 17th century. Ebony with silver ornament. Hours, minutes, days of the month. H. 30, W. 20 cm. Private Collection, Paris

Pl. 127 The back of the clock illustrated in plate 126. Copper plaque engraved with scrolls and cupids framing a bust of Mercury; a huntsman with quiver and bow between cornucopiae full of flowers. Private Collection, Paris

Pls. 128 & 129 Ebony clock by Elias Weckerlin, Augusta, 1680. The dial Augsburg, late 17th century. External dimensions 20 × 20 cm; movement 6 × 9 cm. Private Collection, Paris

Pl. 130 Clock with an automaton by Jaquet-Droz, 1760. The movement is not signed, but the springs bear the mark G.L., for Gédéon Langin, springmaker at La Chaux-de-Fonds. Bronze and tortoiseshell inlay. H. 63, W. 34 cm; D. of dial 22 cm. Collection Dr. Gschwind, Basle

Pl. 131 English clock of ebony, with embossed silver ornament; two hands recording hours and minutes. H. 28, W. 17 cm. Private Collection, Paris

124

125

126

127

128

129

130

131

133

134

135

136

137

138

139

140

141

fully observed by Charles Le Brun (1619–1690), great painter, architect, designer and courtier; he guided the style of all the artists serving the king.

Craftsmen and artists worked in collaboration on clocks—clockmakers, woodcarvers, cabinet-makers, bronze-workers—and men like Martinot, Bidault, Gribelin, du Tertre, Gaudron, Baillon, Porte and Minuel were among the famous clockmakers. Of the cabinet-makers and bronze-workers Caffiéri, Martincourt, Duplessis and Gouthière were the most famous. It was, however, André Charles Boulle (1642–1732) who played a major role at this time by bringing his art of inlay and marquetry to the highest point of perfection. He applied red or brown tortoiseshell inlay to the wood, inlaid fine strips of pewter or brass, or using the opposite process, inserted shell, bone, ivory or mother-of-pearl into the metal. Decoration grew ever more luxurious; richly tooled bronze was applied to the wooden surface, following the outline up to the capital, which was surmounted with a figure: Mars, Minerva or Time resting on his scythe. Towards the end of the reign of Louis XIV the martial trophies were replaced by more appealing subjects: female figures in flowing robes, Cupid stringing his bow and flat surfaces would be decorated with mythological or allegorical subjects in bronze. The simple engraved Louis XIII dial was replaced by a tooled bronze face with enamelled inlays of the Roman figures. The long delicate hands were of tempered steel.

Pls. 132-141 all show clocks of this period; some were to be hung on the wall and were known as cartel clocks; the type illustrated in pl. 134 is a type known as "doll's head", whilst those of pls. 137 and 138 are bracket clocks with a base. The striking clock, (pl. 141) is English; it is surmounted by a graceful peristyle with figures and above the dial has a decoration of a waterfall set in motion by the striking of the carillon.

It must be stressed that decorative clocks were never made to be placed alone, but were rather designed for a special position, the center of a chimney-piece for instance, with a mirror or pier-glass. Nor did the styles known as Louis XIII, XIV and XV die out with the death of the king, but jostled one another in turn, rising to the heights of fashion and declining as taste changed and they fell from vogue.

THE RÉGENCE AND LOUIS XV PERIODS

The second half of the reign of Louis XIV was a financial disaster for France and, after the death of the king, great changes were to be seen in the court of

Pl. 132   Clock by Gaudron of Paris who was made master in 1673. Time disarmed by Cupid. Ebony with copper and tortoiseshell marquetry. This piece was formerly in the Elysée Palace and a replica can be seen in the Palace of Versailles. H. 88, D. 25, base 65×31 cm. Garde-meuble national, Paris

Pl. 133   Clock designed for a study. Ebony and gilt bronze with the three Fates. 50×55×32 cm. Ben Simon Collection, Paris

Pl. 134   Doll's tread clock, Louis XIV. Marquetry of copper, brass and tortoiseshell. 48×28×17 cm; D. 18 cm. Palais de Fontainebleau

Pl. 135   Boulle clock by Mynuel, Paris, about 1700. Black lacquer with brass and copper inlay and very fine gilt bronze ornament. 110×48×21 cm; D. of dial 25 cm. Palais de Fontainebleau.

Pl. 136   Clock of black lacquer with gilt copper inlay. H. with base about 100 cm. Palais de Fontainebleau.

Pl. 137   Large bracket clock with marquetry of copper and gilt bronze chiselled by Duru, Paris, last quarter of the 16th century. 85×42·5×17 cm. Garde-meuble national, Paris

Pl. 138   Large bracked clock with marquetry, copper and engraved and gilt bronze ornament. H. 85 cm. Palais du Sénat, Paris

Pl. 139   Watch-stand, Louis XIV. Made of card-board and folded, embossed paper in gilded relief, on a green and red ground, with gilt mouldings and finials. 34×18×9·5 cm. Serge Roche Collection, Paris

Pl. 140   Elephant clock by Jean Baptiste Baillon. The base of black lacquer and leaves in gilt bronze. H. 50, W. of base 40 cm. Kugel Collection, Paris

Pl. 141   Clock from a palace in Peking, 1780. English. Gilt bronze, automaton and carillon, with a fountain above the dial. H. 54, W. 24 cm; D. of dial 11 cm. J. Fremersdorf Collection, Lucerne

Versailles. When the duc d'Orléans (1715–1723) became Regent the system was already swiftly changing.

The immense salons, grandiose staircases and enormous châteaux were being replaced by exquisite boudoirs, delicate and more intimate drawing-rooms. Monumental chimney-pieces gave way to marble mantels with pier-glasses, on which the clock became an indispensable element of the decoration. Clockmakers and other decorators produced fine and elaborate works of art.

The Régence clock, somewhat smaller than its predecessors, still preserved some of their symmetry, but the artists, freed from the absolute power which had imprisoned them in the grandiose, could now give free expression to their several ideas of beauty. So they created rich models with curving lines in contrast to the austere profiles of the preceding style.

During the reign of Louis XV (1723–1744) the severe style in clocks was abandoned and became much more light-hearted; flowing asymmetrical lines and rounded curves offered the finest inspiration to the engraved and gilded bronze of a Gouthière.

The Marquise de Pompadour, a woman of impeccable taste, lent her patronage to encourage artists in the creation of delicate and beautiful pieces. Sèvres and Meissen porcelain, Vernis Martin and other painted lacquers all played their part in the decoration of clocks. Boucher, Pillement, the decorator Meissonier, the cabinet-maker Cressent and Germain the silversmith, were among the most famous names of the period.

Pls. 143 and 144 are clocks of the Régence period, one a table clock. Pls. 145, 146, 147 and 149 are cartels and a small musical clock in the Louis XV style.

Pl. 130 is attributed to Pierre Jaquet-Droz and dates from 1760. It is of special interest because it is furnished with automata.

Pierre Jaquet-Droz, the son of a farmer, born at La Chaux-de-Fonds in 1721 was given an excellent education and, like many of his compatriots, took an interest in horology. After studying philosophy in Basle, then theology in Neuchâtel he decided not to take Orders and became a clockmaker instead. He rapidly became a master of his art and in 1758 at the age of thirty-seven he travelled to Spain to show Ferdinand VI seven elaborate clocks furnished with music and automata. They were very successful and sold at a high price.

Jaquet-Droz, in collaboration with his son, Henry Louis, and his adopted son, Jean Frédéric Leschot, later made several very fine complicated clocks and automata, the most famous of which are: L'Ecrivain, Le Dessinateur, and La Musicienne which were renowned throughout Europe in 1770. They can be seen today in the Musée d'Horlogerie in Neuchâtel.

Although rectangular in shape, the Ferdinand Berthoud clock is also of the period (pl. 148). It is remarkable for its rich case and its mechanism,

Pl. IX Long-case clock of black lacquer, mounted in bronze with Chinese decoration and an enamelled dial. 238 × 38 × 21 cm

counting the days of the month and indicating different astronomical data.

The middle of the eighteenth century is marked by that extravagant flowering of the Louis XV style, rococo; clock-cases did not escape this fashion which affected furnishing generally. Chiselled bronze in curving, asymmetrical scrolls rises from the base of the console to the capital crowned with a leafy motif. Philippe and Jacques Caffiéri, Roy, and Grimpelle, were the finest bronze-workers of this period.

The dials with scrolls, where bronze and enamel intermingle, are always particularly finely worked, whilst the hands, cut as thin as possible and finely engraved are works of art in themselves.

Magnificent marquetry clocks, illustrated in pls. 150, 152 and 153–156 were also made in the first half of this century. Pl. 152 is especially fine and has a complicated movement with astronomical data and a calendar. The clock made of rosewood with inlays of precious woods and bronze is also a very remarkable example (pl. 155).

THE LOUIS XVI PERIOD

Style changed once more in the reign of Louis XVI, leaving behind the curving asymmetrical lines of the rococo, symmetry and classicism return. This was the period when the most magnificent models were created, each more graceful than the last. Every imaginable form of clock—with pillars, a lyre or vase-shaped, with a revolving dial, with music, carillon or organ notes, wall, cartel, architectural and mural and long-case clocks is to be found.

This was one of the greatest periods of French art, the time of Gouthière, Thomire, Clodion, and Riesener, of Pigalle and Falconnet, at the Sèvres Factory, all creating delicate works of art in the Pompadour style. Clocks were embellished and enhanced to suit the pretty boudoirs of the day. With the last two artists mentioned, sculpture attained a moment of balance and synthesis. They played an important part in the decoration of French clocks of the period and in the creation of small sculpture. Pigalle's work was virile, Falconnet's more feminine. From 1757–1766, when he was Director of the manufactory of Sèvres, Falconnet created several hundred figures of great charm and beauty. Some were used to adorn clocks. The musical clock shown in plate 170 is a fine example of this. Collaboration between clockmakers and artists—sculptors, bronze-workers, enamellers and cabinet-makers—became even closer.

Pl. 142 Mystery clock by Etienne Pomé. Engraved, chased, pierced and gilt copper. The dial painted enamel showing the date. Strikes on the hour. Works when placed either horizontally or vertically against a wall, but the small dial only records the time when vertical. The hand of the small dial showing the cardinal points makes one turn in twenty-four hours. H. 7·5, D. 9 cm, arm 16·5 cm long; D. small dials 3 cm. Private Collection, Paris

Pl. 143 Table clock of silver and silver-gilt, with embossed fruit and foliage. It records the hours and minutes and the date. Kugel Collection, Paris

Pl. 144 Large Régence clock by Julien Le Roy, Paris. Black lacquer and magnificent gilt bronze decoration, with Jupiter surmounting the whole. 105 × 60 × 26 cm; D. of dial 25 cm. Ben Simon Collection, Paris

Pl. 145 Wall Cartel clock with its bracket, rococo decoration of gilt bronze. On either side are the wings often seen on pieces intended for the royal family. The whole is surmounted by a cupid pulling his bow. This splendid piece seems to have been made after a design by Meissonnier (recorded in Britten). Signed Stollwerck, Paris 1750. 95 × 40 × 20 cm; D. of dial 18 cm. Ben Simon Collection, Paris

Pl. 146 Wall Cartel clock, Louis XV by Gudin, Paris, in rococo style. 90 × 45 × 28 cm; D. of dial 18 cm. Ben Simon Collection, Paris

Pl. 147 Cartel clock by Julien Le Roy with bronzes by Caffiéri, 1757. 75 × 40 × 15 cm; D. of dial 18 cm. H. Brault Collection, Paris

Pl. 148 Clock of gilt copper and rock crystal by Ferdinand Berthoud. It records months, days and the date; the center dial shows the hours, the four smaller ones in the angles show the month, the date, the days and the planets. The dial, doors, balance, the twisted pillars, the top, the urn and the finials are of rock crystal. The chime has two bells, one striking on the half-hour, both on the hour. H. 60 cm; base 38 × 33 cm; D. of dial 6 cm. Nathan Collection, Binningen

Pl. 149 Large Chinoiserie clock by Gudin, Louis XV, 1750. It has a chime of thirteen tones in the base. 78 × 53 × 25 cm; D. of dial 18 cm. Ben Simon Collection, Paris

Pl. 150 Long-case clock by Furet, Paris, early 18th century. Rosewood, brass and bronze. Silver-plated dial showing hours and minutes, solar time and the date. The case attributed to Cressent. 225 × 40 × 20 cm; D. of dial 26 cm. Samy Chalom Collection, Paris

Pl. 151 Dial of the clock by Furet, Paris, about 1740. Silver-plated dial showing the hours, the date and solar time.

142

143

144

145

146

147

148

149

150

151

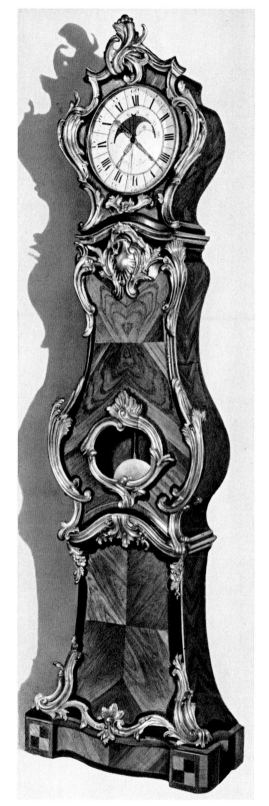

152

153

154

155

156

157

158

159

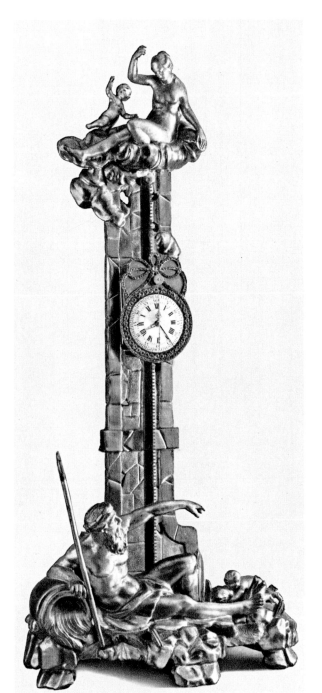

160

161

Pl. 152 Long-case clock by Lamy, clockmaker to the Dauphin, Régence period. Marquetry and gilt bronze. 230 × 45 × 22 cm; D. of dial 25 cm. Ben Simon Collection, Paris

Pl. 153 Long-case clock by Audinet. Black lacquer with gilt bronze ornament. Overall H. 220 cm; top H. 60 cm; W. of base 50 cm; D. of dial 27 cm. Private Collection, Paris

Pl. 154 Long-case clock, Régence. Phases of the moon. H. 225 cm. Private Collection, Paris

Pl. 155 Long-case clock by Henry Voisin, Paris, mid 18th century. Rosewood with inlay of other fine woods, gilt bronze, silver dial. Samy Chalom Collection, Paris

Pl. 156 Dial of the clock by Voisin shown in plate 155

Pl. 157 Lyre-clock by Dorgueil, Louis XVI. Oscillating pendulum, dial in the suspension-bob, thermometer of the Académie. Gilt wood. H. 200, W. 70 cm; oval window containing suspension-bob 33 × 22 cm. Kugel Collection, Paris.

Pl. 158 Clock by Johan Peters Latgens, Solingen, 1791. The whole mechanism is contained in the cylindrical box below the armillary sphere. It records hours, the date, months and the course of the sun and moon, the phases of the moon and the positions of the planets. Wood, painted metal and gilt garlands. Chime and organ. Overall H. 50 cm; base 7 cm; D. 19 cm. Charliat Collection, Paris

Pl. 159 Clock with a singing bird. Different tunes for each hour. D. 30, H. 45 cm. Kugel Collection, Paris

Pl. 160 Clock with rack and pinion in gilt bronze. Eight-day movement. 77 × 35 × 28 cm; D. of dial 7 cm. J. Fremersdorf Collection, Lucerne

Pl. 161 Cartel clock by de Causard, clockmaker to Louis XVI, 1760 (recorded in Britten). Gilt bronze. H. 120 cm; D. of dial 25 cm. Private Collection, Paris

Pl. X Cartel clock of dark and gilt bronze. H. 56, W. 25, D. of the dial 12 cm. Formerly in the Collection of Madame Bouvier, Paris

The most famous French clockmakers of the period were:
Jean Baptiste Baillon
Caron the elder and his son Pierre-Augustin who wrote under the name of Beaumarchais,
Antide Janvier, Antoine Lépine,
Julien and Pierre Le Roy,
Martinot, one of a line of watchmakers,
Le Loutre, de Rivaz, Robert Houdin, Romilly,
Ferdinand Berthoud and J. A. Lepaute, who was the greatest clockmaker of the century.

Other forms of the Louis XVI clock are also interesting. Pls. 159 and 160 are drawn from the realm of fantasy: a clock surmounted by a cage in which one or two birds sing and flutter their wings on the hour, and is a rack and pinion clock of German make. The brothers Maillardet, clockmakers of Neuchâtel, and former workers of Pierre Jaquet-Droz at La Chaux-de-Fonds, were renowned for their special clocks with mechanical singing-birds.

Pls. 162–164 show three very different ormolu cartel clocks, made to stand on a bracket or chimney breast. Pl. 164 is a mantel clock of terracotta decorated with a hunting scene. Pl. 166 shows a splendid mantel clock of the type described as "skeleton", an exceptional little piece with a constant force escapement and calendar.

Pl. 167 shows a musical clock in marble, alabaster, and gilded bronze of the type known as *à colonnes*. Pl. 161 is a classic Louis XVI clock, of which many fine examples were made in Paris and at Neuchâtel.

The reader interested in clocks made at Neuchâtel but cased and decorated in Paris is recommended to refer to Alfred Chapuis' fine work, *Histoire de la Pendule Neuchâteloise* (Paris and Neuchâtel, 1917).

THE EMPIRE PERIOD

The triumph of the ornamental clock was brought to an abrupt end by the Revolution and the First Republic (1792–1799) and manufacture revived only fitfully throughout the Consulate of 1799–1804. Many foreign artists returned to the land of their birth, whilst the aristocracy and rich bourgeoisie could no longer afford to take an interest in luxurious objects. The Convention decreed that a Republican calendar should supersede the old, and the Gregorian calendar

Pl. XI Cartel clock, Louis XV, signed Thiéry, Paris. Ornamented with laurel leaves and wings. H. 46, W. 56 cm. Ben Simon Collection, Paris

only returned under the Empire. The clock typical of this period is therefore very simple, often of the skeleton type depicted in pl. 180, with the dial divided into ten hours to fit the decimal day.

In the relatively calm period that followed the Revolution and preceded the Empire, new clock-cases, not unlike those of Louis XVI, were made. These were known as Directoire clocks and many were made in Neuchâtel. No longer twisted in shape, their simple lines were thrown into delicate relief by restrained bronze mounts. The case itself is the most attractive part of these clocks, with its fine marquetry carried out in various exotic woods. The movement and the dial and the brass hands, which were cut and engraved by hand and terminated in a rosette, were all made in Neuchâtel.

17th-century clocks showing the date

Pl. 162 Clock by Ferdinand Berthoud. The earth turns once in twenty-four hours. Twenty-four hour dial. 42 × 30 × 24 cm; D. of globe 12 cm; D. of dial 6·5 cm. Ben Simon Collection, Paris

Pl. 163 Clock made by Favre, Louis XVI. Gilt bronze on a bronze ground. The two winged figures, the vine-leaves and the feet are gilt bronze. H. 56 cm; base 34 × 15 cm; D. of dial 12 cm. Private Collection, Paris

Pl. 164 Clock by Lieutaud, Louis XVI, Paris, 1770 (recorded in Britten). In terracotta with a band of gilt bronze showing a boar hunt. Perhaps the model for a later bronze piece. 40 × 40 × 18 cm; D. of dial 9·5 cm. S. Roche Collection, Paris

Pl. 165 Clock by Lepaute with enamelled porcelain. H. 30 cm. Ben Simon Collection, Paris

Pl. 166 Skeleton mantel clock, Louis XVI, 1775. Parts of gilt brass, without ornament and an enamelled dial. Dead-beat escapement, thermometer on the pendulum, and with two pointers recording the date, the day of the week. 50 × 25 × 22 cm. Private Collection, Paris

P. 167 Musical clock by J.S. Bourdier, late 18th century, Louis XVI style. Marble, alabaster and gilt bronze. It records hours, minutes, the date and strikes the hours. The springs are signed Richard, août 1792. 115 × 58 × 27 cm. From the Victorien Sardou Sale, Palais de Fontainebleau

Pl. 168 Clock by Jean Baptiste Mayet, Morbier. The case is signed L.F.D.C., Louis Frédéric du Commun of Le Locle, 1775. Fluted enamel dial. D. 25 cm; H. 97 cm. Collection Dr. Gschwind, Basle

Pl. 169 Clock from the Emperor's chamber by Bailly, 1790. From the Tuileries. Gilt bronze on a marble base with a figure of Astronomy holding a telescope and compass, the celestial sphere, the zodiac and an astronomical frieze. 89 × 60 × 27 cm; D. of dial 13.5 cm. Palais de Fontainebleau

Pl. 170 Clock with the Three Graces. H. 77, D. of base 21 cm; D. of the sphere containing the movement 19 cm. Palais de Fontainebleau

Pl. 171 Empire clock, engraved and gilt bronze. 50 × 25 × 15 cm. Garde-meuble national, Paris

Pl. 172 Clock in the form of the Chariot of Venus. attributed to Ravrio. Gilt bronze and sea-green marbles This clock formed part of the decoration of Napoleon I', study in the Elysée Palace. 44 × 63 × 17 cm; D. of dial 8·5 cm. Garde-meuble national, Paris

163

164

167

168

169

170

171

174

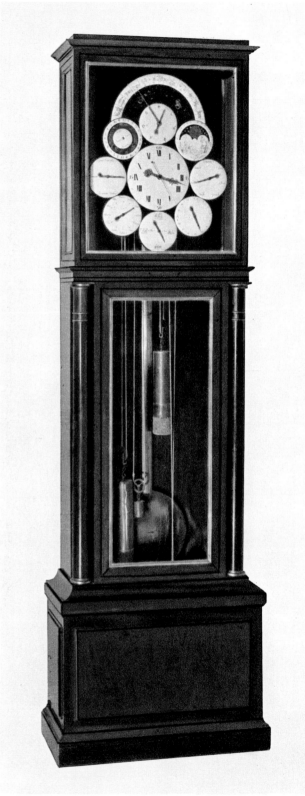

175

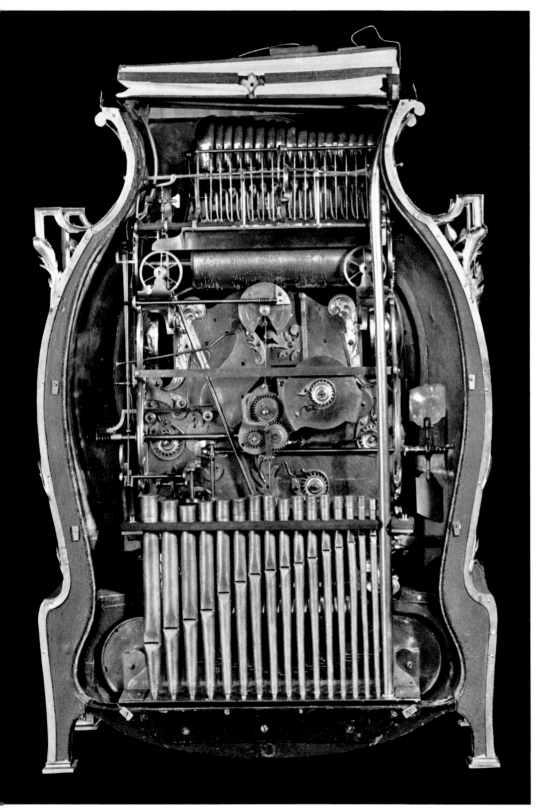

178

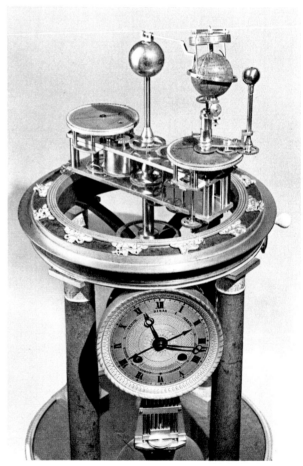

179

180

181

182

183

Pl. 173   Empire clock by E. Leroy (in the Palais Royal). Gilt bronze. In the background the bill of sale and guarantee for this clock, dated 27.VII.1814. 43 × 24 × 10 cm. Kugel Collection, Paris

Pl. 174   Long-case clock by Samuel Stevens, London. Dark green lacquer ground with gold painting. Hours, minutes, the date and a chime on the hour. 217 × 45 × 25 cm. Gilbert Suc Collection, Paris

Pl. 175   Imperial regulator by Petiet fils (Year 13) showing hours, minutes, seconds, months and the signs of the zodiac; the date, day of the week, leap years, and the times of sunrise and sunset; the moon and its phases. It chimes the hours and the quarters, has two driving weights, a mahogany case and rings of gilt copper. H. 225, base W. 66 cm; D. 51 × 46 cm. Palais de Fontainebleau

Pl. 176   Mantel clock by Antide Janvier, 1805-1810. Gilt bronze, revolving hour dial; shows minutes, seconds, the date and phases of the moon. Mahogany case inlaid and decorated with gilt bronze. 52 × 28 × 22 cm. Private Collection, Paris

Pl. 177   Regulator clock by Antide Janvier, 1812. The dials show: hours, minutes, seconds, phases and age of the moon; months, the date and the days of the week. Thermometer in the pendulum and repeater-strike. Original mahogany case. 200 × 45 × 27 cm. Formerly Gélis Collection; Private Collection, Paris

Pl. 178   Musical clock by Johan Peters Latgens, Solingen, 1791. It records the hour, the date, the month, leap years, the course of the sun and the moon and is furnished with the signs of the planets. A striking and organ mechanism are repeating. Charliat Collection, Paris

Pl. 179   Planetarium clock by Raingo showing the hour, the day of the week and the phases of the moon. Charliat Collection, Paris

Pl. 180   English skeleton clock, early 19th century. Lever escapement. 39 × 27 × 13 cm; D. of dial 16 cm. Au Vieux Cadran, Paris

Pl. 181   Oxidised bronze clock, partially gilt. 56 × 27 × 16 cm. Garde-meuble national, Paris

Pl. 182   Japanese foliot clock, 18th century. The hour is divided into ten sections of six minutes. Alarm and striking mechanism. 17·5 × 13 × 9·5 cm; D. of dial 6·5 cm. Private Collection, Paris

Pl. 183   Japanese pendulum clock supported on a four-footed stand. The carved weight and motor are visible. Striking mechanism. 46 × 25 × 15 cm. Private Collection, Paris

The Empire period produced yet another style. Under the all-pervading influence of Louis David (1748–1825) French artists forsook tradition and turned for their inspiration to antiquity. The clockmakers Percier, Fontaine, Ravio, Thomire and others rendered the new style with a pure classical line.

Although at this period clocks did not attain the importance of the preceding style, Master clockmakers, nevertheless, continued to make their appearance. A. L. Bréguet took pride of place, representing his period by the variety and ingenuity of his inventions. He made few clocks, but some very beautiful small travelling clocks, more or less complicated as seen in Pl. 107.

Among Bréguet's clocks one of the most interesting is his Mystery clock, in which the mechanism is placed in the moving bob of the pendulum, beating the seconds apparently freely. The dial, with centralized hands for hours, minutes and seconds is on the visible side of the bob, whilst on the other face a fourth hand, reflected in a mirror placed against the bottom of the oscillator cage, indicates the day of the month. Another calendar clock made by Bréguet with equation of time and the Revolutionary calendar has only three wheels in the whole mechanism.

Pls. 169, 171, 172, 179 and 181 show Empire mantel clocks. Pl. 179, signed by Raingo, is surmounted by a planetarium which shows the respective rotations and phases of the earth and moon. It also shows the months, the days of the month and various astronomical phenomena. A bell sounds the hour and the half hour.

THE POST—EMPIRE PERIOD

The period which followed the Napoleonic era produced no remarkable changes in the decoration of clocks.

During the Restoration of Louis XVIII and later Charles X and Louis-Philippe, new styles and types of clocks were created. 1850 saw the dawn of a new era of mechanization and mass-production, but the noble styles of the past were still imitated in quality clocks.

PART TWO

Ancient Measuring Instruments

Measuring the height of a tower with an astrolabe

Introduction

THE SENSE OF MEASUREMENT is, in the higher animals, instinctive and perhaps inborn. A cat that jumps onto a piece of furniture, or the bird perching on a twig have both measured their movements with great precision. Man also possesses this intuitive sense and is capable of developing it. The billiard-player can instinctively solve an equation that would take a mathematician days to resolve.

Must we conclude that the science of measurement is only a development of this vague feeling? Far from it: we have only the most elementary instinctive sense of measurement. Technology has led to the posing of far more complex problems and has made progress only when we have given attention to measuring exactly. This can be seen if one considers that even today certain phenomena exist for which no standards have been established, and which cannot, therefore, be measured. For instance, we have no means of comparison between smells, no degree of intensity or quality, and hence we have almost no use for our sense of smell. The scent of the dog or the sensitivity of bees give us an idea of the vast resources that the measurement of smell would give us.

In order to be objective every measurement implies the adoption of exact and easily established standards against which we may compare our observations. The manifest desire to establish accurate standards of measurement came with the Renaissance and led to the emergence of modern technical civilization. Standards of measurement may be absolute or relative. Angular measurement, for instance, is absolute. It is based on the division of any circle into 360 segments, or degrees, which require no other definition, and which can be reproduced anywhere at any time.

On the other hand linear rule is relative. From remote Antiquity man everywhere has sought to fix standards of length to which merchandise, buildings and land could be easily compared. And in every country these standards have had their origin in parts of the human body. In this sense, the foot, the cubit, the ell and the fathom are universal, but, they are not fixed and are subject to considerable local variations. At the beginning of the Christian era the Chinese foot was the equivalent of 23·4 cm; the foot used in the Tyrol during the sixteenth century 29·9 cm, and the English foot, still in use, equals 30·5 cm. The ell, which measured, in theory, the length of the outstretched arm was so variable that at the end of the eighteenth century no fewer than 112 variants existed in the Duchy of Baden alone.

Some geometricians resorted to averages for the fixing of standards of measurement. The sixteenth-century writer Jacob Koebel made the suggestion that sixteen men should be chosen at random "both large and small, as they come out of church" and placed in line, foot against foot. This would give the length of a rod for measuring fields. But even this delightful suggestion fails, because at that time the rod used by Tyrolean miners was three feet, not sixteen.

In fact the simplest solution is to construct an artificial unit of measurement. Hence one can find occasionally a bar of iron sealed into the wall near the door of some ancient churches, fixing the length of the foot or the ell for the benefit of traders in the nearby market. Sometimes there is in the same place a stone container which settles the standard volume for grain or liquids without argument.

Modern scales scarcely differ at all from this simple method. The French Revolutionary reformers thought that their new definition was absolute, and that, by declaring the unit of length to be linked to the terrestial meridian, and the meter to be one ten-millionth part of the quadrant of this meridian from the pole to the equator, they had established an immutable scientific fact. Nothing of the kind; modern science has proved that this measure is not absolute. The meter, then, is nothing more today than a platinum rule lodged in the Pavillon de Breteuil at Sèvres.

The advantage of the metric system is that this arbitrary unit is linked with other standards of size. Plane, volume and weight are calculated metrically and nearly all physical values are related to the system.

However, a good many measurements are still non-metric. Temperature, for instance, at least what we call temperature in everyday parlance, is measured by quite a different standard. The unit known as a thermometrical degree is one hundredth part of the length of a column of mercury extended between freezing and boiling point of water, and it is only a means of comparison. Specialists work with their own nomenclature: color, kinetic, electronic, ionization, excitation, rotation, vibration temperatures and so on, none of which has anything in common with the ordinary thermometer.

One physical measurement dating from remote antiquity is weight. In this field too the first units were linked with natural standards. This produced an astonishing lack of consistency still to be seen in English measurements: one pound, *avoirdupois*, in use in commerce, equals 453 grams, whereas the pound *troy* (used for precious metals and drugs) equals 373 grams. Flour is sold in pecks or stones, equal to fourteen pounds, whereas cheese is sold in "cloves" of eight pounds. Doctors calculate in *troy*, pharmacists in *avoirdupois*.

In an attempt to unify such measures in some way standards have been established in every country. The best known in France is the stack of bronze cups; each one of them consists of a series of cups diminishing in size, the total weight of which is equal to the containing cup. These so-called columns of Charlemagne date, not from his time, but from the time of Jean le Bon (1350). The container holding them is usually finely decorated. These standards were kept in cases with a double or triple lock, the keys of which were held by different officials for security (pl. 191).

The weight of coins was tested by ingots cast in replica of the piece to be measured. This function was reserved for officers of the king.

In the seventeenth century the scope of these boxes of master-weights was enlarged, but their use was still restricted to apothecaries, who were the only people allowed to keep them to verify merchants' scales.

Boxes of this kind contained a very delicate balance. Small auxiliary weights would be used to represent the permitted values (pls. 192, 193).

Several museums still preserve big municipal standard weights which served to verify commercial scales. They sometimes weigh up to tens of kilograms and are often richly decorated.

Measurement of time is very different today from what it used to be. Originally the unit of time was the length of the day from sunrise to sunset. The length of the night was a matter of complete indifference to our remote ancestors because all human activity ceased after dark. Like peasants today everyone stopped work at sundown, the labourer laid down his tools, the traveller looked for a night's shelter and even the soldier sought his billet. The day is, of course, a very elastic unit of measurement. In northern countries a summer day is twice as long as one in midwinter. Although this difference is less noticeable in the Mediterranean—the cradle of civilization—it still exists, and one must look for a different reason to explain our ancestors' indifference to this variation. In fact, the slow tempo of life was responsible: at a period when men travelled on foot, on horseback or in a chariot, measurement of the exact hour was a haphazard affair. One only needs to recall the vague expressions used in Genesis: "And it was morning, and it was night, and it was the first day." According to Censorinus, a Roman chronologer, even the word hour was unknown in Rome before the Christian era, and, in the *Law of the Twelve Tables* (451 B.C.), the hours are not once mentioned. Until the seventeenth century hours were counted everywhere in Europe in "temporaries", that is periods of time, reckoned in groups of twelve entirely variable days. It is the speed of our life which has forced us to count in minutes, seconds, then fractions of a second, as we have to measure the ever-increasing speed of movement. The development of the railway gave the minute its importance, the automobile, that of the second, whilst radio communications calculate in fractions of a second, and electronic computers in micro-seconds. In sum we implicitly obey the law by which time is measured by speed and speed by time. Neither the one nor the other is absolute, although they can be measured.

Since the sixteenth century scientific humanism has been responsible for checking and controlling our knowledge, and our sense of measurement became thereby more accurate. Man looked for greater and greater accuracy and we shall see over a period of three centuries how rapidly the so-called mathematical instruments developed. At that time the State and the sovereign were one; what we now call the cabinet was the personal entourage of the ruler. These keepers of official measurement had to have instruments worthy of their owner. They were therefore made by master craftsmen who were responsible for the technical perfection and splendid decoration alike. Hence all the admirable pieces which enrich our museums and give the mistaken impression that instruments of former days were all masterpieces.

Of course there must always have been working instruments, were they only for the personal use of poor scholars; but they have not come down to us. Only the finest with the most splendid decoration are now the joy of our collectors. And it is to these that this book is devoted, in the hope that it may describe more accurately the history, use and genius of the works it sets out to describe.

Pl. 184 Frontispiece to the Rudolphine Tables, 1627. This is an imaginative representation of the Temple of Astronomy supported by ten columns. Those in the background are simple, almost untrimmed tree-trunks while those in the foreground become gradually more architectural. The columns symbolize the successive achievements of Aratus, Meton, Hipparchus, Ptolemy, Copernicus and Tycho Brahe and each bears one of the instruments invented by these astronomers. Bibliothèque de l'Observatoire, Paris

Pls. 185 to 189 Standards of length. These rulers, usually made of wood but sometimes ivory, were used in trade. Some are plain, others more decorated and subdivided according to local practice. They are only accurate enough to serve the needs of a pedlar. Musée de Cluny, Observatoire de Paris and Private Collections

Pl. 190 Standards of capacity. These stone bowls, usually placed in front of the church door were used to check measurements of liquid or corn sold in the market. Cordes, France

Pl. 191 Set of cup weights, the so-called "Charlemagne's Column". These standards were in the shape of bronze bowls fitting one into the other and constituting a series rising from a few grammes to several kilos. Musée des Arts décoratifs, Paris

Pls. 192 & 193 Jewellers' and money-changers' balances. These small balances, which were very accurate for their time, were often elegantly decorated. Money-changers' balances were accompanied by discs fixing the weight of local coinage. Musée des Arts décoratifs, Paris

184

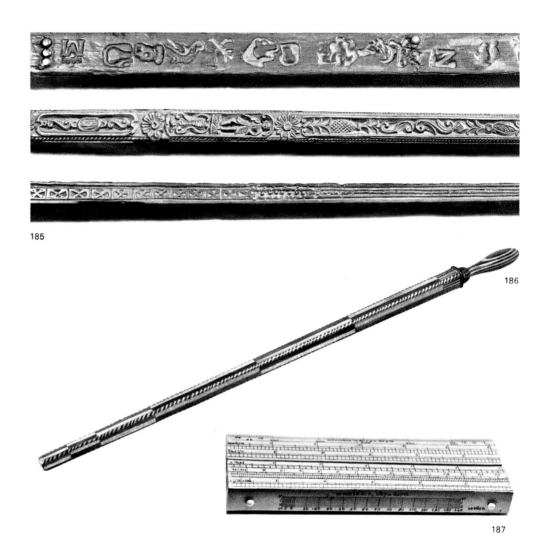

185

186

187

188

189

190

191

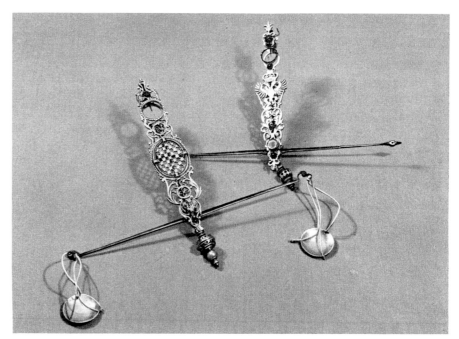

192

193

194

195

Measuring Instruments
before the Renaissance

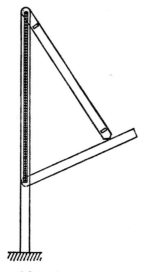

Triquetrum of Copernicus

Pl. *194   Portrait of Father Schall, S.J. Father
Schall was a missionary in China in the 17th century
and was elevated to the position of President of the
Tribunal of Mathematics of the Academy of Science
of the Celestial Empire. Jealous Mohammedan
astronomers attached to the Court caused him to be
imprisoned. He narrowly escaped torture and died in
prison in 1660. Private Collection, Paris*

Pl. *195   Portrait of Father Verbiest, S.J. Father
Verbiest was at first thrown into prison with Father
Schall but was reinstated in 1669 and went on to
receive the highest Chinese scientific honors. The
Japanese painter, Kuniyoshi, faced with the task of
painting portraits of the two famous men, gave the
more venerable one the features of Father Verbiest.
The splendid instruments made by the Jesuit Father
for the Peking Observatory have been preserved.
Private Collection, Paris*

BEFORE TURNING TO THE MOST interesting pieces in our collections it is relevant to sketch in the history of the earliest means of measuring. Very few examples remain from Antiquity or the Middle Ages, most having disappeared through war or neglect. Nevertheless buildings could never have been constructed without plans and human communities have always been interested in the division of land. All these things had to be measured and the instruments must have existed (pl. 184).

These are many obvious reasons why so few pre-Renaissance pieces have survived: first, they were often of wood, crudely made and ill-adjusted, they have not withstood the passage of time. Even at the beginning of the sixteenth century Copernicus was still using a large articulated triangle made of three graduated planks.

Another reason is the rudimentary technique of mechanics. The drawings of their inventions are notoriously bad and were a poor guide to those who had to make them. Tools were clumsy and no machines existed. To get an idea it is enough to watch craftsmen of Morocco or Thailand today operating a primitive lathe for turning wood, holding it in their feet and working it by a hand bow. Our ancestors had to make do with poor quality material. The Chinese used jade, the Assyrians terracotta, materials which needless to say allowed no adjustment. Bronze shrinks after it has been poured, changing the design and its dimensions; brass beaten into strips varies in thickness up to 100 % and the hardness of the surface successfully prevents accurate engraving; laminated metal dates at the earliest from the sixteenth century.

It is true that one finds a mention now and then in literature of such instruments, but these documents should be treated with extreme caution: Chinese books and Greek writings have come to us in later transcriptions and fidelity to the text was not a strongpoint of the translators. We are, for instance, constantly regaled with the story of a Chinese chariot with a jade figure on its pole shaft, the arms of which always pointed to the south, whence the story, repeated *ad nauseam*, that the Chinese had discovered the compass a thousand years before the West. Today it is recognized that the Compass chariot never existed anywhere save in the imagination of the compilers and that the pictures of it are much more recent. In the first treatise on the compass written in 1269, Pierre de Maricourt starts out by saying that experience is more important than anything and that one must have built an instrument oneself to be capable of describing it. That does not prevent him from following this excellent maxim with a description of perpetual motion which is absurd and unworkable. Even Ptolemy, the mentor of all astronomers till the sixteenth century, describes a kind of sphere which he used to list the positions of 1,028 stars, whereas Tycho Brahe, fifteen hundred years later, said he could not use this machine with any kind of precision. Nor should the miniatures illustrating medieval manuscripts be forgotten, and especially the *Chronicles of Alexander*: there are flying machines and underwater boats in which no one believes, but let it come to a Chinese stele and scholars will write pages about the marvellous instruments they think they have discovered.

Chinese 'south pointing' chariot

These remarks may seem harsh, but the real history of measuring instruments is picturesque enough without such extravagant embellishments.

Nothing remains of the mass of Egyptian instruments which must have existed. However, many wall-paintings and bas-reliefs supply documentary evidence, showing surveyors armed with a cord and architects checking alignments. Chaldea on the other hand, the birthplace of astronomy, has left only tablets with calculations. China, traditionally supposed to be the oldest civilization of all, but which after all turns out to be contemporary with the miracle of Mycenæan Greece, was only interested in agriculture and its astronomy hinged on knowledge of the calendar. For this purpose China used jade instruments to determine the New Year and the auspicious moment to plough. The famous instruments of bronze which are the pride of the Peking and Nanking museums were made in the fourteenth century under the supervision of Persian scholars and reconstructed in the seventeenth by Jesuit missionaries.

From Greece we have inherited several marble sundials, though their date is uncertain; but in any case it would be late, for the idea of such instruments seems to have originated in Asia Minor. Greek science, so much cultivated in Alexandria towards the beginning of the Christian era, was mostly acquired from books: the Greeks always had great scorn for applied science and were really theoreticians. One example, always quoted with admiration, is Eratosthenes' calculation of the circumference of the earth. In 200 B.C.

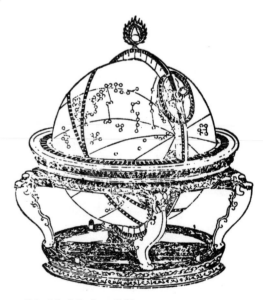

Celestial globe from Peking

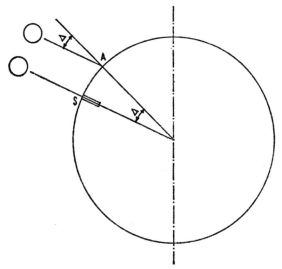

Diagram of method used by Eratosthenes to measure the size of the earth

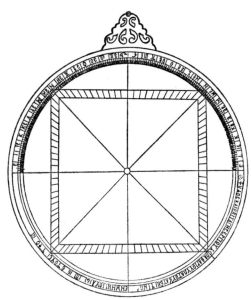

Byzantine astrolabe

this geometrician is supposed to have calculated the circumference of the earth with extraordinary accuracy. He may indeed have discovered the method, but his success depended on chance.

Christian refugees, escaping from Alexandria after the Arab Conquest, were responsible for bringing what was left of Greek scholarship to Asia Minor. Nestorians, retreating towards Antioch, carried Alexandrian traditions with them, and knowledge of the astrolabe, the most important instrument of the period, to which we shall turn later. In the middle of the ninth century the school of Antioch had only two pupils, who finally went to Harran near the head of the Euphrates. A kind of university had gathered there, Christians, Jews and Sabeans. At that moment the Arab Caliphs, sated with conquest and avid for glory, inaugurated a nationalist policy for science, which may perhaps be compared with events in eighteenth-century Germany; for it will be remembered that in 1740 to encourage learning in a somewhat backward country, Frederick the Great of Prussia founded an academy, most of whose members were French. By generously subsidizing scholarly publications Germany attained an international scholastic reputation in the course of a century. Using the same tactics Haroun-al-Raschid and his son Al-Mamun summoned all the scholars of Harran to Baghdad and encouraged by every possible means the arabization of Greek science. In 814 Al-Mamun made it a condition of peace between him and the Emperor Michael III that all the Greek philosophical books preserved in Byzantium should be handed over.

The oldest astrolabes we have date from this period. Some are Byzantine, the rest Arab. Mohammedan interest in this instrument arises from the rigorous rules laid down in Islamic ritual for the hours of prayer. Mohammed had decreed, somewhat vaguely, that the daily prayers must be said: "first, when a man can distinguish his neighbour; secondly, towards noon as the sun passes its zenith; thirdly, when the sun, shining on A'isha's chamber, casts no shadow within; fourthly when a man may still discern the place where his arrow fell; fifthly when the first third of the night is passed." The naïveté of these rules shows just how arbitrary was time-measurement in the seventh century. Subsequently the exegetes tried to make clearer and more precise laws. The astrolabe which was in the keeping of a specialist in the principal mosque in each town, determined the hour of religious ritual which was then announced to the other mosques. Even today, despite the numerous clocks enshrined in Moroccan mosques (most of which do not work) the astrolabe is still in use.

The invasion of Spain was a fortunate thing for Western knowledge; the Jews, driven from the peninsula by the Reconquest, escaped to Provence where they translated Oriental texts and gave us the Greek heritage. A few documents on the subject of mathematical instruments written in the thirteenth century by these refugees have been preserved. A corpus of writings of varying quality copied in the monasteries describes a number of these objects, many of which can never have been constructed. Then an English monk, John de Hollywood called Sacrobosco, published a work which was to be tremendously popular for three hundred years: the *Treatise on the Sphere* which was issued in dozens of editions with many commentaries. It described in a methodical way the elements of spherical astronomy, from which a more logical idea of the measurement of time and the construction of chronological instruments was conceived. At this period the sundial with an axial gnomon was discovered and we shall return to this below. It replaced the very inaccurate old sundials and indicated a regular hour throughout the year.

The shadow cast on the sundial by the gnomon made a complete circle in twenty-four hours at a constant speed. From this arose the idea of reproducing the movement mechanically and of building clocks furnished with a needle, which, like the shadow on the sundial, turns round on a flat disc numbered round its circumference. The efforts of mechanics resulted at the end of the thirteenth century in the production of this amazing piece of mechanism. However, the world was still waiting for the unknown genius who could think of substituting many short and reiterated movements for the continuous movement. The extraordinary invention known to us as the clock-escapement has the effect, as we shall see, of blocking the mechanism and releasing it for a very short but constant interval. This idea must be considered to be one of the most astonishing manifestations of the genius of its time.

Necessity created the organism and technology succeeded in perfecting the materials, by producing suitable metals and more precise systems. Scholars combined with craftsmen and craftsmen with artists. Improved communications allowed fruitful exchanges between scholarly minds, and put the craftsman in contact with his colleagues elsewhere. Europe was simmering with the desire to develop its culture. The dawn of the Renaissance was at hand.

Reconstruction of the clepsydra according to Gazari (the clock of Gaza)

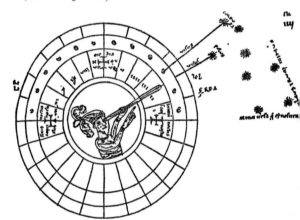

Locating the Pole

Terrestrial and Celestial Globes

TERRESTRIAL GLOBES

The idea that the earth is a sphere is, contrary to general opinion, very old. The measurement made by Eratosthenes discussed in the previous chapter would be senseless if the earth were supposed to have been flat. Some texts refer to terrestrial globes, although the Middle Ages, setting aside any doctrine that questioned scholastic dogma, forbade all representation of a spherical earth. It was not until the fifteenth century that the earliest globe we possess was constructed, that is the "apple" of Martin Behaim, which dates from 1492 and which is now preserved in the Germanisches Museum, Nuremberg.

Before that date several planispheres had been drawn, using the information provided by earlier voyages. One of these, prepared by the Italian geographer Paolo Toscanelli was to have unexpected results: as was usual with maps of the time it ignored the Pacific Ocean and put the coasts of Japan and China much closer to Europe in the west. This fortunate mistake caused Christopher Columbus to look to the west for the Indies. The Portuguese mariner Vasco da Gama having sailed right round Africa reached the Spice Islands by the eastern route, hence Spain had much to gain in seeking a shorter route to the west. When he set foot in the New World Columbus was certain it was Japan, quite close, therefore, to the fabled land of India. The everyday use of the name Indian to describe the aborigines of equatorial America perpetuates this error.

Undoubtedly one would have hesitated to look for the Indies in that direction and the discovery of America would have consequently been greatly retarded if, at that period, a means had existed of measuring lines of longitude. The problem had been recognized for a long time and its theoretical solution

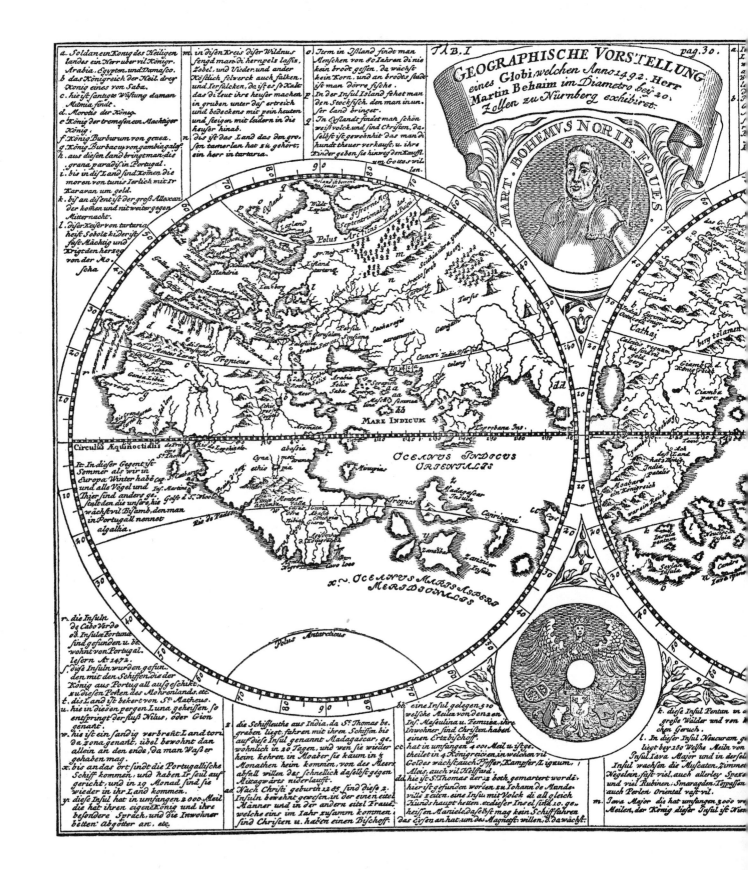

TAB. I   pag. 30.

GEOGRAPHISCHE VORSTELLUNG eines Globi, welchen Anno 1492, Herr Martin Behaim im Diametro bej 20. Zollen zu Nürnberg exhibiret.

MART. BOHEMVS NORIB. EQVES.

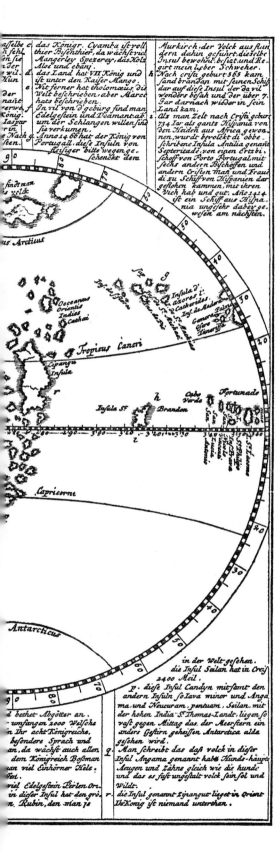

would still have to wait a good fifty years or more, while a method of making the actual measurement was not worked out till another two hundred years had passed, by the Belgian cosmographer Gemma Frisius, professor in the University of Louvain, in 1530. This is described in detail elsewhere in this book. Briefly it consists in comparing local time at the point where one is, with the local time at an initial, conventional meridian. This requires the use of a chronometer capable of keeping time from the point of departure with the greatest precision, however long and difficult the voyage. This horological achievement was not attained till 1769 and then by the Englishman John Harrison, after thirty-three years of effort.

Thus it is not at all surprising that these early globes were full of errors in distance. Nevertheless, after the sixteenth century they were produced in increasing numbers and inscribed with ever-growing detail. The great interest in globes was stimulated by the rise of great empires, and the many expeditions which were aimed at extending European dominion overseas. No library was complete without one of these very decorative instruments.

The largest globe of all was the one made by Coronelli in 1683 for Louis XIV; 4·75 meters in diameter, it stood on a gilt-bronze base as large in proportion, and this gigantic globe, now in the collections of the Palace of Versailles, still waits its companion, a celestial globe of the same size.

The great noblemen of the seventeenth century, in their anxiety to imitate the Sun King as far as their means allowed, commissioned the same Vincenzo Coronelli to make globes of 1·10 meters round, some of which have fortunately survived owing to their fine engraving and luxurious mounts (pl. 196).

On most globes made after the seventeenth century two calibrated metal circles, one parallel to the horizon, the other passing through the poles and forming a meridian, enabled elementary problems to be solved at once; (pl. 197); for instance, the local time at a given point, the length of the day, the hours of sunrise and sunset, etc. Terrestrial globes were not solely decorative, but true instruments of measurement.

CELESTIAL GLOBES

It is rather surprising to learn that celestial spheres preceded by a long time their terrestrial counterparts. The reason is that the earth does not immediately present itself to the human eye as a sphere, whereas the starry sky looks like

Planisphere after the globe by Martin Behaim, 1492

a hemispherical arch. So that the idea of its representation followed naturally on the apparent facts of observation. By watching the stars traveling the night sky, astronomers were able to fix them and mark their positions on the globe. In the Mediterranean regions the whole of the northern, and more than half of the southern, celestial hemispheres are visible at some time during the year. The constellations had been observed and classified in remote Antiquity and their positions in relation to each other noted.

The stars appear to our vision as more or less well-defined groups. In order to recognize them the constellations were given names, often of animals. With a little imagination one can see in the outlines of a constellation the shape of a lion, a swan or a bull and by degrees every cluster of stars was observed and classified. Four centuries before Christ, Eudoxus of Cnidus is said to have drawn onto a globe the constellations known in his time. The only description remaining of this ancient sphere is that of the poet Aratus, about 270 B.C. We do, however, possess one made a little later: the Farnese globe in the Naples museum. This marble monument, 2·40 meters tall, represents the giant Atlas holding up the heavens. On this globe 65 cm in diameter, the position of certain constellations is indicated and also of several circles of reference. Actually it is not an instrument of measurement at all, because the globe is fixed, and there are no calibrations. At the time when it was made, about 200 B.C., other more interesting instruments may well have existed. Cicero, in his *De Re Publica* describes a mobile celestial sphere, constructed by Archimedes, showing the movements of the sun and moon, as well as the daily rotation of the starry heavens.

The Arabs, inspired by Greek writings constructed numerous celestial globes, the oldest of which to survive date from the eleventh century (pl. 198). These instruments are finely engraved (pls. 199 and 200). Generally the axis on which they turn can be changed at will from the ecliptic to the equatorial pole. This allowed the coordinates of the stars, in the ecliptic as well as the equatorial system, to be measured. These terms must, however, be explained.

When one looks at the stars in the sky one sees that certain stars, in fact some of the brightest ones, slowly change their position in the field of stars. The early astronomers said that there were fixed and moving stars. The latter, which they called the planets, were named Mercury, Venus, Mars, Jupiter and Saturn; the sun and the moon joined their ranks. When one observes these seven stars it becomes clear that they follow one another on a narrow path, fixed by the position of the constellations along its edge. These constellations, most of which have animal names, constitute the Zodiac (< Gk. *zōon* = animal). The longitudinal axis of this route is the ecliptic. The ecliptic is the apparent path of the sun through the stars during the course of the year, and as the planets all revolve round the sun in almost the same plane they therefore

Arab zodiac

Pl. *196   Terrestrial and celestial globes by Coronelli, 1688. Father Vincenzo Coronelli, an Italian Franciscan monk, became famous in Venice, and was commanded by Cardinal d'Estrées to make two immense globes for Louis XIV, and many people wanted reductions of them. Beautifully engraved even the reduced spheres of Coronelli were 107 cm. in diameter. They were fitted with ornate stands and formed part of nearly every royal and noble library. Musée d'Histoire Naturelle, Paris*

Pl. *197   Terrestrial globe by W.J. Blaeu, 1622. Blaeu was cartographer to the Republic of the United Provinces in 1633, and constructed many globes. They are of papier-mâché covered with plaster and are engraved with the time-zones. D. 67 cm. Kugel Collection, Paris*

198

199

200

keep to this same narrow band in the sky. The ecliptic is inclined at about 23 ½ degrees to the Equator and was originally so called because it was found that the eclipses only occurred near the times when the moon crossed this great circle.

The ecliptic, which is a great circle on the celestial globe, serves as a fixed point when calculating the position of the stars. If one takes a conventional point of departure, the longitude (< Lat. *longitudo* = length) can be measured in degrees along this line. To facilitate the notation the early astronomers subdivided the ecliptic into twelve equal parts and called them after the most important constellation in their range: these were the signs of the Zodiac. Every sign is divided into thirty degrees. For instance, the longitude of a certain star may be the 22nd degree in the sign of Leo.

If a large calibrated circle is passed through the poles of the ecliptic so that it cuts the ecliptic at a right angle, one can read on it the latitude (< Lat. *latitudo* = breadth) which separates a star from the ecliptic base. In this way every star's latitude and longitude could be fixed.

The astronomers of Antiquity measured, by means of rules of alignment, the angular differences between the stars and traced a kind of network which determined the position of all the stars. The first catalogue of stars was thus composed by Hipparchus about 150 B.C., and Ptolemy adapted it to his period about three centuries later. Ecliptical coordinates were to be used for fifteen hundred years. In the seventeenth century they were replaced by equatorial coordinates. We shall see the reason.

If we look at the vault of the sky at night for an hour or two, we shall be able to see that it turns, more or less, round a point marked today by a brilliant star called Polaris or the Pole Star which indicates the north. The sphere of the heavens seems to turn on an axis passing through this heavenly pole. This daily movement can be reproduced on any sphere, all that is required being to put an axis through its two poles. The great circle perpendicular to this axis is called the equator (< Lat. *aequare* = to measure) and this circle allows the formation of new coordinates called equatorials. To make measurements, the circle is divided into 360 degrees which mark the *right ascension*.

If the celestial globe, balanced on its axis is arranged so that the two poles are on the horizon, a picture of the hemispherical arch as it would appear to a man standing on the equator is devised. This sphere is called the *right sphere*. If we now turn this right sphere on its axis we shall see all the stars rise vertically. This movement was called *rising in the right sphere*, or more simply, right ascension.

Since the equator was marked in degrees every star passed over the horizon at the same time as a certain equatorial degree. Henceforward it was defined by this degree, which is known as the right ascension of the star. The

Path of the stars round the Pole

Pl. 198 Celestial globe in brass, Persian, 1144. This is the earliest globe to have survived from the Near East. It is signed by Yunus ibn al-Husain and dated 539 A.H. It has the 1022 stars of Ptolemy's heaven in the form of pieces of inlaid silver. D. 17·5 cm. Private Collection, Paris

Pl. 199 Celestial sphere of bronze, Arabian. This sphere is inlaid with silver stars. D. 20 cm. Private Collection, Paris

Pl. 200 Celestial sphere of gilt bronze, Arabian. D. 11 cm. Private Collection, Paris

point where the equatorial gradation commences is the point where the equator crosses the ecliptic and is known as the Vernal Equinox.

A meridian circle graduated in the same way cuts the equator at a right angle. At that point, one can measure the angular distance separating the star from the equator: this is called the *declination*. Right ascension and declination together define the position of the star on the sphere.

Since every star circles the earth once every twenty-four hours the right ascension can be counted in hours instead of degrees, fifteen degrees being equal to one hour. It is, in fact, far easier to observe the time at which a star crosses the meridian than to measure its angle in relation to others. Thus as soon as it was possible to calculate time exactly, equatorial coordinates were substituted for ecliptics. This transformation in celestial measurement dates from the middle of the seventeenth century, the period when the first reliable clocks appeared.

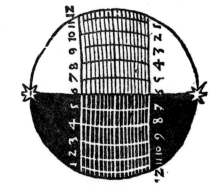

Upright sphere after Sacrobosco

It was also about this time that celestial spheres with automatic movement were invented, reproducing the apparent movement of the stars. Of course, the oldest of these cannot be considered to be very precise: their clock mechanism is not regular enough. Certain Chinese writers discuss a moving celestial sphere, constructed in China about 1090 by Su-sung, which is said to have been kept at the top of a tower and worked by a fountain. This must be treated with caution, as must most of the Chinese annals, especially as Chinese celestial maps, even though they are more recent than this, are highly inaccurate and border at times on the fanciful. This eleventh-century Chinese globe cannot, in any case, be considered a precision instrument.

On many of the Western mechanical spheres built in the seventeenth century one can see a small sun which follows the ecliptic line and makes a complete circle in a year. The sun actually moves across the firmament of fixed stars at the rate of about a degree each day. This movement was not difficult to reproduce and enables one to see, for instance, at what date the sun "entered the sign of Cancer" and so on.

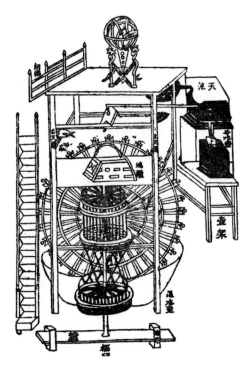

Water-clock by Su-sung, 1090

The use of celestial globes is similar to terrestrial ones: by attaching a horizontal and a meridian circle, the hours of the rising of a star, the direction in which it would be visible and the sign of the Zodiac passing across the horizon at the same time, could be calculated. This last observation was essential for astrologers. It was believed that every sign had certain physiological dispositions and its height at the moment of birth determined the future of the child. Without commenting here on the methods of astrology it must be recognized that in trying to penetrate the secret of the stars the astrologers laid wide the heavens to all observers.

Armillary Spheres and Planetaria

Armillary sphere

IN THEORY IT IS EASY to make a model of our cosmic system. Since the earth was formerly believed to be at the center of the universe it was quite sufficient to place a small globe of the earth in the center of the celestial sphere. Under these conditions it would have been invisible, however, and so the sphere of the fixed points had to be symbolized as a series of overlapping rings. Hence the name armillary sphere (< Lat. *armilla* = bracelet).

The circles used here to represent the celestial sphere are those used in astronomy to locate stars: first the ecliptic and the equator, and then the meridians, particularly those which pass through the two points of intersection of the ecliptic and equator and those at 90 degrees from these points. These are the *colures*, marking the dates of the equinoxes and the solstices on the ecliptic (pls. 201, 203; pl. xii).

To these are nearly always added the two *tropics*. These are the two small circles which run parallel to the equator and are situated at the places where the ecliptic is at its farthest distance from the equator, *i.e.* at the solstices. They mark the entry of the sun into Cancer at the summer solstice and into Capricorn at the winter solstice. Some of the finer armillary spheres also have an index marking the position of the most important stars.

The designers, as they grew more skilful, added rings showing the orbits of the sun and moon between the globe of the earth and the sphere of the stars. They even worked into these rings some extremely complicated devices to account for the eccentricity of the orbits, or to show the movement of precession which displaces the *colures* at the rate of one complete circle every 25,780 years. Such refinements were, of course, of purely academic interest, and in the end the armillary sphere became so complicated as to be practically useless.

Pl. XII   Armillary sphere in bronze by D. Heckinger, Augsburg, about 1650. D. 19·5 cm. Private Collection, Paris

Pl. 201   Armillary sphere of bronze, 17th century. This sphere borne by Atlas is furnished with an auxiliary ring counting the hours according to the daily revolution of the firmament. Overall H. 45 cm. Private Collection, Paris

Pl. 202   Demonstration planetarium, 18th century. A simple instrument with no mechanism representing Copernicus' solar system. The positions of the nine planetary bodies made of small ivory balls are arranged by hand. H. 36 cm. Private Collection, Paris

Pl. 203   Armillary sphere of bronze, 17th or 18th century. It has the principal circles indicating the position of the stars, the sun and the moon. D. 38·5 cm. Private Collection, Paris

201

202

203

204

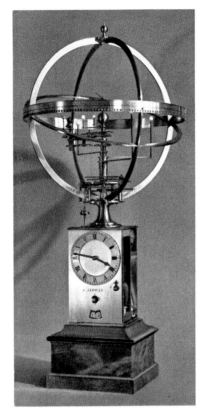

205

207

206

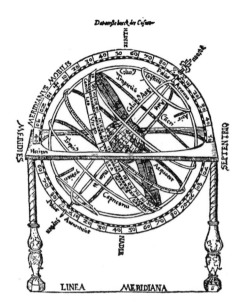

The rings of the sphere

Pl. XIII Armillary sphere of papier-mâché, late 18th century. This armillary sphere, constructed on the system of Copernicus was intended for teaching rather than for exact measurements. The care lavished on its decoration shows that it was designed for some gentleman's library. H. overall 54 cm. Gilbert Suc Collection, Paris

Pl. 204 Armillary sphere after the system of Copernicus, 1714. Design for a sphere worked by clockwork and constructed by Jean Pigeon of Lyons and G. Le Roy, his stepson, for the Duc d'Orléans. Bibliothèque de l'Observatoire, Paris

Pls. 205 & 206 Clock with a planetarium, 1774. This is a remarkable instrument by Antide Janvier, one of the finest clockmakers of all time. His mechanical planetaria reveal an extraordinary aptitude for designing the gear mechanism of these instruments. H. 60 cm. Private Collection, Paris

Pl. 207 Astronomical clock and planetarium, 18th century. In this instrument the planetary system is driven by the clock mechanism. It is enclosed in a crystal sphere and the stars in the heavens are engraved on it. D. of globe 28 cm. Samy Chalom Collection, Paris

Thus the great sphere of gilded wood made in 1590 by Antonio Santucci for the Grand Duke of Tuscany had a diameter of 2·20 meters with no less than twelve concentric spheres which are almost impossible to distinguish from each other amongst the jumble of rings. Nevertheless it is a highly decorative piece, and Santucci was instructed to reproduce it for the Escorial Library where it stands to this day. Between the sixteenth and the eighteenth centuries no Cabinet of curiosities could afford to be without one of these expensive and fragile pieces.

The first cosmic system as conceived by Eudoxus in the fourth century B.C., limited its aims to attributing to the stars a perfectly circular movement round the earth. Further study led to more and more complex orbits with the planets occupying eccentric circles, the centres of which themselves moved in an eccentric circle. The construction of such an elaborate armillary sphere would have resulted in a machine enormously expensive and indeed impossible to make. In 1543, when Copernicus suggested that the sun should be at the centre of the universe the problem was simplified (pl. XIII). Armillary spheres became less elaborate, but much less interesting.

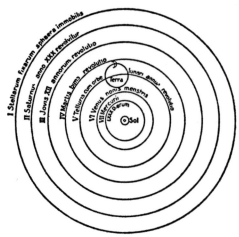

The system of Copernicus, 1543

New instruments consequently appeared, more didactic than mathematical, on which the planets moved freely round a central sun in the plane of the ecliptic (pl. 202). These planets were represented by small globes, and in 1609, when progress in optics had revealed the existence of satellites, (pl. XIV), these were added to their respective planets. Instrument-makers then tried to work the whole system by clockwork. (pls. 205–207). Naturally, since some planets take a considerable time to complete one revolution, twelve years in the case of Jupiter, thirty years in the case of Saturn, these planetaria stopped working a long time before they were able to indicate the exact position of the planets. In fact they are only curiosities and can hardly be used for measuring.

As we have said, Ptolemy claimed to have used a large armillary sphere to locate the 1,028 stars which he used in his catalogue. This instrument is described under the name of *astrolabon organon* (machine for fixing the positions of stars), and must certainly have included the circles we have listed above; but he would also have needed, besides a sighting-tube, an alidade which he could point at a star. It is doubtful that this instrument really existed, as it is too complex to have been made in Ptolemy's time. It was left to Tycho Brahe to make it fifteen centuries later, which he did then only with great difficulty. The famous Danish astronomer, who spent his life and fortune on making the most perfect instruments of the sixteenth century, admitted that this sphere only led to disappointment in use and that the measurements which could be taken were inaccurate.

Furthermore from the thirteenth century on, a more exact and less costly instrument, the *torquetum*, had been available. Here each element is separate,

Pl. XIV   Mechanical planetarium, end of the 18th century. In the 18th century in England elegant planetaria were made that worked by trains of gears. The one shown here has a central sun surrounded by the planets Mercury, Venus, the Earth and the Moon, Mars, Jupiter and Saturn. Since Uranus was not discovered till 1781, this instrument must have been made before then. Apparently the positions of Jupiter and Saturn were transposed when it was constructed. D. 24 cm. Private Collection, Paris

the measure being taken on its own plate, firmly attached to the others. The first plate is horizontal and is used for observing the azimuth—the angles formed along the horizon. The second is sloped according to the terrestrial latitude at the point of observation and is thus parallel to the equator and measures right ascension. The third plate, mounted obliquely on the equatorial table, is in the plane of the ecliptic: this gives celestial longitude. Perpendicular to this plate a sector comprising an alidade and a plumb-line is used for measuring heights, celestial latitude and declination. Most of the problems of spherical astronomy can thus be solved.

Although the torquetum was a robust instrument it had little success and only a few examples survive. This is probably because its use demanded greater skill than the astrolabe and it was thus reserved for astronomers. Geometricians had become sufficiently skilled at the beginning of the thirteenth century to devize an even more schematic instrument: this was the *rectangulus*. It was substantially the framework of the torquetum, the multiple planes of which had been reduced to two rectangular shafts. The makers never really overcame the problems of adjustment presented by this construction and the rectangulus probably never left the drawing-board.

With the advent of the seventeenth century, direct observation of right ascension with the meridian telescope rendered obsolete the use of the torquetum and similar instruments. Now it was easier and far more accurate simply to note the exact time when the star crossed the meridian while at the same time the mural circle gave the declination. Given these two coordinates, mathematical trigonometry could calculate with precision all that the sphere showed imperfectly, and the instrument was afterwards built only for decorative or didactic reasons.

The meridian telescope and mural circle were the forebears of modern equipment. They lacked all decoration and were built solely as precision instruments. They appeared at the same time as the refracting telescope, and, as soon as the superiority of the optical instrument over the simple alidade was established, it was adopted wherever positional accuracy was required. Instruments were no longer experimental oddities, and became the tools of astronomers and observatories. Precious materials, gilding and engraving were abandoned. The eighteenth century saw the last of the fine pieces described, whilst the nineteenth century turned to purely utilitarian ends.

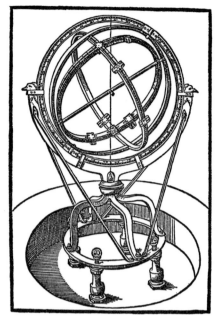

Astrolabon Organon of Ptolemy reconstructed by Tycho Brahe

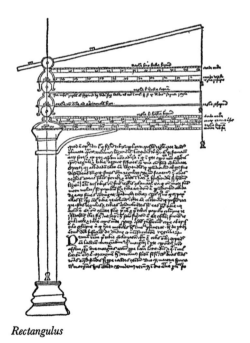

Rectangulus

Astrolabes

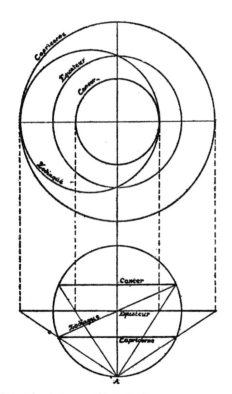

Principle of stereographic projection

The PLANISPHERIC ASTROLABE is among the finest achievements of Greek geometry. It is unfortunate that its educational value is ignored today as it is the easiest instrument on which to reproduce the movement of the sky and positions of the stars. If students of elementary astronomy were taught to handle the astrolabe in the way they learn to read an atlas some remarkable results would follow, because the instrument very clearly indicates celestial phenomena which are only vaguely comprehensible to most non-specialists.

The astrolabe is, in fact, a flat representation of the armillary sphere. It locates the stars at any given moment, past present or future, enabling their apparent movement to be reproduced and the principal problems of spherical astronomy to be solved at a glance. To give only a few examples: one can read off the position of the sun, both in height and in direction; the time; the times of rising and setting of any star; the length of the day or night; the time and duration of twilight and the direction from which to expect the appearance of any imminent celestial phenomenon.

In theory the astrolabe projects onto a flat surface the different elements of the sphere: the equator, the tropics, the *colures*, the ecliptic and so on, by the technique known as stereographic projection. This alarming name is its only complication. The method shows the universe as we would see it if we were observing from one of the poles of the celestial sphere, and if we then marked on a surface parallel to the equator the position of the stars as we saw them. This method of projection has two remarkable qualities:

(a) every circle on the sphere is shown as a circle;
(b) the angle of alignment between two bodies is projected in its actual size.

The importance of these two theorems will be immediately apparent: the first means that the design for the astrolabe can be made entirely with a ruler and compass, ensuring greater accuracy. The importance of the second is self-evident since all astronomical measurements are based on angular measure. The direction of the stars, their height above the horizon, the hour-angles and the distances between stars can all be measured on the astrolabe.

The instrument consists of two parts: on a fixed plate called a *tympanum* the circles which give the astronomical positions are engraved: the equator, the tropics, the horizon, the hour-circles and so on. Above this plate is a second pivoted disc, representing the sky, with the principal stars and the circle of the ecliptic covered by the sun in a year (pls. 209, 210).

So as to allow the tympanum to be visible under the disc representing the sky, the latter is cut away to a large extent, leaving only a network known as the *rete*, which is often called "the spider's web." By revolving this network the apparent movement of the sky in relation to the earth can be seen, and similarly the position of the stars in relation to us.

To measure this position the tympanum is engraved with circles, the centres of which are at the same height above the horizon. Depending on the accuracy needed, the number of circles is increased or diminished, for instance one every three degrees, or ever six, or every ten. Two circles are added below the horizon, the first at 6°, the second at 18°. These are the twilight circles and official twilight begins when the sun is 6° below the horizon, just as the brightest stars begin to appear. When the sun has sunk to 18° below the horizon all stars visible to the naked eye can be seen, and this is the hour of astronomical twilight.

To these circles on the tympanum are added the *azimuths*, radiant arcs converging at the zenith and showing the directions along the horizon.

This means that a different tympanum is needed for each geographical latitude, since the position of the horizon in relation to the pole varies according to this latitude. Every astrolabe is therefore provided with numerous tympana, each one marked with the latitude of the place for which it was drawn.

The idea of stereographic projection dates from the Alexandrian school of the second century B.C., but whether the principle was immediately applied to the construction of the astrolabe is less certain. It is only in the fifth century A.D. that we have proof of its existence, when a certain Synesios claimed to have invented it by combining Hipparchus' projection with Ptolemy's. After the fall of Alexandria to the Arabs the tradition moved to Syria, and thence to Byzantium and Bagdad. Tenth-century astrolabes made in these towns still exist in modern collections (pl. 208).

From then on the astrolabe began to spread, particularly among the Arabs, where its use was held to be a prerogative of rank (pls. 211, 214;

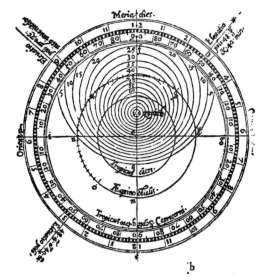

Plan of the circles of height

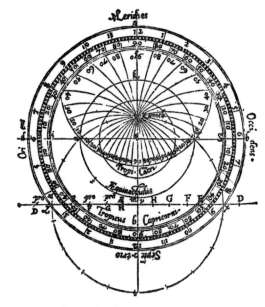

Plan of the azimuths

pl. xvi). No prince would undertake a journey or make an important decision
without first consulting his astrolaber. When Kaiser Wilhelm II was touring
the Middle East with a view to making an alliance with Imperial Turkey, he
had himself preceded by an astrologer, for whose use he sought out the best
astrolabe in existence. He finally decided upon the one made in 1647 for
Shah Abbas, but the owners of this splendid instrument—an English Museum—
declined to lend it.

By the sixteenth and seventeenth centuries, the astrolabe was structurally
perfect, both in the East and the West (pls. 212–216). In Persia specialized

studios grew up where the work was divided between the scholar who made the calculations, the designer of the instrument, the engraver who traced out the lines and the chiseler responsible for the inscriptions. The astrolabe seems to have been introduced to the West by the Jews who brought the Spanish tradition to France in the twelfth century. During the fourteenth and fifteenth centuries a true French style made its appearance (pls. 217, 218), and astrolabes were not beneath the attention of the great Renaissance artists. (pl. 219; pl. xv). By the eighteenth century the astrolabe was falling into disuse, calculations having replaced measurement. However, the ease and speed with which it solves some problems has brought it back into use, in a simplified form, for aviation. Since it allows immediate, if approximate, fixing of astronomical positions, light-weight instruments have been made in which the rete is replaced by a transparent plastic disc (pl. 220). These are not artistic, but purely utilitarian objects which are consequently not destined for the great collections of art.

In Moslem countries, on the other hand, the astrolabe has not entirely disappeared. The hours of the five daily prayers are easily marked on the astrolabe. The instrument was an essential part of the ritual trappings of the mosque: it was a sacred object kept apart from the gaze of the impious. It is therefore sometimes difficult to acquire one of these astrolabes if its owner happens to be a practising Muslim.

Of course perfection of the instrument made it more complicated. The tympana were now lodged in a hollowed-out, thick plate called the *matrix* which left the back of the astrolabe free for the addition of a number of extra lines. Every measurement has, as its starting-point, the height of the star above the horizon, therefore the back of every astrolabe was equipped with an alidade with a sighting-tube; a scale of heights was engraved on the limb. Tables were added for conversion of the hours according to the various methods of the day, as well as trigonometrical tables and, most important, astrological scales. Moroccan astrolabes also have a Julian calendar, which shows the daily position of the sun in the Zodiac.

Some mathematicians enjoyed designing variants on the type of astrolabe described above (pl. 222) chiefly by devising new methods of projection. One of these is still based on stereographic projection, but assumes the observer to be on the equator at the point where its circle crosses the ecliptic. The plan of projection is the colure of the solstices. This arrangement was conceived by the eleventh-century engraver Ibrahim-al-Zarqali, of Cordova, hence the name *Saphaea* (scale) *of Arzachel*. Rediscovered by Gemma Frisius in the sixteenth century it had little success, even though its use enabled the avoidance of a profusion of tympana. For this reason Gemma called it *Astrolabium catholicum*, the universal astrolabe.

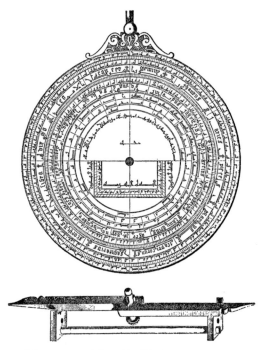

Moroccan astrolabe with alidade

Pl. 208 *Carolingian astrolabe, brass, 10th century. This is the oldest Western astrolabe that has come down to us. It was probably made at Barcelona where there was an important school of Hispano-Moresque science. This instrument marks the transition between the school of Cordova and the Provençal School of the early Middle Ages. The inscription is particularly interesting, showing the very early use of Arabic numerals in the West. D. 15·2 cm. Private Collection, Paris*

Pls. 209 & 210 *The principal parts of two astrolabes: one, of the Gothic period, has a matrix, a spider and four tympana; the other, Oriental, a spider and five double-faced tympana. D. 10 cm and 5 cm. Private Collection, Paris*

Pl. 211 *Astrolabe, brass, Indo-Persian, about 1650. Signed by Muhammad Maqim, the royal astrolabist at Lahore, this is the work of one of the most famous instrument-makers in the service of the Great Mogul. D. 25 cm. Charliat Collection, Paris*

208

209

210

211

212

213

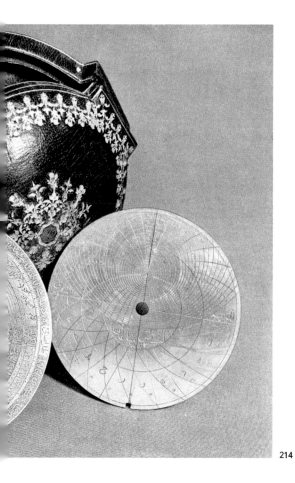

214

215

216

217

218

219

220

221

Pls. 212, 213 & 215 *Astrolabe, brass, Indo-Persian, 17th century. Neither signed, nor dated, this instrument was probably made at Lahore by one of the family of astrolabists who lived there during the 17th century. It may have been Diya al-Dîn, brother of the famous Muhammad Maquim (cf. Pl. 211) D. 9 cm. Private Collection, Paris*

Pl. 214 *Astrolabe, brass, Persian, about 1690. This is the work of a famous astrolabist, Muhammad Khalil (or Djalil) ibn Hasan 'Ali who worked at Isfahan at the end of the 17th century and who was praised by Chardin in his report of a journey made in 1674. This magnificent instrument is still in its original case, a very rare occurrence. D. 11·4 cm. Observatoire de Paris*

Pl. 216 *Astrolabe, brass, Syro-Egyptian, 1326. This astrolabe, constructed at Damascus by Ali ibn Ibrahim ibn Muhammad, is a good example of a school of craftsmen, whose work we have few examples. D. 16·2 cm. Observatoire de Paris*

Pl. 217 *Astrolabe, brass, Gothic, 15th century. Western astrolabes of this period are remarkable for their freedom of construction, simple arrangement and the elegant engraving of the inscriptions. D. 16·5 cm. Private Collection, Paris*

Pl. 218 *Astrolabe, brass, Gothic, 16th century. At this period Western astrolabists began to cover the backs of their instruments with different graduations, many of which are astrological in character. D. 10 cm. Private Collection, Paris*

Pl. 219 *Astrolabe, brass, Antwerp, 1557. This astrolabe, signed by Giles (Aegidius) Quinniet, who was mentioned by Plantin as 'Old Gilles the sphere-maker', is an important example of the work of a school regarded at the time as the best in the world. D. 15·6 cm. Musée de Cluny, Paris*

Pl. 220 *Astrolabe, cardboard, 18th century. Some instrument-makers, and not by any means the least, published printed astrolabes on paper stuck on board. They were very fragile and consequently now rather rare. Owing to their relative cheapness they could be made to a large scale and allowed more accurate readings. D. 28 cm. Private Collection, Paris*

Pl. 221 *Astrolabe, brass, Hispano-Moresque, 1721. Muhammad ibn Ahmad al-Batuti constructed this instrument for the Great Mosque of Fez, where astrolabes were in use till the beginning of the 20th century for fixing the hours of prayer. The Moroccan astrolabists carefully preserved the model of instruments made at Toledo eight centuries before, even using the fine Kufic script. They also still use the Julian calendar, a relic of the Roman occupation of North Africa. D. 23 cm. Private Collection, Paris*

A pupil and friend of the eminent Louvain professor, Juan de Roias, invented a variant of his master's method by moving the center of projection back to infinity in a right perpendicular to the plane of the colure of the solstices. In this way he obtained the so-called orthogonal projection, which was slightly easier to draw but which did not make the instrument any more practical. Roias's astrolabe was never generally used.

The astrolabe is now something of a rarity: perhaps rather less than two thousand are in existence. It is, however, strong, and its beauty has always demanded careful handling. It has quite functional lines and apart from a few decorative features in the manner of suspension, there is not one superfluous detail. This gives it a strict balance and controlled harmony which are immediately apparent. The astrolabe, a somewhat clinical instrument, yet provides a link between art and the dry science it serves.

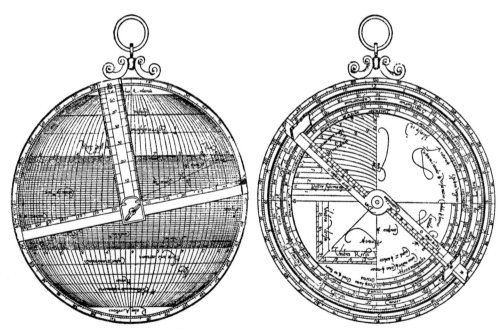

Universal astrolabe by Roias, Lisbon

*Pl. XVI   The face, case and two tympana of the
astrolabe in plate 214. Built by Muhammad Khalil
about 1690. It is a beautiful instrument, designed and
calculated by one of the most famous Persian astrolabe
experts and probably decorated by Abd al-a'immah,
who signed many instruments at that time. Private
Collection, Paris*

Sundials

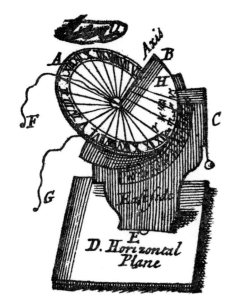

Equatorial sundial

W HEREAS THE ASTROLABE is comparatively rare, very many sundials have survived. Such is their variety that any thorough treatment of the mathematical, historical, esthetic or narrative aspect would fill several volumes.

From the earliest times it was realized that the regular movement of the sun in the course of the day could be used as a method of measurement of time; sundials work on this principle.

The following are important points which should be noted. In the lower latitudes nearer to the equator, the movement of the sun appears to be almost vertical and during the day the most noticeable variation is the height above the horizon. A native of equatorial Africa, if asked how long it will take to reach a certain place, will raise his arm above his head to indicate the height the sun will then be above the horizon. Ask the same question of a native in higher latitudes and he will stretch out his hand in a horizontal direction to indicate the position of the sun. Thus a southerner describes the course of the sun across the sky by moving his arm through the vertical plane, and a northerner, by moving it in a horizontal plane.

It therefore follows that there will be two systems for instruments which measure solar time, sundials of *height* and sundials of *direction*, the first originating in the lower latitudes and the second, which are more recent, in the more northerly latitudes.

SUNDIALS MEASURING HEIGHT

The height of the sun may be measured directly by pointing a straight edge at it and measuring the angle which it forms with the horizon. A simple instrument using this principle has the shape of a quarter circle, or *quadrant* (pl. 223). Hence comes the generic term for all chronometrical instruments even if the quarter circle has disappeared and even if, like our clocks, the dial no longer measures the height of the sun.

The quadrant dates from remote Antiquity. It is formed by two straight-edges at right angles to each other with a limb between in the form of a quarter circle. At the apex of the angle a plumb-line is attached. When the instrument is held vertically with one of its edges pointing at the sun the plumb-line shows the angle of the sun to the vertical on the circular edge. It is then a simple matter to graduate the limb in the opposite way so as to make the line indicate the angular height.

From the time of rising at the horizon and its maximum height, at the zenith, the sun never forms an angle greater than 90°. At one time the hour of dawn was considered to be the first hour of the day, and culmination naturally marked the middle of the day or noon. Between these two moments the half day can be divided into as many units as are required. We have already touched on the rudimentary conception of hours in primitive civilizations. Egyptian quadrants divided the quarter circle into six equal segments, and in sub-tropical regions the time between these divisions could be said to be nearly the same. It is a different matter in the north. However, some churches have quadrants graduated in the same manner. Chronometry in the Middle Ages was not much better than the gropings of the Egyptians on the subject.

In our latitudes the quadrant was used without modification until the eighteenth century, when changes were introduced to account for variations in the length of the day, and for daily variations in the length of the hour.

It is generally known in northern latitudes that the sun is higher in summer than in winter, and that for any given moment its height will daily vary. So two sets of lines are traced on time-keeping instruments, one showing the date, the other the time. The latter, called *hour-lines*, may be straight, curved or arcs of a circle, depending on the pattern adopted by the maker. A head is threaded onto the plumb-line and adjusted according to the date so that when the whole instrument is pointed at the sun it shows the time on the hour-lines (pl. 224).

The *solar ring* is another instrument for direct measurement of the height of the sun, and specimens survive from the days of Imperial Rome. They are small cylindrical bracelets, wide in relation to their diameter, which are hung up facing the sun. Light rays passing through a small hole bored in the proper place strike the inside wall of the ring. It is sufficient to mark the hour lines at this spot. It is of course possible to add date lines as well.

Direct observation of the sun is made difficult by its dazzling glare, and it was thus a great advance when measurement of the shadow thrown by a

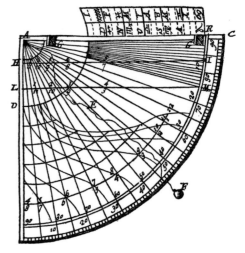

Quadrant with curved lines

Pl. 222 Astrolabe-quadrant, brass, about 1680. This is an astrolabe which could be folded into four. It is signed John Prujean, an Oxford instrument-maker according to information provided by Professor Edmund Gunter of Christ Church. Radius 11 cm. Private Collection, Paris

Pl. 223 Solar dial quadrant, wood, 17th century. Radius 8 cm. Private Collection, Paris

Pl. 224 Universal dial for measuring height, ivory, 17th century. This is a rectangular version of the old quadrant. It allows the instrument to be used for various geographical latitudes. 4·5 × 8 cm. Kugel Collection, Paris

Pl. 225 Shepherd's sundial, 18th century. Although this dial is only made of wood covered with paper, its very careful workmanship sets it apart from the much simpler instruments still to be found among the Pyrenean peasants. It is contained in a fine multi-colored box of woven straw. H. 10·5 cm. Private Collection, Paris

Pl. 226 Shepherd's sundial, ivory, 18th century. This is a far more elegant instrument, engraved with the hours in color and some gilding. H. 12 cm. Private Collection, Paris

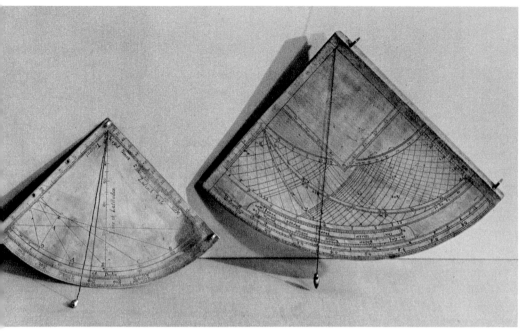

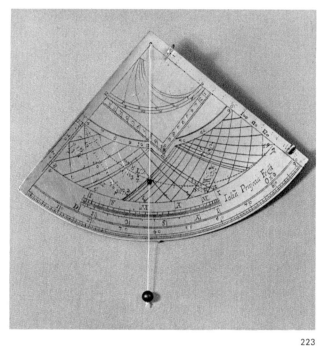

222

223

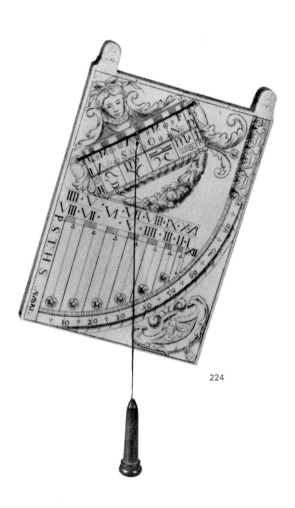

224

225

226

227

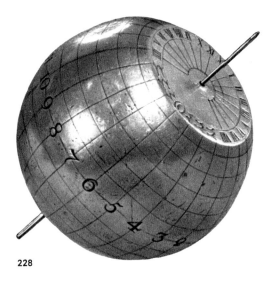

228

229

230

gnomon was introduced instead. This term, which in Greek simply means "indicator", is the origin of the term gnomonics, the science of the sundial.

The gnomon can have any shape or arrangement, the tip alone marking the hours on lines drawn for the purpose. We possess Egyptian sundials to measure height and these use gnomons, the oldest example must date from the fifteenth century B.C. They consist of a horizontal bar which is pointed towards the sun. A short, vertical gnomon on one end casts a shadow onto the bar, and the length of the shadow indicates the time. Five hour-points are marked on the horizontal bar, the first of which, at the foot of the gnomon, indicates

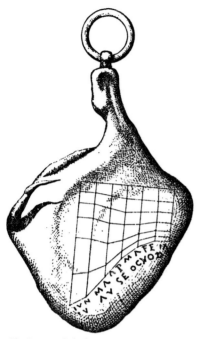

Portable Roman dial, first century A.D.

Pl. 227 Sundial with analemmatic projection; 18th century. Signed by F. Briot, it combines a French dial of the type called Butterfield (cf. Pl. 247) with an analemmatic dial and can consequently be used without a compass. It is one of the many gnomonic ideas which were curious rather than practical. L. about 10 cm. Private Collection, Paris

Pl. 228 Equatorial Sundial, brass, 18th century. It is not difficult to draw the successive meridians on a sphere through which the sun passes hour by hour. The sphere is inclined with its axis parallel to that of the earth and the shadow of this axis shows the time on a parallel plane at the equator. This is the easiest sundial to make. D. 6 cm. Private Collection, Paris

Pl. 229. Magnetic dial by Bloud, about 1670. The art of inlay developed at Dieppe produced a school of dial-makers, one of whom, Charles Bloud, invented a special kind of solar watch in which the compass needle told the time. It disappeared after a few years. 8 × 8 cm. Private Collection, Paris

Pl. 230 Magnetic dial by Bloud, about 1670. This exceptional sundial is in a tortoiseshell case still in its original cover. Its octagonal shape is also unusual. W. 7.3 cm. Observatoire de Paris

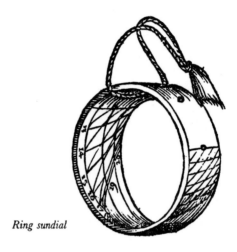

Ring sundial

noon. The distance of the others is in the progression 1 : 3 : 6 : 10 : 15, which means that the distance between two successive points follows the progression 1 : 2 : 3 : 4 : 5. These proportions bear no relation to the sequence of hours as we understand them, and serve to show the arbitrary nature of Egyptian chronometry.

A small Roman sundial from the third century B.C. discovered near Bratislava, is based on this same principle, but in this case the horizontal bar has been replaced by a curved sector of bronze, which can be adjusted according to the date. The readings made on this instrument are therefore slightly more accurate than on the earlier Egyptian model.

Another portable bronze sundial was found in the ruins of Portici near Naples, during the first excavations in the ashes of Vesuvius. It must therefore date from at least the beginning of our era. About 12 cm high it has a curious shape like a ham and is known as the "Ham Dial". It hangs from a ring with a horn-shaped gnomon; vertical lines traced on the body mark the months, whilst another series of curved lines mark the hours.

The three instruments just described are portable sundials; a form of traveling clock. Larger, fixed sundials existed in Classical times and as these were made of marble a good many have survived. They have hollow dials, hence the name *scaphes* (< Gk. *skaphé* = a hollowed-out boat) and they originated in Greece in the third century B.C.

These scaphes are drawn on the inside of a hemisphere and are neither more nor less than the inverted image of the sky. A gnomon with its point at the center of the hemisphere sets the center of symmetry. Whenever the sun's rays strike this point a shadow is projected onto the marble opposite the position of the sun. The hollow surface may be graduated with hour-lines and the "arcs of the signs", the first giving the time, the second the signs of the zodiac and the path of the sun and hence the date.

Later sundial-makers were to construct similar hollow dials right up to modern times, using bronze or ivory, and in all sizes. After the eighteenth century the Japanese used European sundials as models to engrave *hidokei*, some of which are only a few tenths of an inch in diameter.

We now come to a very common, though very attractive, sundial. This consists of a small vertical column with a horizontal gnomon attached to a pivoting capital. The gnomon can be brought into line with one of the verticals drawn on the shaft of the column. Each vertical represents a certain month. The length of the shadow telling the time is read off on spiral curves. To tell the time it is only necessary to point the gnomon at the sun; when it is in the correct position its shadow covers the vertical line exactly.

Simply, yet strongly made, these columnar sundials are both elegant and practical. They date from the beginning of the eleventh century. Pyrenean shepherds are supposed to use them still, hence their name, "shepherds' dials" (pls. 225, 226; pl. XVII).

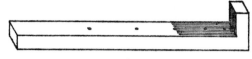

Egyptian dial

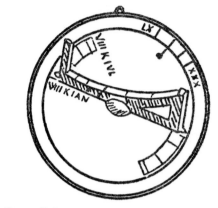

Roman dial

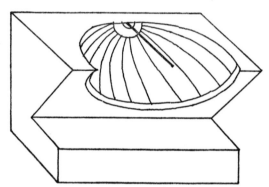

Roman sundial or scaf, *with a hollow dial*

SUNDIALS MEASURING DIRECTION

If a gnomon, a simple rod, is stuck vertically into the ground it will be immediately apparent in northern latitudes that the shadow pivots on the foot of this stick and in the course of the day traces a semicircle. Hence the idea of deducing the time from the angle of this shadow.

Because of this fact many authors writing on gnomonics have stated repeatedly that the first sundials were the Egyptian obelisks. In fact, the obelisks of Egypt stood close to the temple walls which they adorned and

Pl. XVII   Pocket sundials: 17th and 18th centuries. Topl ine: Shepherd's dial (see Plate 225); mine compass, marked Johan Oberhauser, Schwaz (Tyrol) and made of wood with ivory; 11·5 × 8 cm; magnetic dial by Bloud. Bottom line: Diptych dial in ivory 6·7 × 5·7 cm; five oval dials in ivory, Dieppe type, about 6 × 4 cm. Private Collection, Paris

239

could not therefore project a shadow on the ground. According to Egyptologists they were symbols of solar radiance, not clocks.

The Romans, who had only the vaguest notions of chronometry, erected obelisks looted from Egypt in their public squares, and then used them as gnomons without realizing their mistake. As has been said the position of the shadow of a vertical pole varies from day to day at the same hour, as does the length of the shadow. Many sundials made during the Roman Empire display the same fault. A small rod cast its shadow on a horizontal or vertical slab, but such sundials were quite small and their inaccuracy therefore less pronounced. A careful division of the day into hours was, besides, never a particular concern of the Romans.

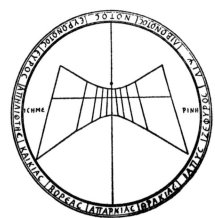

Graeco-Roman dial with a gnomon

The problem was solved in 1644 by the French geometrician Vaulesard. The passage of the sun's rays over the tip of the gnomon traces a cone; the intersection formed on a flat, horizontal surface is an ellipse (pl. 227). After a few days, when the declination of the sun has changed, the shadow of the tip of the gnomon traces a like ellipse, now shifted from the first in the direction of its minor axis. Instead of drawing a new ellipse it would be better to move the gnomon and the new shadow would be cast nicely onto the first ellipse.

An interesting, so-called *analemmatic* sundial is thus made. One of the most famous of these is in the forecourt of the church at Brou in France. The part of the gnomon is played by the observer who stands on a line marked with the dates so that the shadow of his head shows the time on the analemmatic ellipse.

A clever variation of this was the magnetic sundial conceived by Bloud of Dieppe. Here the ellipse is slid along its minor axis by means of a cam

Pl. 231   Equinoctial table-dial, about 1685. The dial is made of a large cylinder, either of silver or silver plate, which is arranged parallel to the equator. Ulrich Harvolck, its maker, may have been Austrian. An axial thread throws a shadow on the interior of the cylinder, which is graduated. H. 20 cm. Private Collection, Paris

Pl. 232   Two ivory dials used as equatorial dials. Left: diptych dial from Nuremberg, signed Hans Ducher (late 16th century). Right: dial by Bloud (17th century). When the cover of these dials is inclined so as to be parallel to the earth's equator a perpendicular needle on the shutter shows the time by throwing a shadow on a circle divided into 24 equal parts. Left: 9.5 × 6.5 cm. Right: 8.2 × 9 cm. Private Collection, Paris

Pl. 233   Equinoctial sundial of the French type, 17th century. This silver dial has a circle, the angle of which can be adjusted according to latitude. It is furnished with a compass and plumbline. 7 × 9 cm. Private Collection, Paris

Pl. 234   Equinoctial sundial of the Augsburg type, about 1650. This very pretty dial by Rugendas is the prototype for many solar watches made in South Germany for more than a hundred years. Its simplicity and excellent workmanship distinguish it from imitations of later date. 6.5 × 6.5 cm. Private Collection, Paris

Pl. 235   Despite the fashion for Butterfield (cf. Pl. 247) dials the Augsburg type were copied by several French instrument-makers, but they were rather heavy and replaced the complete equinoctial circle by a segmented circle. This one is signed Dubois. 8 × 8 cm. Private Collection, Paris

Pls. 236 & 237   Equinoctial dial, French, 18th century. In this case the octagonal plate is elongated in a way similar to the dials made by Butterfield (cf. Pl. 247). It also has a device for transposing into solar time the hours read by the light of the moon. 6.5 × 5.5 cm. Private Collection, Paris

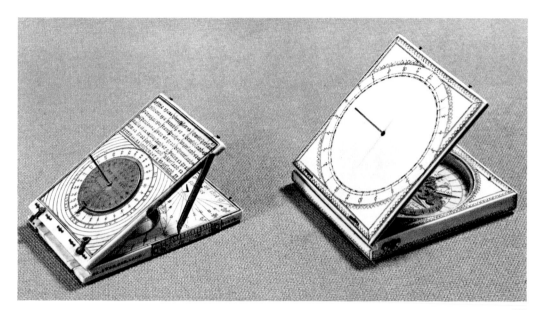

232

231

233

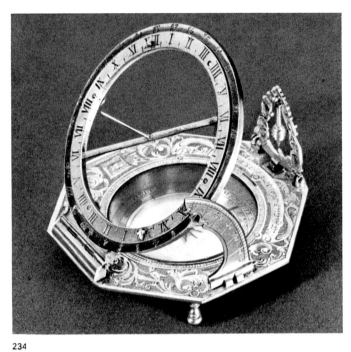

234

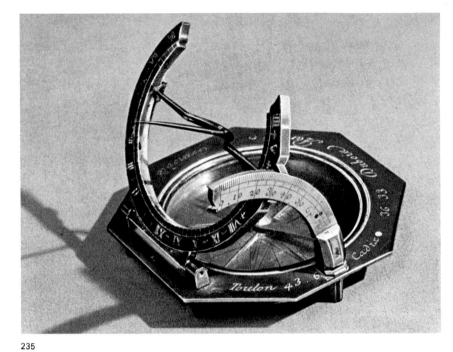

235

236

237

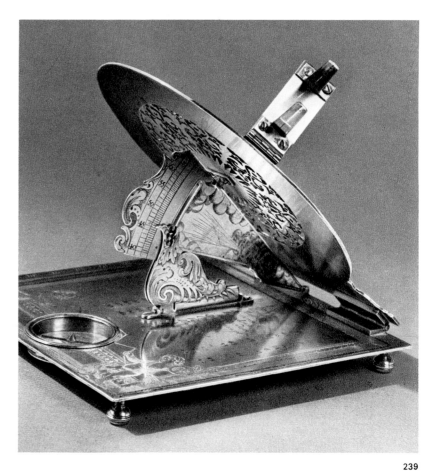

238

239

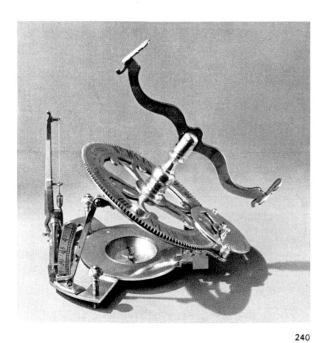

240

241

242

243

244

graduated according to the calendar. But, instead of the ray of the sun turning round the gnomon, the whole instrument turns towards the sun. The directional reference is given by a compass needle which shows the time on the ellipse (pls. 229 and 230). Bloud's sundial was, of necessity, portable and in effect a solar watch. These magnetic sundials were generally mounted in an ivory box, although tortoise-shell examples are known.

Pl. 238 Equinoctial dial, silver, 17th century. This instrument is the work of Chapotot who was one of the most skilful dial-makers at the end of the 17th century. This dial comprises an inclined plate in the plane of the equator. An alidade, turning on this plate, is directed towards the sun. Across the end of the alidade is stretched a thread which will cast a shadow on the plate in the axis. The other end of the alidade has a pointer which marks the time. D. of plate 17 cm. Private Collection, Paris

Pl. 239 This illustration shows the thread which indicates the direction of the sun, and the regulating device for setting the angle of the plate. It is interesting to compare this construction with the sundials of Butterfield (cf. Pl. 247).

Pl. 240 Equinoctial dial with gear mechanism, 18th century. This dial of polished brass is signed by Gaspard of Lunéville. King Stanislas supported a brilliant school of dial-makers at his residence there. The alidade in this case is geared to move a small auxiliary dial which shows the minutes. D. of the plate 13.5 cm. Private Collection, Paris

Pl. 241 Equinoctial dial with gear mechanism of the German type, 18th century. This elegant geared dial bears witness to the skill of its maker even though it was made in the middle of the 18th century. D. of plate 12 cm. Private Collection, Paris

Pl. 242 Equinoctial ring, English, 18th century. This ring of gilt brass is characteristic of a type which was widespread for over a century due to its robust design. It is signed by Heath, a skilled London maker. D. 24 cm. Charliat Collection, Paris

Pl. 243 Equinoctial ring, German, 18th century. The German method of construction is lighter than the English shown in Pl. 242. It also smaller. The ring is gilt copper. D. 8 cm. Private Collection, Paris.

Pl. 244 Equinoctial ring, French, 18th century. Signed Langlois, this ring is rather heavier than the German one. It is in gilt copper. D. 10 cm. Private Collection, Paris

STYLE-AXIS SUNDIALS

We have described how the concept of the sun revolving round the axis of the earth became more specific in the thirteenth century, after the publication of Sacrobosco's *Treatise*. This axis of the earth points towards the celestial pole, the Pole Star. When a rod, a style-axis, is aimed in this direction the sun turns round it in a regular movement in the course of one day. Whatever the date, the shadow of the style-axis will point in the same direction at any given time, and so the direction of the shadow can be traced as it varies from hour to hour. These hour-lines then hold good throughout the year (pl. 228).

Let us take the case of a surface perpendicular to the style-axis. This surface will be parallel to the plane of the equator, and the dial is therefore known as an "equatorial dial", or "equinoctial dial" since the sun moves in the plane of the equator on the days of the equinoxes. On these dials the shadow moves at a constant speed with the hour-lines at an equal distance from each other. They are thus easy to draw (pl. 232).

Of course the sundial must be set with its style-axis parallel to the axis of the earth. If the instrument is moveable it must be equipped with a compass set in the stand. A moveable sundial must also be adjustable for the latitude of observation. For this purpose the style and dial are jointed on a hinge with a graduated sector supporting them and controlling the angle of inclination (pls. 233 and 234).

Equinoctial sundials are easily made into small solar clocks which are both light and strong. One very successful contrivance appears to have been invented by a French clockmaker of Auch called Rugend, sometime towards the end of the seventeenth century. Like so many other craftsmen he was probably forced to emigrate to Germany during the Wars of Religion, and to change his name. In fact a family of sundial-makers lived in Augsburg during the eighteenth century, and signed some excellent dials of this type with the name Rugendas (pl. 234). These dials were afterwards copied with varying skill and style by several German makers.

French craftsmen were not slow to copy these Augsburg dials (pl. 235), but they chose a more elongated base than the regular octagon favored by the Germans (pls. 236–239).

They finally made this plate in the shape of a tooth wheel which engaged with a smaller wheel joined to an indicator, which made a complete circuit for an angular deplacement of 15 degrees. This base plate also had an alidade

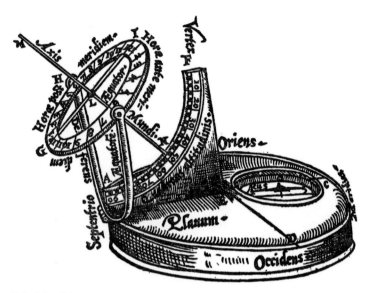

Principle of the gnomon

which the observer pointed at the sun. Thus the indicator marked off the minutes (pls. 240 and 241).

A curious variant on the equatorial sundial is the equinoctial ring, not to be confused with the solar ring described above. Invented in the first years of the seventeenth century it enjoyed great success for it made an excellent pocket-dial thanks to its compactness and strength. Here the style-axis is replaced by a rectangular channel fixed across the diameter of a suspended ring. The inclination of this groove corresponds to the height of the pole, so that if the ring is in the plane of the meridian the groove is parallel to the axis of the earth. In the groove there is a slide, pierced with a small hole, which is moved along a graduated scale according to the declination of the sun at the date of the operation. A second ring perpendicular to the first, and thus parallel to the equator, is marked with the hours. When the instrument is accurately orientated the ray of sunlight passing through the little hole on the slide falls

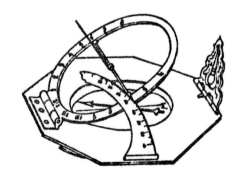

Equinoctial dial from Augsburg

on the equatorial ring and gives the time. Conversely, when the ray falls on the ring, instrument is truly orientated and is now a compass (pls. 242-244).

Quite large sundials of this type were made, especially in England; they are not suspended but stand on a pedestal placed on a table. They are highly decorative and fairly accurate instruments (pl. 245).

The sundials which just described have their plates in the plane of the equator, and it is not at all difficult to project the shadow of their gnomons onto any vertical or horizontal surface. The outside walls of churches and public buildings are often decorated with large vertical sundials with a style-axis consisting of a simple iron bar or metal triangle; equally familiar are the horizontal sundials engraved on pieces of slate, lead or bronze and set on a column in the garden (pl. 246). The small portable sundials for traveling are more interesting and, at a time when mechanical watches were erratic to say the least, these miniature instruments proved their worth. On the first watches the hands could be reset whenever necessary by making use of very small sundial as a check, the ancestor of radio time-signals, no less.

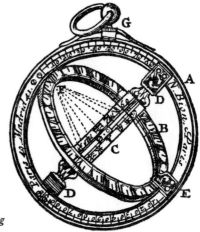

Equinoctial ring

One prototype of the portable horizontal sundial was invented in southern Germany at the beginning of the fifteenth century. It is a graduated horizontal plate holding a vertical rod that can be folded back flat for traveling. To indicate the time the rod is raised supporting an oblique wire. This joins the rod to the dial and forms the style-axis.

After numerous variants had been tried, a portable sundial was made in an extremely elegant version by Michael Butterfield, a craftsman, probably of English origin, who settled in Paris about 1680 and was given the title of

Ingénieur du Roy. His pocket sundial is in the shape of an elongated octagonal, with a small compass and folding triangular style. To use the dial the style had to be erected to the vertical and adjusted for latitude. A typical feature is the scale which supports the style and shows its inclination. It is in the shape of a bird whose beak indicates the latitude. This sundial was such a success that it was given the name Butterfield despite the fact that it was copied for nearly a century by French makers (pls. 247 and 248).

There were also local fashions for solar clocks. Apart from the Augsburg equinoctials and the Butterfields, collections contain a number of diptych sundials made at Nuremberg during the sixteenth and seventeenth centuries. At first they were made of fruit-wood, later of ivory (pl. XVII). They consist of two plates on a hinge which can be opened like a book and fixed at right-angles, so that one of the plates forms a vertical disc, the other a horizontal. Between them a slanting wire forms the style-axis (pls. 249–252).

Gnomon of a Butterfield dial

The surface of the diptych left plenty of space free and the Nuremberg makers were inspired to cover this with calendars, compass-cards, conversion-tables for the various types of hours in use, and even maps; and, not satisfied with all this elaboration on the one instrument, both a horizontal and a vertical sundial, they added little dials with vertical, horizontal and hollow

Pl. 245   Table hour-ring, about 1710. English instrument-makers, and notably J. Rowley who made this dial, made some very large rings with consequently increased precision. H. 40 cm. Private Collection, Paris

Pl. 246   Horizontal sundial, slate, 18th century. No gentleman's garden of the period would have been complete without a decorative sundial. Slate allowed very accurate engraving and being impervious to weather was a perfect material. 30 × 30 cm. Private Collection, Paris

Pl. 247   Horizontal sundial, so-called Butterfield, about 1730. Butterfield was probably English but he settled in Paris and soon became attached to the court of Louis XIV. He was the first to make these robust solar watches, both practical and elegant. The chiselling and engraving is of a high order. 7·5 × 6·1 cm. Private Collection, Paris

Pl. 248   So-called Butterfield sundial, silver, 1730. Many French instrument-makers made these small solar watches in imitation of Butterfield, sometimes in silver or gilt brass which were in great demand. This one is signed Lemaire, who made some excellent instruments. 8 × 7 cm. Private Collection, Paris

Pl. 249   Diptych dials from Nuremberg, ivory, 17th century. At first these multiple dials were made in fruit wood, then ivory was used and they became a speciality of Nuremberg. They are usually rectangular, sometimes oval, and more rarely, round. Left to right: dial by Hans Ducher (Tucher) about 1590. 9·5 × 6·5 cm. Oval dial, unsigned, in the style of Ducher, 6 × 3·5 cm. Round dial, the metal parts of gilt copper. D. 4·7 cm. Rectangular dial by Hans Troschel, about 1600. 8·5 × 4·5 cm. Private Collection, Paris

Pl. 250   Diptych dials from Nuremberg, ivory, 17th century. This is the upper face of the diptych which generally has a plan of the winds or a conversion table for lunar into solar hours. Left: dial by Leonhard Miller about 1620. 9 × 7 cm. Right: Unsigned dial, about 1600, 12 × 7 cm. R. Gest Collection, Beauvais

Pl. 251   Diptych dial from Nuremberg, ivory, 17th century. This photograph shows the interior arrangement of the two leaves, where there are several different kinds of dial and a list of the latitudes of various towns. 10 × 7 cm. R. Gest Collection, Beauvais

Pl. 252   Diptych dial of the Nuremberg type, wood, 18th century. During the 18th century several instrument-makers made series of diptych dials in wood, and covered with prints on paper. Although the method was cheap it has a certain charm. 9 × 7 cm. Private Collection, Paris

245

246

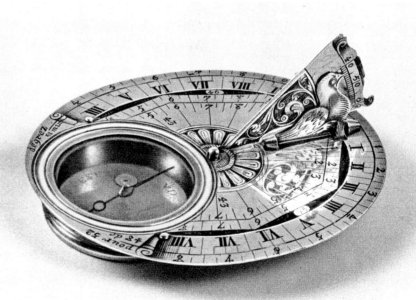

247

248

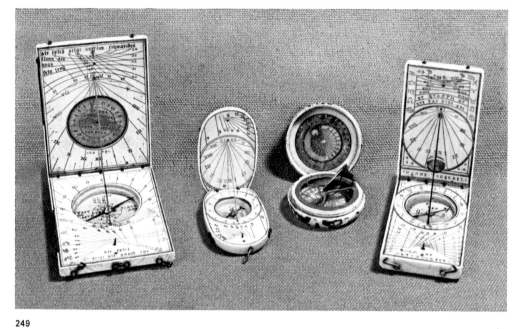

249

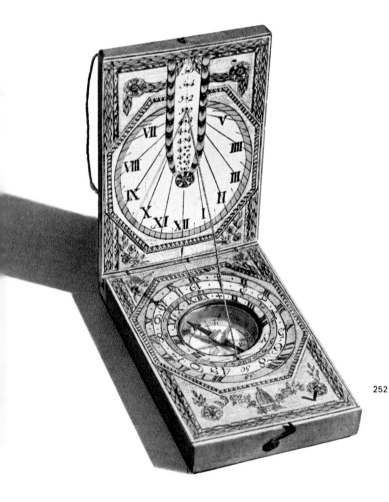

252

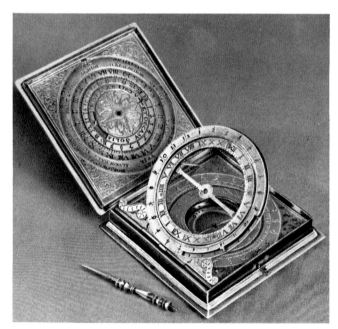

253

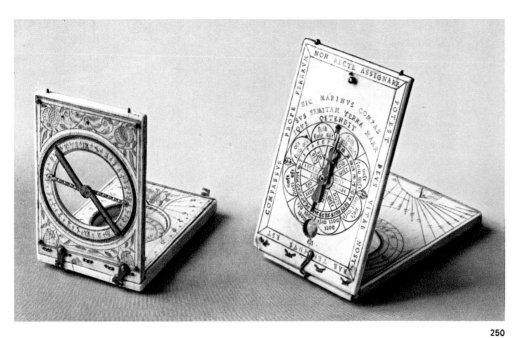

250

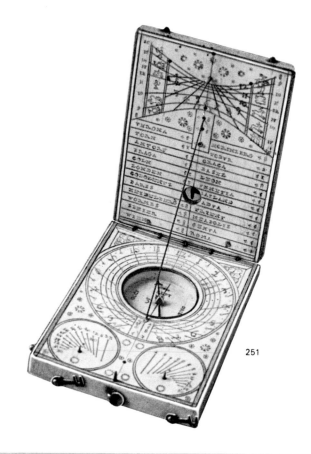

251

254

255

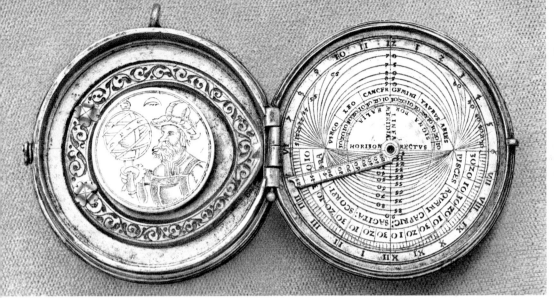

256

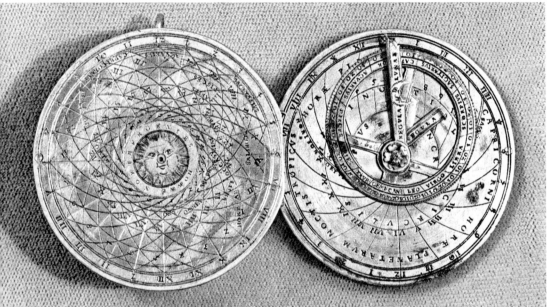

257

259

258

260

261

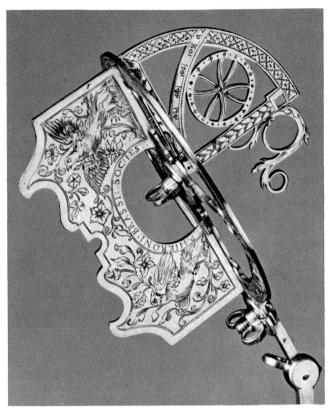

262

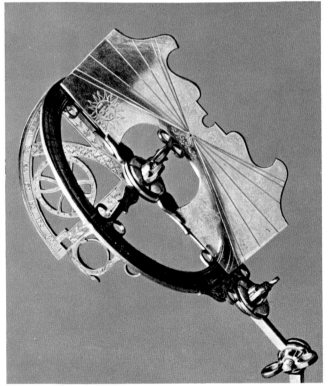

263

266

267

Pls. 253 & 254   Astronomic compendium in gilt cop-
per, 16th century. Some instrument-makers, usually
those attached to one of the minor courts of southern
Germany, distinguished themselves by making small
gilt copper boxes containing a solar dial and finely
engraved on every surface with astronomical tables.
This one shows the style of Ulrich Schniep of Munich,
one of the best instrument-makers of the period. 9 × 9
cm. Private Collection, Paris

Pl. 255   Astronomic compendium in gilt copper, 1600.
This case is signed by Juan Cocart, a Brussels
clockmaker who worked for the Emperor Charles V
after his retirement to Yuste, and took the Spanish name
Juanin. This is one of the smaller dials made by
this great instrument-maker. 6 × 6 cm. Observatoire
de Paris

Pls. 256-259   Astronomic compendium in gilt
copper, 1562. This astronomer's outfit was made by
Christopher Schissler, a master in this field. The
interior comprises several layers with different instru-
ments, and the outer case is covered with ingenious
diagrams. D. 5·5 cm. Observatoire de Paris

Pl. 260   Stone dial in the form of a polyhedron.
This is a true collector's piece containing several
different dials. W. 28 cm. Historisches Museum,
Basle

Pl. 261   Polyhedron dial, 1617. This multiple
dial, signed by N.M. Gumnor of Nuremberg, is
after a design published by Oronce Fine in his book
"De Solaribus Horologiis" (Paris 1560). L. 20 cm.
Private Collection, Paris

Pls. 262 & 263   Sundial, 18th century. This
instrument was intended to facilitate the drawing of
solar dials on walls; the beautiful engravings on the
instrument point to its having been a presentation piece
intended for the royal collections. D. 11 cm. Observa-
toire de Paris

Pls. 264 & 265   Nocturnal of gilt brass, 1584.
This "Star-dial" wasde dicated to Albert, Archduke
of Austria, and its maker only added his initials,
B.H., not enough for us to identify him. However
he was clearly a great craftsman, a contemporary of the
Habermel family, who made some of the finest
instruments of the century. D. 18·8 cm. Observatoire
de Paris

Pls. 266 & 267   Multiple dial, bronze, 1677.
This piece contains eight different solar dials and is
decorative rather than practical. On the upper part the
figure carries a sphere, or hollow hemispherical dial
which is the most interesting part of the instrument.
H. 20 cm. A. Davidson Collection, London

gnomons, as their fancy dictated. The effect is very decorative, bordering on the luxurious.

Some yet more ambitious craftsmen in southern Germany made what can only be described as pocket astronomical kits splendidly engraved in gilded copper, with sundials and all manner of instruments including astrolabes, all in a small round or square box, now collectors' pieces (pls. 253-259).

On the subject of multiple dials, mention should be made of the polyhedral sundials which caused rivalry among geometricians from the sixteenth to the eighteenth centuries. Ranging from miniature to monumental dials, these pieces concentrate the greatest possible number of chronometrical data on all sides of a polyhedron (pls. 260, 261, 266 and 276). At best their use can only be justified by the fact that one can dispense with a compass when all the dials show the same time and are therefore correctly orientated. Actually all this elaboration is the result of a kind of scholarly vanity which led the craftsmen to complicate their work so as to show their skill.

Drawing the hour-lines on a given surface presents no difficulties, however. A special *sciatheric machine* was devised which made drawing of the hour-lines a simple matter on mural sundials. Basically this is an equatorial dial fixed in the stonework of a wall. Using threads to reproduce the sun's rays which hourly strike the surface to be calibrated, the terminal points of the rays are marked. All that is then needed is to draw straight lines from these points to the foot of the style-axis, and with no special skill the hours can be marked. Even the "arcs of the signs" can be drawn, showing month-by-month the hyperbola traced by the end of the shadow throughout the day (pls. 262 and 263).

LUNAR DIALS

It is clear that, up to a point, the light of the moon can replace the sun's rays: its light throws a more or less intense shadow. The path of the earth's satellite, however, does not coincide with that of the sun: the positional difference between the two varies from zero at the time of the New Moon up to twelve hours at Full Moon and returns to zero after twenty-nine-and-a-half days. Daily correction is therefore necessary. Some dials are equipped with an engraved table which indicates the amount to be added or subtracted each day.

NIGHT DIALS, OR STAR DIALS

These dials are called *nocturlabes* (pl. xviii) or more usually *nocturnals*, and are based on a completely different principle. The celestial clock, the night sky, turns slowly round the heavenly pole and any star will serve as a reference point, but usually the two brightest stars in the constellation of the Great Bear are used. These are easily seen and a line drawn through these two stars passes very close to the Pole Star, and for this reason they are known as the "Pointers". A disc, pierced with a central hole, enables the Pole Star to be fixed; the handle is held almost vertically with the top tilted back towards the observer and an arm pivoted on the center can be rotated until these two stars are lined up along the edge, the arm thus imitates the hand of a clock.

The disc is graduated into twenty-four hours around the edge and the arm thus indicates the time. It must, however, be remembered that the sky

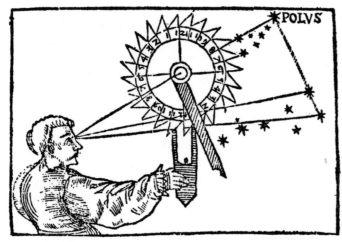

Use of the Nocturnal

Sundial

Pl. XVIII Nocturnal in gilt copper. 16th century. This instrument is signed D. Alcino Faelae of Verona and Io. Paulus Cimerlinus, who were probably monks. In the late 16th and 17th century a number of such gnomons were designed and made by monks. The engraving here is not that of a professional, though technically the piece is well made and the whole is highly decorative. On the back is a dial of universal height invented by Regiomontanus and sometimes known as a capuchin, as the device governing the setting resembles a monk's hood. D. 14·5 cm. Private Collection, Paris

rotates once in every twenty-three hours fifty-six minutes (approximately), so that the nocturnal gives sidereal time. There is, however, a supplementary disc marked with the months and days of the year and this is set for the date of the observation and automatically corrects the reading into mean solar time (pls. 264 and 265). Because it has to be read at night, the hour disc is bordered with broad indentations, so that the time can be told by touch.

Sixteenth-century nocturnals are most decorative objects with a very characteristic type of ornament; nearly all are of copper gilt and their strong construction has helped them to survive.

Roman sundial

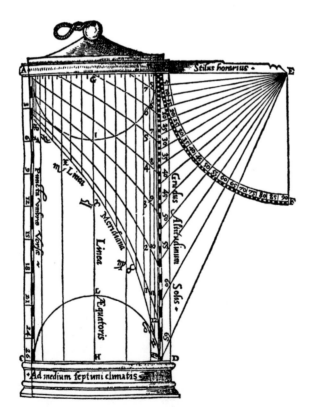

Shepherd's dial

Clepsydras and Hour-glasses

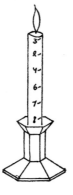

Candle divided into hours

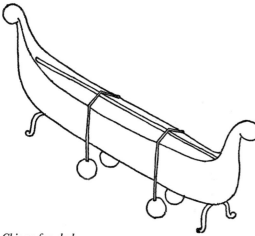

Chinese fire-clock

IN THE PRECEDING CHAPTER instruments to tell the time were described. They fix a definite moment in the passage of a day. Time can also be measured in a different way: time-keepers actually mark duration, that is, starting from a given moment they count the time that has elapsed since they were set in motion. Our clocks and watches, for instance, once they are set right—say at noon—record the passage of the hours, one, two, four-and-a-half, since that time. So we say that it is one, two or four-and-a-half hours after noon.

Mechanical clocks are fully discussed in the first part of this work, but before they appeared many more or less ingenious ways of keeping time had been invented. For example, a burning stick or candle serves to mark the passage of time. For centuries the Chinese have used a long rod covered with a combustible paste which slowly burns out. The time was read from the amount burned up. Some forms of this fire-clock have a long cradle, often carved in the form of a dragon, supporting the rod. Astride the rod threads are placed, one after another, which ignite and burn as the fire reaches them. From these threads are suspended small metal balls, which sound the hour by dropping on to a piece of metal which forms a gong. Alarm-clocks of this kind from China were described in the seventeenth century.

Another kind of Chinese fire-clock, dating from the next century, was a flat metallic box containing a labyrinth of narrow grooves. These were filled with a long string impregnated with combustible powder, which burned through in several hours.

Slow-burning candles have been used for time-keeping in the West ever since candles were invented. Charles V of France (1364) was said by Christine de Pisan to have kept "a lighted candle in his chapel, which was divided into twenty-four sections, and there were attendants appointed to tell him what he had to do at a given time." Later, when oil-lamps were used, they were furnished with a calibrated glass reservoir, in which the level of the oil marked the hour.

Long before, the idea of measuring water flowing from a tank had been conceived. This is the principle of the *clepsydra*, a contrivance that has been recorded in every country from earliest times. Obviously they must have been very inexact time-keepers, principally because their starting was never accurate; also the various changes in the size of the orifice—impurities, calcification, evaporation and wear—were fatal. Clepsydras could only in fact record a very short duration, perhaps as little as one hour, and accounts of all those traditional monumental clepsydras are probably apocryphal. The clock of Ctesibius dating to about 150 A.D. (pl. 269), and the one which was sent by the Theodoric the Visigoth to Gondebaud, Duke of Burgundy in about 430 A.D., and that offered by Haroun-al-Raschid to Charlemagne must all have actually been constructed, but the important thing is to know if they worked. Ruins are still to be seen at Fez of a building erected to house an immense hydraulic clock; it would undoubtedly have demanded the undivided attention of a clock-keeper, like the monumental clocks of the fifteenth century.

The famous clepsydra in the Cairo museum, which dates from about 1400 B.C., is a kind of huge flowerpot with a pierced base; it could never have been at all accurate, nor can have it worked throughout a whole night as has been claimed. The likelihood is that it actually only checked much shorter periods of time, for instance, the hours when the irrigation flood-gates were opened for individual farmers. Apparently a similar object is still in use in Algeria.

More common is the hour-glass, in which the flow of water is replaced by sand. Everyone knows these instruments because they are still used today as egg-timers. The hour-glass is composed of two conical phials placed one above the other; the sand in the upper phial flows slowly through a narrow, calibrated throat into the one below. Kitchen hour-glasses pass the sand in three minutes, whilst the large hour-glasses formerly used by the Navy lasted a half-hour. Some have been made to last two, or even four hours. These periods of time should not be taken literally. In 1703, a French fleet of five warships, under the flag of Admiral Duguay-Trouin, was caught in fog near Spitzbergen and, as the sun did not appear for nine days it was impossible to tell at that latitude whether it was day or night. Measurement of time relied absolutely on the hour-glass. When the sun finally reappeared it was found that the sand-glass was eleven hours out.

Until the end of the eighteenth century when a two-coned glass phial could be accurately blown, the hour-glass was made up of two separate phials

Sand-glass, 16th century

Pl. 268 Sand-glass, 18th century. This large sand-glass mounted in ivory gives an idea of the glasses used by the navy, though this one is too luxurious to have served such a purpose. H. 20 cm. R. Gest Collection, Beauvais

Pl. 269 Reconstruction of the clepsydra of Ctesibius. The only information we have about this clock, invented about 200 B.C, is from late written sources. At the end of the 17th century Perrault reconstructed it but there is nothing to prove that the original instrument was ever made. Private Collection, Paris

268

269

270

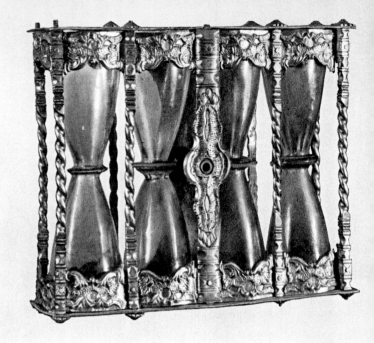

271

272

Pl. 270 *Multiple sand-glass with four phials, 17th century. Set in a rich silver mount the four phials, each 22 cm tall, tell the quarters, half hour, three quarters and the hour. Overall height 47 cm. Private Collection, Paris*

Pl. 271 *Multiple sand-glass with four phials, 17th century. This is probably a church hour-glass, for the gilt bronze mount allowed it to turn on a horizontal axis, now lost, so as to repeat the flow of the sand when the phial was empty. H. 25 cm. Gilbert Suc Collection, Paris*

Pl. 272 *Three different hour-glasses, 18th or 19th century. Left to right: Rosewood mount, H. 36 cm; metal mount, H. 45 cm; in a leather case, H. 24 cm. Kugel Collection, Paris*

Pl. XIX *Large sand-glass for the table. 17th century. This magnificent instrument was probably for a nobleman's study. It is made of ebony and ivory with gilt bronze and amber and is composed of a stand for writing materials, a reversible sand-glass with three phials and a clock, the whole being richly decorated. It may be Italian work, and was almost certainly intended for the court of the Grand Duchy of Tuscany. H. overall 56 cm. Private Collection, Paris*

which terminated in a flat lip. Where they were joined a small piece of metal pierced with a tiny hole was inserted between them. Of course the friction of the running sand gradually wore away this hole and consequently the time required for its flow diminished.

Once the upper phial was empty the hour-glass was reversed to measure another period; with this in view, some instruments were set in a pivot. As naval hour-glasses served to keep the watch, that is the division of the working-hours of the crew, it was not unusual for the ship's boy in charge to "swallow the sand", that is turn the glass before it was quite empty. On the other hand, in church and the law courts hour-glasses were useful for stemming the prolix orator's flow of words. And on occasion a skilful gesticulation might increase one's own time at the expense of an opponent.

Some church hour-glasses are multiple (pls. 270 and 271), that is, they are provided with four glasses to mark the quarter, the half, three-quarters and the hour. Some have a phial with six strangulated bulbs: when they are made to mark the half hour, each of the six lasts a period of five minutes and can be used as a standard for an ordinary instrument (pl. 272).

Hour-glasses are often splendid instruments—Holbein, for instance, designed some monumental hour-glasses for presentation to Henry VIII.

Topographical Instruments

A pace according to Koebel, 1550

THE ART OF SURVEYING can be traced back to man's earliest social organizations. Farmers, for example, always sought to mark the boundary of their land. Rulers too, although in principle lords over all, still had to have a plan of their inherited possessions. Hence very early a corps of men was formed to measure distance, and geometers, or surveyors, to measure area, by elementary methods.

One of the first units of measurement was the pace, which can be taken as two strides of three or four feet according to local custom; in the Renaissance distinctions were made between the "woman's pace" of three feet, the "simple pace" of four feet and the "geometrical pace" of six feet. A pace-counter, or *pedometer*, was invented as soon as mechanics were far enough advanced. These instruments were worn attached to the belt and linked to one leg by a cable. After two strides a ratchet moved, advancing the gear by one tooth on the clock.

Another gadget was the *hodometer*, worked by a wheel, ancestor of the modern taxi-meter. The wheel was run along the length of the road be to measured, and every turn registered on the meter. Vitruvius, the Roman architect, who lived at the beginning of the Christian era, invented a device which dropped a small pebble onto a sounding-board after a certain number of turns of the wheel, probably about a thousand.

We possess standards of the Chinese foot made of jade and bronze, and standards of the Egyptian cubit in wood, bronze and even gold. Greater lengths could be measured by the perch or by means of cords made of hemp, covered with resin or pitch to resist damp. The surveyor's chain of metal dates only from the beginning of the seventeenth century.

Orientation was of no great concern to the first surveyors. Much has

267

been written on the orientation of temples and pyramids, but measurement has proved that these alignments are often very inaccurate and haphazard. The use of the compass in surveying is a late development. Its invention has long been attributed to the Chinese, but actually the presence of this instrument in China before the thirteenth century has never been proved and by that time it had been long known in Europe. It is probable that the Norsemen had some kind of compass; it is indeed said to have been brought to France with the invading Normans, and introduced by them also to the Mediterranean. It did not take the Arabs long to discover the secret and Marco Polo probably carried it to China. In any case the instrument was used solely by sailors and it was only in the fifteenth century that the magnetic needle was adapted for use on topographical instruments.

Although measurement of angles had been understood for centuries, almost the only angular measurement at the time of the Pharaohs was the right-angle. At first they worked with simple squares, then traced two arcs on the ground joining the centres, and the intersections, by two straight lines; and finally they applied the theorem that a triangle, the sides of which are as 3: 4: 5, is a right-angled triangle. These primitive methods required no complicated instruments but on the other hand they were of little use for larger areas.

Although a graphic representation of measurements, that is a plan or map, could sometimes be worked out fairly accurately for small areas, it was entirely defective over any considerable distance. Tyrolese miners, even in the seventeenth century were unable to draw surveys of their concessions and traced the plan of their galleries full size on the ice of a frozen lake. No faith can be placed in the fantastic geographical maps and estate plans of the Middle Ages.

Once again it was the men of the early Renaissance who introduced seriously workable methods. The expanding kingdoms and empires, the voyages that they inspired and the development of communications forced attention on the drawing of boundaries—instruments and methods were invented for this purpose.

As often happens, these first instruments were complicated and fragile, but practice brought simpler and more robust designs. The oldest devices are rare—those that were used for the most urgent work. When it came to working for the State, however, instrument-makers produced works to add to the prestige of their rulers, beautifully made, no expense being spared. The Emperor Charles V commissioned from the workshop of the famous Mercator at Louvain for his personal use a fine set of topographical instruments which were always with him on his campaigns. Unfortunately, the collection was destroyed when the imperial tent was burned down in the Siege of Ingolstadt.

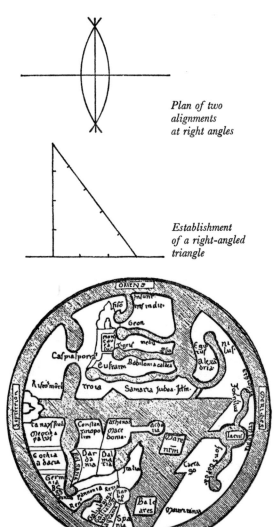

Plan of two alignments at right angles

Establishment of a right-angled triangle

Map of the world by Guido, 1119

Pl. XX   Artillery tangent-scale in gilt brass; 1614. This is the work of Christopher Trechsler the Elder, who was one of the most eminent designers of military instruments of the century. It comprises a flat base which was placed on the tube of the cannon; a small compass, a level and a graduated quadrant for measuring the angle of the site; the apparatus is further complicated by various regulating devices. H. 28·5 cm. Observatoire de Paris

Fortunately many other splendid instruments never saw a piece of land and, from the day they were made, remained safely within the royal cabinet. Today they are treasured museum possessions. Most of them serve for the measurement of angles, because large areas had to be measured indirectly by triangulation. The principle is simple: having fixed a base of a known length, the point to be measured is viewed from either end of the base. The angles made with the base thus determine a triangle and by a proportionate calculation or a scaled drawing, one can work out the distance of the point. Thus little by little a whole territory could be covered.

MEASUREMENT OF SURFACE ANGLES

The first instrument designed for this purpose, the *recipiangle*, was a simple pair of compasses made of two flat arms. At the ends of these arms, and at their joint, sights were fixed in the form of small, vertical slots; one of the arms was pointed towards the base alignment, and the alignment of the point to be fixed was sighted along the sight-pins of the other arm. The angle between the arms is the angle between the two points, and a graduated sector beneath the pivot of the compass gives the measure of this angle.

Sometimes the graduated sector is replaced by a rod which bisects the angle between the two arms. A scale can be moved on this rod by means of a parallelogram, and this scale shows the aperture of the compasses. Readings taken in this way are simpler and more precise.

Towards the middle of the sixteenth century the instrument was modified by doubling it, that is by fixing two recipiangles at either end of a straight-edge which served as a base-line. A triangle which resembled a sighting-triangle was thus obtained. By engraving a graduated scale on the base and on the arms the distances sought could be found by simple proportion.

The interest aroused by this method is proved by its numerous variants. Danfrie's *trigonometer* of 1597 reproduces its plan exactly (pl. 273), and Bürgi's *triangular instrument* of 1592 is very similar. Purbach's *geometrical square* (1561) and Abel Foullon's *holometer* of 1562 are complicated solutions to the problem (pl. 274).

However, given a relatively short base-line, it is impossible to measure large distances with any accuracy. The base-line must be in proportion to the distance to be measured, and a base-line of several yards or sometimes even several hundred yards may be required. In this case separate instruments

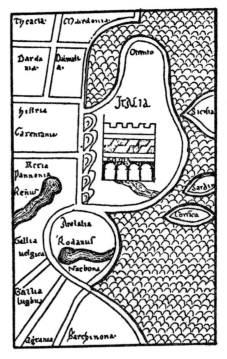

Map of Italy by Guido, 1119

Pl. 273 Trigonometer in gilt bronze, 1597. This instrument was invented by Philippe Danfrie, instrument-maker of Paris. The engraving is excellent but th. instrument could only be used over short distances and was not therefore very successful. It was soon replaced by the graphometer, invented by the same man, which became an essential tool for surveyors. L. 31.5 cm. Musée des Arts décoratifs, Paris

Pl. 274 Geometric Square, gilt bronze, 1599. This splendid instrument formed part of a series made at Prague by the finest instrument-maker of the 16th century, Erasmus Habermel, who was attached to the Court. The engraving is perfectly executed with simple lines and decoration, and the gilding is superb. Habermel amused himself by combining different topographical aspects on the same instrument. H. 60 cm. Observatoire de Paris

Pl. 275 Goniometer in gilt brass, 18th century. Signed by Picart at Cambrai. It should be noted that the alidade is furnished with an additional graduated segment forming a vernier. In theory therefore one should be able to read the angles to within one minute of arc. D. 16.8 cm. Private Collection, Paris

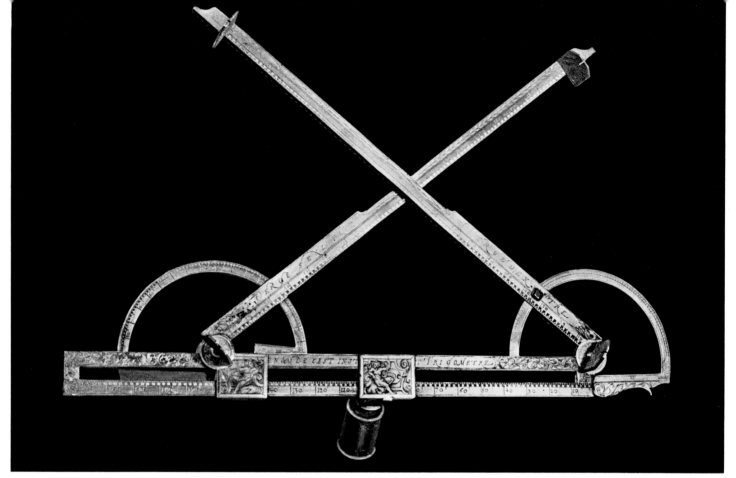

273

274

275

276

277

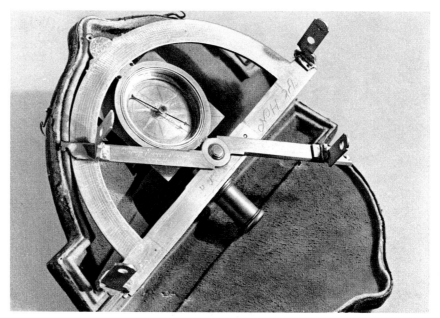

278

279

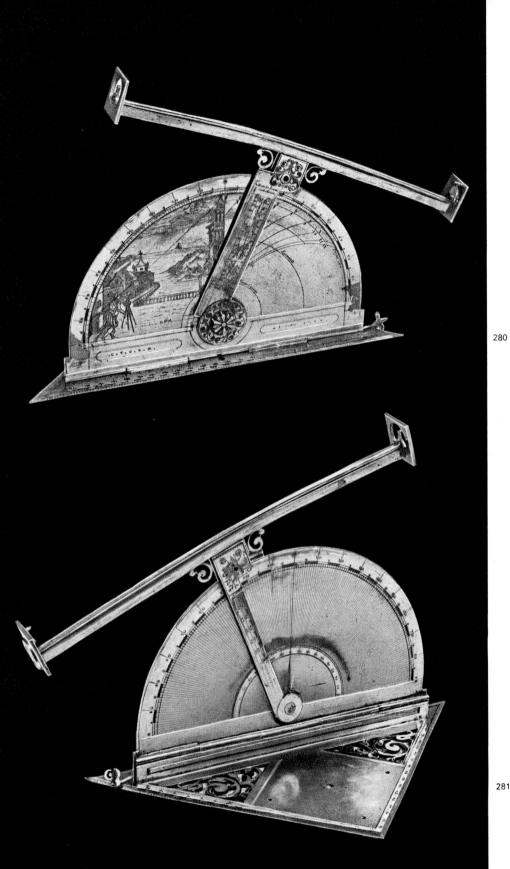

280

281

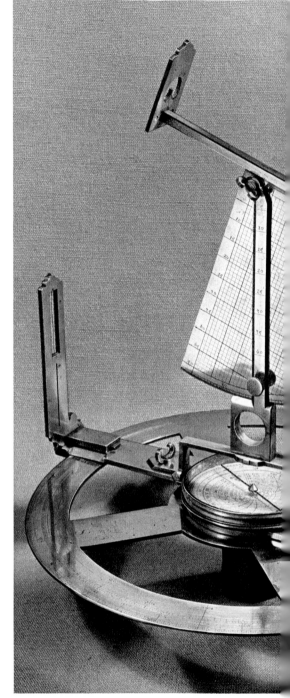

282

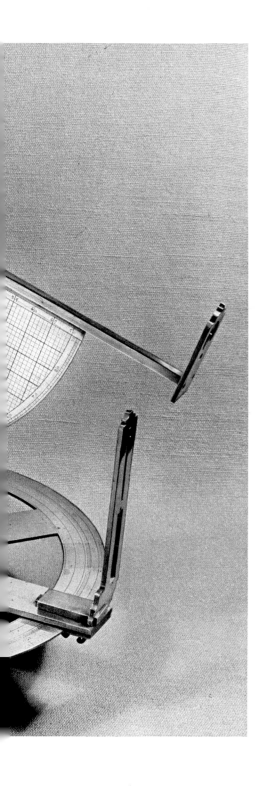

283

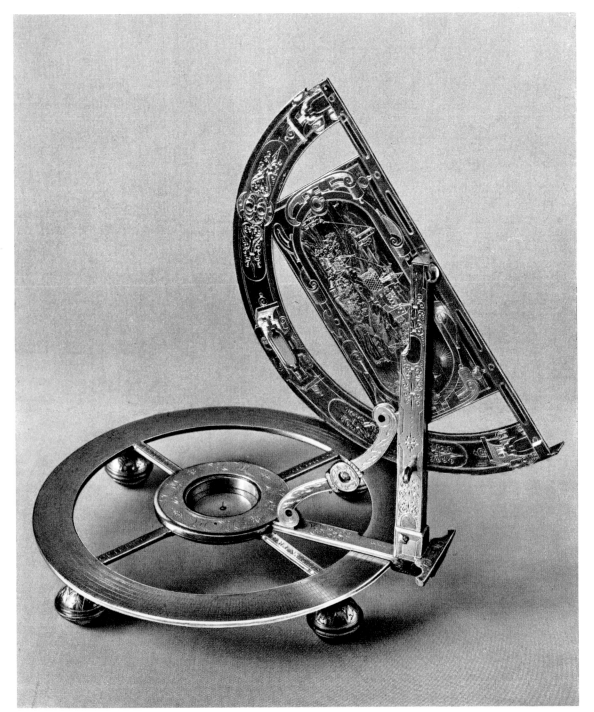

284

285

Pl. 276   Goniometer in gilt brass, 17th century. The construction of this instrument is exceptionally fine and it apparently has the Papal Arms. It is signed by Franciscus Continus, a name that does not figure among the famous instrument-makers, and may even have been the owner. The subdivision of the rim into transversals allowed a reading to within 10 minutes of arc. D. 22 cm. Private Collection, Paris

Pls. 277 to 279   Three graphometers, brass, 18th century. The first is signed by J. Rochette, Paris; the second by Huguet, Paris and the third by Lordelle of Paris. During the 18th century there were several dealers in topographical instruments who did not always make the instruments they signed. As can be seen the instrument was becoming larger and stronger and no longer confined to scholars, was now used in surveying. D. 19·6 cm., 22 cm., and 16 cm. Private Collection, Paris

Pls. 280 & 281   Theodolite of gilt copper, about 1590. This instrument constructed by Christopher Trechsler at Dresden was made for a survey known as "by the plane table". It allowed an immediate diagram of alignments to be drawn up and probably served for the lay-out of military camps, in common with other instruments made by Trechsler. L. 23 cm. Private Collection, Paris

Pl. 282   Theodolite, gilt brass, about 1645. This theodolite made by Elias Allen of London, whose instruments are remarkably precise, has the disadvantage of allowing the siting of horizontal angles only when the vertical quadrant and its support are detached. Butterfly screws are provided for this and the pins can be folded down. D. 22 cm. Private Collection, Paris

Pl. 283   Artillery tangent-scale, gilt bronze, about 1670 It is signed by Johann Koch, who was born in Cologne but worked in Vienna and Berlin. He was responsible for some fine sundials. H. 27 cm. Private Collection, Paris

Pl. 284   Theodolite, gilt brass, about 1590. In this topographical instrument, Erasmus Habermel elegantly demonstrates the skill of his period in matters of geometrical measurement. These de luxe prototypes were probably intended for a nobleman's study. D. 21·9 cm. Observatoire de Paris

Pl. 285   Small theodolite, 16th or 17th century. This beautifully constructed instrument has a sighting tube instead of an alidade for measuring horizontal angles. Length of the oblique alidade 15·5 cm. Private Collection, Paris

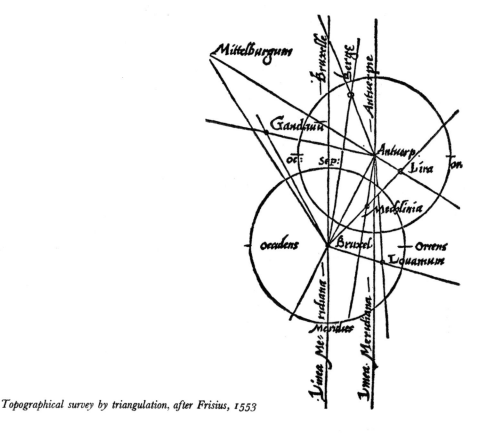

Topographical survey by triangulation, after Frisius, 1553

must be installed at either end of the base. These instruments comprise a graduated plate with a sighting alidade pivoting at the center. Two other sights are permanently fixed to the plate and give the alignment of the base. If necessary a compass was mounted either on the plate or on the stand.

The first *goniometers* thus constructed were complete circles graduated on their limb from 0°–360°. They were invented by Gemma Frisius around 1550, who recommended them for his methods of topographical survey by triangulation, a method which remains standard to this day. Gemma's circle is also known as the *Dutch Circle*, because a Dutch geometrician, Jan Pieterszoon Dou, used it in 1612 to make a survey of his country (pls. 275-276). Soon it was realized that a semi-circle was sufficient, and the instrument became less clumsy. Thus the *graphometer* was conceived in 1597, an instrument which for the last four centuries has been one of the basic tools of the surveyor (pls. 277–279).

MEASUREMENT OF VERTICAL ANGLES

Everything we have just said applies also to the vertical when heights are to be measured. The line is then placed in the direction of the object to be sighted and at its two ends a measurement is made of the angle of altitude of the point to be measured. The result, as for surface angles, is calculated by means of proportional triangles.

In gunnery it is essential to know the angle of sight precisely, that is the vertical angle between the direction of the target and the horizontal, and elevation will be added to this according to distance. The instrument which measures the angle of sight is the *clinometer*. This has an alidade with sights moving vertically, and graduated sectors for the angle of sight and for elevation. The horizontal plane is indicated by a spirit-level, or better still, a plumb-line, which is stronger. In this case the graduated sector gives the direct measurement of the angle to the horizontal—the complement of the angle to the vertical.

The instrument can, of course, be made more complicated. Some artillery sights have as well as the clinometer, a series of adjustable devices which are mechanical masterpieces, apart from their esthetic value.

Sixteenth- and seventeenth-century instrument-makers often combined several topographical instruments. The idea of uniting the measurement of surface with vertical angles is a logical step. It was followed by the development

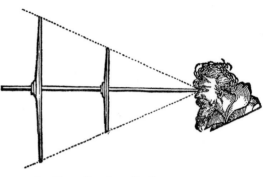

Jacob's staff or Cross Staff

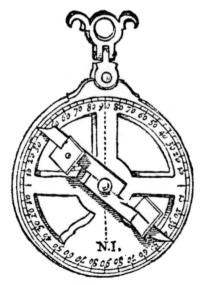

Mariner's astrolabe

Pls. 286 & 287 Goniometer, gilt copper, about 1600. Another splendid instrument by Erasmus Habermel (see Pls. 274 and 284) where the artist sought to introduce elaborations, particularly by articulating the circle on a graduated sector so as to allow the measurement of angles in every plane. H. 36 cm. Observatoire de Paris

Pl. 288 Quarter-Staff by Davis, wood, 18th century. An instrument for measuring the height of the sun at sea. It was carried on the shoulder, with the observer's back to the sun. One of the pins was aligned towards the horizon, the shadow of the other fell across a small screen; the height was read off from graduated sectors. L. 53 cm. Gilbert Suc Collection, Paris

286

287

288

289

290

291

292

293

294

295

of the *theodolite*, which Leonard Digges claims to have invented in 1572 (pls. 280–282), though similar instruments made in Italy, France and Germany at about the same period can be seen in museums (pls. 284–285). Since they have a horizontal and a vertical circle it is possible to take measurements from the same station.

The method was developed to the point where the two instruments were mounted on a ball-and-socket joint so that they could operate in all planes, but they were too unsteady and were not very successful. However they are very decorative and interesting collectors' pieces (pls. 286 and 287).

MEASUREMENT AT SEA

Nautical calculations serve to pinpoint the ship in geographical longitude and latitude. They can thus be linked to topographical measurements, although none of the instruments described above is suited to installation aboard ship.

Longitude is calculated by observing the difference between local time at a starting meridian and local time at the point whose position is to be determined. It is therefore a problem involving time-keeping and its solution requires a perfect clock, which will keep exact time from the ship's departure to her return, notwithstanding the conditions experienced on the voyage. This has been treated elsewhere in this work. The theory of this method had been put forward by Gemma Frisius as early as 1530, but the necessary chronometer was not perfected till 1762.

Geographical latitude is easy to determine. Tables are published giving the sun's declination north or south of the equator for each day of the year. The figure is added to or subtracted from the sun's angular distance from the zenith. It is therefore only necessary to obtain the zenith distance to obtain the latitude. There are, of course, corrections and allowances to be made, but this is the method.

These calculations can be made with an astrolabe. A simplified version, the *Mariner's astrolabe* was constructed, better suited to conditions at sea. This consists of a large graduated circle provided with an alidade across its diameter. It was intentionally made heavy, and much of its surface was cut away to avoid being caught by the wind. The instrument had to be suspended from a rope, but in spite of this, one sixteenth-century navigator admitted that errors of measurement could be as great as 5°. Attempts were made to make a lighter instrument, one that could be used for sighting the sun and the

Pl. 289   Three octants, gilt wood, 18th century. The use of reflecting mirrors reduced the angle of height by half, and one-eighth of a circle would suffice to measure the height of the sun, which never exceeds 90°; hence the name octant. In 1757 Campbell reduced the section to one-sixth, which made it more manageable in some cases and the instrument became the sextant used today. L. between 30 and 43 cm. Gilbert Suc Collection, Paris

Pl. 290   "Le Dict de l'Astroloc", fresco in the castle at Verneuil l'Embon. The subject is treated somewhat fantastically, but strongly evokes the atmosphere of darkness and mystery surrounding an astrologer immersed in the occult

Pl. 291   Astronomy, high relief on the Cathedral of Sens, 12th century. Cathedral architects liked to depict the sciences and liberal arts among other subjects on their façades. The instruments are however purely imaginary and useless as documents

Pl. 292   The Angel of Chartres, 12th century. The portal of Chartres Cathedral contains this angel carrying a sundial, which had an oblique gnomon added in the 16th century without changing the initial, clearly wrong graduation. In the 12th century a semi-circle was divided into equal parts with a gnomon throwing its shadow from the center

Pl. 293   Lapis Polaris, Magnes; 16th century engraving. In 1580 J. Galle engraved a collection of plates after the drawings of Stradanus showing new inventions. This one has the principal instruments used for measuring distances at sea

Pl. 294   Clavius: 17th century engraving. Father Christopher Clavius was the moving spirit behind an enormous compilation which defined astronomic methods and the construction of instruments. In 1582 he played an important part in the reform of the calender

Pl. 295   Tycho Brahe; 17th century engraving. At the end of the 16th century this famous astronomer devoted all his fortune to the building of an observatory where the most accurate instruments supplied new astronomical measurements. These enabled Kepler to formulate the laws governing the celestial bodies

horizon at the same time. The *Jacob's staff*, *Cross-staff* or *arbalestrilla*, devised in 1342 for measuring the angular distance between stars, was sometimes used. This was a cross-shaped instrument, as its name implies, with a long graduated handle, one end of which was placed to the eye, while a cross-bar, or hammer, was slid along it until one of the hammer tips touched the horizon, the other the star to be determined. The scale on the handle provided the answer.

The *arbalestrilla* is adequate for determining star-positions, but as soon as the observer aims it at the sun he is necessarily dazzled. This problem is elegantly solved by the *Davis quadrant* or *back-staff* invented in 1594. Here the observer turns his back to sun and aims the instrument at the opposite horizon, and the position of the sun is determined by a shadow cast by a small screen on a cursor moving on a sliding scale (pl. 288).

Finally in 1731 an English astronomer, John Hadley, contrived to align the image of the sun with the horizon by a system of mirrors, and the angle needed for one of the mirrors was read on a graduated scale. This device, after two centuries of improvement, resulted in the modern sextant, which is still an indispensable navigational instrument.

Instruments of navigation were not often designed for their beauty. What is more, they were exposed to the hazards of the sea and are usually in poor condition today. A few were made for display and have therefore never been used. Others are documentary pieces with a definite historical value.

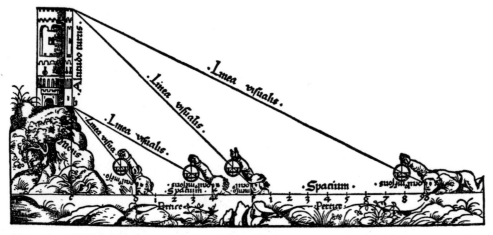

Measurement of the height of a tower by means of a goniometer

Conclusion

Scarcely a hundred years have elapsed since museums first took an interest in "industrial art". Into this category fall all the objects formerly considered unworthy of the collector. The History of Art deals with painting, drawing and sculpture; everything else is scornfully dismissed as "the minor arts". Precious metals and tapestries have preoccupied great masters in vain; enamels, glyptics and glass have produced their marvels and all for nothing, they are set down as minor arts as if they were the result of second-class artistic feeling.

The aesthetic value of these crafts is at last beginning to be appreciated. We have learned to distinguish styles, to recognize a school or a period, and to look beyond the value of the material or the perfection of the work, and to find there an undeniable beauty.

This beauty is also to be found in products which are still more industrial. Several decades have passed since the term "functional esthetics" first appeared. One of the earliest examples is ship-building—the curves of the Canadian canoe, or the lines of a yacht have been brought to perfection by rejection and adaptation. Even the uninitiated are moved by the sight of a great sailing ship—the sweeping hull, taut rigging and the billowing sails make it a thing of beauty.

The instruments described above fall into the same category. Of course it is an advantage to know their history and use, but once familiar with these little-known objects we should learn to appreciate their beauty. As in the other industrial arts, the style and taste of a country or a period is apparent to the experienced observer. As a rule mathematical instruments are not made for display; they are rarely to be found overloaded with pointless flourishes or heavy ornament. During the High Renaissance they were sometimes gilded, engraved or chiselled, but always with a restraint appropriate to their scholarly function. The finest sixteenth-century instruments were made in southern Germany by Erasmus Habermel, a master-craftsman who never allowed decoration to take first place: the instrument itself was the work of art, and Habermel embellished it with graceful, restrained, almost geometrical, yet elegant lines. What is more the artist refused to put himself in the limelight, and his signature, if not limited to two initials, is in tiny concealed letters. Schissler too, and his friends Rückert and Schniep, decorated gilt-bronze astronomical instruments with fine scrollwork in the style of Virgil Solis, ignoring the mythological subjects so common on contemporary clocks. In Persia astrolabe-makers aimed at balance of line and grace of form, and the splendid engraving on the minor parts was limited almost wholly to Arab script. Rugendas was surrounded by the Augsburg gold- and silversmiths who created so many elaborately-worked pieces and heavily decorated hanaps, yet he could produce the most restrained sundial, its shining silver enhanced by delicate gilding.

It is doubtful whether modern manufacturers can follow their example and pay attention to the esthetic aspects of their products. Mass production leaves no room for the craftsman. The demand is for accurate, strong, practical instruments. Can it be true that no one expects them to be beautiful?

The answer is of course, that it depends on what we mean by "beautiful". I have tried to show that beauty lies, not in the decoration, but in functional expression and purity of line. This is no obstacle to good design and indeed a new phrase has been coined—"industrial design"—to describe the application of clear esthetic principles to manufactured wares.

This movement began sixty years ago when the German architect Behrens studied form in relation to steam turbines. Since then we have seen an even more marked evolution in the field of automobile construction. One only need recall the strange, illogical, almost ridiculous appearance of the early automobiles, mere caricatures of the horseless carriage, and the first tourers, with lines suggesting speeds that were rarely attained, to recognize the important part played by artists in the development of modern aerodynamic shapes.

If we turn to modern instruments of the topographer we feel the same urge, perhaps subconsciously, to simplify their line and to ennoble them by giving them a less elaborate, more balanced shape. This belongs wholly to the field of esthetics. This work may perhaps encourage that tendency and prove a stimulating example to modern manufacturers, so that industrial life can be embellished and the work of the scientist accompanied by a certain beauty.

Art-lovers may be inspired to collect an unusual class of object. Neglected, and often lost, antique instruments of measurement can teach us a valuable lesson in esthetics. The history of their evolution is instructive and logical —their perfect execution shows an exemplary discipline and regard for quality.

General Index

alidade 224
arbalestrilla 284
astrolabe, mariner's 283
astrology 212
astronomic compendium 257
azimuth 220, 222
balance 11, 78, 122
– bimetallic 121, 122, 143, 144
– spiral 104, 121, 137
bristle, pig's 78
caliber 122
Cardano's suspension 103
Charlemagne, columns of 195; Pl. 191
clinomemeter 278
clock, with automata 19-26, 162
– with bells 19-26
– bracket 161
– carriage 65, 66, 151
– cartel 162, 174
– crucifix 56
– lantern 56
– long-case 152
– monstrance 54
– table 53, 54, 80, 162
– weight-driven 36, 40
clockmakers of Blois 90, 151
– England 124, 149
– France 124, 149, 164
– Geneva 90
– Lyons 89-90
– Neuchâtel 174
– Switzerland 124, 129, 149
cock 78, 86, 106, 107
compass, geometer's 268
– magnetic, in sundials 245, 257
– in watches 68
coordinates see latitude, longitude
cross-staff 284
day, lunar 31
dead point 78
dial, anelemmatic 240
– diptych 248
– equinoctial 245-6
– lunar see nocturnal

dial, magnetic 240, 241
– polyhedral 257
– shepherd's 238
dialmakers of Augsburg 245
– Dieppe 240, 245
– Nuremberg 248
Dutch circle 277
enamel 87, 89, 130, 132
equinoctial dial see dial
escapement 15, 16, 18, 112-5, 122-3
– anchor 26, 114
– crown wheel 78, 114
– cylinder 112, 114, 138
– detent 115, 138, 144, 149
– spring detent 106
– frictional rest (dead-beat) 114
– lever 115, 137, 138
– pin wheel 27; Fig. 114
– recoil 112
– verge 17, 36, 78, 106
– virgule 114, 122
fire-clock 261
foliot 11, 16, 17, 36, 66
fusee 68, 77, 149
– and chain 77
– and gut 77
gearing 112
globe, celestial 56, 65, 208
– terrestrial 205
goniometer 277; Pls. 275, 276
graphometer 277; Pls. 277, 278, 279
hodometer 267
holometer 270
isochronism 97, 102, 103, 104, 137
jack 20, 24, 32
Jacob's staff 284
jewels 110, 111, 112, 123, 132
latitude 139, 211
Lépine caliber 122
longitude 139, 140, 211, 283
matrix 224
minute mechanism, hand 36, 80, 85, 102, 103
nocturnal 258-60
oil 18, 110, 111

pedometer 267
pendulum cheeks 102, 103
– Galileo's 26, 97
– gridiron 39, 116, 144
– mercury 116, 143
– applied to monumental clocks 18
– in weight-driven clocks 26, 102, 103
– wooden 116
quadrant, Davis' 234, 284
recipiangle 270
rectangulus 220
Saphaea of Arzachel 224
Savonette caliber 122
scaph 238
sextant 284
solar ring 234
spring 44, 68, 137
sphere, armillary 213
– clockwork 56, 65
spider 222
square, geometric 270
stackfreed 66, 77
stereographic projection 221, 222
sundial see dial
surveyor's chain 267
temporaries 196
theodolite 283
torquetum 218, 220
triangular instrument 270
trigonometer 270
triquetrum 201
tropic 213
tympanum 222
watch, Chinese 130
– flat 130
– pocket 66, 67, 77, 109
– repeating 29, 104, 132, 137
– Roskopf 138
– subscription 112, 132; Pl. 108
– turnip 106, 123
wheels, train of 16, 18, 68, 80, 85
winder, key 137
– pendant 137
winding, automatic 130

Index of Names

al-a'immah, Abd   Pl. xvi
al-Batuti, Muhammad ibn Ahmad   Pl. 221
Ali ibn Ibrahim ibn Muhammad   Pl. 216
Allen, Elias (London)   Pl. 282
Archambaud, John (London)   Pl. 57
Archimedes   16
Arland, Henry   Pl. 65
Arnold, John   115, 124, 149
Audinet   Pl. 153
Baillon, Jean Baptiste (Paris)   Pl. 95; 140
Bailly   Pl. 169
Ballard (Bourd)   Pl. 50
Barberet, J. (Paris)   Pl. viii
Barlow, Edward   39, 104, 114
Barroneau (Paris)   Pls. 83, 84
Beaumarchais, P. A. Caron de   114, 124
Behaim, Martin   205
Benoist, Mathurin   25
Bernouilli, Daniel   142
Berthoud, Ferdinand   111, 112, 143, 144, 162;
   Pls. 105, 119, 120, 148, 162
Blaeu, W. J.   Pl. 197
Blakey, William   68
Bloud, Charles (Dieppe)   240, 245; Pls. 229,
   230, 232
Bodecker, Jost   25
Bonbruict (Blois)   Pl. v
Boulle, André Charles   161
Boulliau, Ismaël   97
Bourdier, J. S.   Pl. 167
Bouvier, Charles François (Paris)   Pl. 80
Brahe, Tycho   42, 202, 218; Pl. 295
Bréguet, Abraham Louis (Paris)   112, 121,
   129, 130, 132, 137, 149, 189; Pls. 100, 102,
   103, 104, 108
Bréguet & Fils   149; Pls. 121, 123
Briot, F.   Pl. 227
Brown, T.   Pl. iv
Brunner, Caspar (Berne)   26; Pl. 3
Burgi, Jost   54, 56, 270; Pl. 36
Butterfield, Michael (Paris)   247, 248; Pl. 247
Cabrier (London)   Pl. 77
Caldiere, Giovanni della   23
Cameel (Strasbourg)   Pl. 46

Cameler, Peter (Olmutz)   Pls. 30, 30a
Ceulen Haghe, Johannes van   Pl. v
Chaptot   Pl. 238
Chesnon, Salomon (Blois)   Pl. iii
Cimerlinus, J. P. (Verona)   Pl. xviii
Clavius, Christopher   Pl. 249
Cocart, Juan (Brussels and Yuste)   Pl. 255
Combret, Pierre (Lyons)   80; Pl. 62
Copernicus, Nicholas   41, 42, 201, 218
Coronelli, Vincent   207; Pl. 196
Coster, Salomon   26, 100, 102
Coudray, Julien (Blois)   67
Cressent (Paris)   Pl. 150
Ctesibios   17
Danfrie, Philippe   207; Pl. 273
Davis (London)   Pl. 58
Debary (Geneva)   Pl. v
Debaufre, Pierre & Thomas   110
De Caudard (Paris)   Pl. 161
Delaulne, Etienne   87
Desargues, Girard   68
Digges, Leonard   283
Diya al-Din (Lahore)   Pls. 212, 213, 215
Dondi, Jacopo de'   22
Dorgueil   Pl. 157
Dou, Jan Pieterszoon   277
Dubois, William   Pl. 235
Du Bois & Fils (Le Locle)   132; Pl. 112
Ducher, Hans (Nuremberg)   Pls. 232, 249
Duchesne, Claudius (London)   Pl. 126
Dufalga (Geneva and Paris)   Pl. 96
Duhamel, Pierre (Geneva)   90; Pl. iv
Duru (Paris)   Pl. 137
Earnshaw, Thomas   115, 149
Emck, Hans Jacob   54
Emery, Josiah (London)   115
Engels, Pierre   22
Engueran, Pierre   25
Eratosthenes   202
Eudoxus of Cnidus   208, 218
Fabron (Geneva)   Pl. viii
Faelae, D. Alicino (Verona)   Pl. xviii
Falconnet   164
Fardoil, Nicolas   68

Favre   Pl. 163
Feau, Nicolas   Pl. 13
Fatio, Nicolas   110
Flant (La Rochelle)   Pls. 59, 60
Formereau (La Rochelle)   Pls. 62, 66, 67, iii
Foullon, Abel   270
Frédéric, Louis (Le Locle)   Pl. 168
Frisius, Gemma   141, 202, 224, 277, 283
Fromanteel   Pls. iii, 72, 73, 74
Furet (Paris)   Pls. 150, 151
Fusoris, Jean   23
Gaspard (Lunéville)   Pl. 240
Gaudron (Paris)   Pls. 125, 132
Gautrin   Pls. iii, 93, 94
Goullons (Paris)   Pl. v
Graham, George (London)   27, 114; Pls. 85,
   86
Grandisson, John of   22
Grégoire, Jean (Blois)   Pls. 43, 44
Grossmann, Moritz   138
Gruber, Hans (Nuremberg)   Pls. 41, 42
Gudin (Paris)   Pls. 146, 149
Guéroult (Avranches)   Pl. 32
Guido, Pietro (Mantua)   67
Habermel, Erasmus (Prague)   Pls. 274, 284,
   286, 287
Habrecht, Isaac   25, 26
Habrecht, Joachim   24
Hahn, P. M.   Pl. 37
Halder, Heinrich   23
Hallaycher, Matheus (Augsburg)   Pl. 69
Hanus (Prague)   24; Pl. i
Hartmann, G. (Nuremberg)   Pl. xv
Heath (London)   Pl. 242
Harrison, John (London)   39, 116, 121, 142,
   207; Pl. 116
Harvolck, Ulrich   Pl. 232
Heckingen, D. (Augsburg)   Pl. xii
Henlein, Peter (Nuremberg)   66
Hessen   Pl. 97
Hipparchus   211
Houghton, William   114
Huaud, Pierre   89; Pl. iv
Hubuer (Bremen)   Pl. 55

Houriet, Jacques Frédéric 124, 129
Huguet (Paris) Pl. 278
Huygens, Christian 26, 85, 98, 100-105, 141, 151
Ingold, Pierre Frédéric, 112, 124
Jamnitzer, Wenzel (Nuremberg) 53; Pl. 23
Janus, Reinhold (Leignitz) 54
Janvier, Antide 124; Pls. 176, 177, 205, 206
Jaquet-Droz, Henry Louis (La Chaux-de-Fonds) 132, 152, 162; Pls. 110, 130
Jaquet-Droz, Pierre (La Chaux-de-Fonds) 152, 162, 174
Jena, Hans of 25
Jolly, J. (Paris) Pl. VIII
Kepler, Johannes 42
Khalil, Muhammad ibn Hasan 'Ali Pls. 214, XVI
Knibb, Joseph (London) 26, 39
Koch, Johann (Vienna and Berlin) Pl. 283
Kreitzererm, Christoff Pl. 28
Lamy (Paris) Pl. 152
Lange, J. (Münster) 23
Langin, Gédéon (La Chaux-de-Fonds) Pl. 130
Langlois Pl. 244
Latgens, Johann Peters (Solingen) Pls. 158, 178
Le Coultre, Antoine (Le Sentier) 137
Lecoultre-Piguet, Ami (Le Brassus) 132; Pl. 115
Lemaindre, Nicolas (Blois) 44; Pls. 10, 11
Lemaire Pl. 248
Leonardo da Vinci 41, 77
Lepaute, Jean André 27, 114, 124; Pl. 165
Lépine, Jean Antoine 122; Pl. III
Le Roy, Julien (Paris) 124, 142; Pls. 88, 97, 144, 147, VII, VIII
Le Roy, Pierre (Paris) 111, 114, 121, 142, 143; Pls. 117, 118
Le Roy & Fils Pl. 106
Leroy, E. (Paris) Pl. 173
Leschot, Georges Auguste 124, 137
Leschot, Jean Frédéric (Paris) 162
Lestourgeon (London) Pls. 77, VII

Liechti, Laurent 24, 26
Lieutaud (Paris) Pl. 164
Lightfoot, Peter (Exeter) 23
Londini, Bouguet Pl. III
Loon, van (Haarlem) Pl. 78
Lordelle (Paris) Pl. 279
Lucas (Amsterdam) Pl. 75
Maquim, Muhammad (Lahore) Pl. 211
Marchand (Geneva) Pl. 76
Marcou (Amsterdam) Pl. 78
Martinot, Gilles 161; Pl. 70
Mayet, Jean Baptiste (Morbier) Pl. 168
Michelin, Samuel (Langres) Pl. 81
Miller, Leonhard (Nuremberg) Pl. 250
Mudge, Thomas 115
Müller, W. 24, 26
Musique, Etienne 21
Naze, Jean (Blois) 44, 90; Pl. 12
Nicole & Capt (London) 137
Oberhauser, Johann (Schwatz) Pl. XVII
Perrelet, Abraham Louis (Le Locle) 129
Petiet Fils Pl. 175
Pfaff (Augsburg) Pl. 31
Philippe, Adrien 173
Philipps, Edouard 137
Picard (Cambrai) Pl. 275
Picard, Jean 39
Pigeon, Jean (Lyons) Pl. 204
Piguet, Henri (Le Brassus) 137
Pironneau (Blois) Pl. 51
Plantart, N. (Blois) Pl. 40
Pohl, Anton 24
Pontevicio, Comino da 77
Pommé, Etienne Pl. 142
Prujean, John (Oxford) Pl. 222
Ptolemy 31, 42, 202, 211, 218
Puiné, Huand le Pl. V
Pureur, Jean 25
Quare, Daniel 39, 104, 106
Quinniet, Giles (Antwerp) Pls. 119, 219, xv
Raineri, J. P. and Carlo (Venice) 24; Pl. 2
Raingo Pl. 179
Raviro Pl. 172

Reinhold, Jacob 54
Reinhold, Janus (Augsburg) Pls. 26, 27
Richard, Daniel Jean (Le Locle) 107
Richard, Louis Pl. 167
Roberts, F. (London) Pl. VII
Rochette, J. (Paris) Pl. 277
Roias, Juan de 231
Roskopf, Georges Frédéric 138
Rousseau, J. (Geneva) 90; Pl. 52
Rowley (London) Pl. 245
Rugend (Auch) 245; Pl. 234
Rumuault, G. (Abbeville) Pl. 56
Rummel, Augustin Pl. 91
Sacrobosco, John of 204
Schissler, Christopher Pls. 256-9
Schmidt, Carl Pl. 20
Schniep, Ulrich (Munich) Pls. 253, 254
Shearwood Pl. VII
Smith (London) Pls. 71, 79
Stevens, Samuel (London) Pl. 174
Stollwerk (Paris) Pl. 145
Tavan, Antoine (Geneva) 121, 122, 123
Thiéry (Paris) Pl. XI
Thuret (Paris) Pl. 124
Tompion, Thomas (London) 114
Toutin, Jean (Châteaudun) 88
Treschler, Christopher (Dresden) Pls. 280, 281, xx
Troschel, Hans (Nuremberg) Pl. 249
Tucher see Ducher
Vaulesard 240
Verbiest, Ferdinand 201
Vic, Henri le 21, 35
Vitruvius 267
Vleesch, Brixius (Ypres) 36
Voisin, Henri (Paris) Pls. 155, 156
Volant (Paris) Pl. 39
Wallingford, Richard of 22
Weckerlin, Elias (Augsburg) Pls. 128, 129
Wetzel (Strasbourg) Pl. IV
Winnerl, Joseph (Paris) Pl. 122
Yunus ibn al-Husain Pl. 198
Zarquali, Ibrahim al (Cordova) 224
Zoller, Martin (Augsburg) Pl. 29

The text of this book was printed by the Presses Centrales S.A., Lausanne. — The illustrations and the jacket in four-color offset were made by Offset-litho Jean Genoud S.A., Lausanne. — The black and white illustrations were printed by Roto-Sadag S.A., Geneva. — The plates for the figures in the text were executed by Busag S.A., Berne-Niederwangen. — The binding was entrusted to Burkhardt, Zurich. — The book was designed by Walter Lachenmann, Munich.

PRINTED IN SWITZERLAND